Joe Barth Abba

Philosophy of Thomas Aquinas on Justice and Human Rights

Philosophie
Philosophy

Band / volume 108

LIT

Joe Barth Abba

Philosophy of Thomas Aquinas on Justice and Human Rights

A Paradigm for the
Africa-Cultural Conflicts Resolution –
Nigerian Perspectives

LIT

Bibliographic information published by the Deutsche Nationalbibliothek
The Deutsche Nationalbibliothek lists this publication in the Deutsche Nationalbibliografie; detailed bibliographic data are available on the Internet at http://dnb.d-nb.de.

ISBN 978-3-643-90909-1 (pb.)
ISBN 978-3-643-95909-6 (PDF)
Zugl.: München, Ludwig Maximilian Universität, Diss., 2016

A catalogue record for this book is available from the British Library

Klosbachstr. 107
CH-8032 Zürich
Tel. +41 (0) 44-251 75 05
E-Mail: zuerich@lit-verlag.ch http://www.lit-verlag.ch

Distribution:

In the UK: Global Book Marketing, e-mail: mo@centralbooks.com
In North America: International Specialized Book Services, e-mail: orders@isbs.com
In Germany: LIT Verlag Fresnostr. 2, D-48159 Münster
Tel. +49 (0) 2 51-620 32 22, Fax +49 (0) 2 51-922 60 99, e-mail: vertrieb@lit-verlag.de

In Austria: Medienlogistik Pichler-ÖBZ, e-mail: mlo@medien-logistik.at
e-books are available at www.litwebshop.de

TABLE OF CONTENT

FOREWORD

Within the area of both the micro and the macrocosm of the globe, people often observe and hear that many nations in the African continent unwisely are infamous regions consequent upon their notoriety and barbarianism regarding human right violations become inevitable. Such awful situations aggravate conflict and could abridge one's life-span and the daily dream for the expected joyful and ordered co-existence.

The challenging question is do Africans in this era of 21st century: as an individual or as a group nations, cherish and heartily accept this type of life as surrounded by atrocious and brutal acts such as constant conflicts, terrorism, kidnapping, killing, corruption etc?

The distracted environment, virile unexamined lives with ill actions of men in their domain and countries negate the objects of justice, and righteous living and rights of others needed for the up-grade and increment of the developmental goals (*cf.Aquinas Summa Theologiae iia, iiae qtn 57, art* 1ff).

The signification of happy and peaceful co-existence is based on the standard of behaviour in line with the principles of rights and wrongs in any reasonable country or nation concerning the good and love of one's neighbor (cf.Matt7: 12). In other words, treating each other as fellow lovely children of God with full rights to happy living till the individual's natural death comes. St. Thomas Aquinas' knowledge and doctrinal relevance of which this research work is all about seek for a strong panacea to the African conflicting nations seeking the way out for resolutions. Holding more practically and meaningfully to his ideologies and notions of justice, human rights, fairness, human life, and dignity for pro-life, will persistently or perpetually give room for peaceful co-existence and greater progressions for both developed and developing nations. These facts if well followed with spontaneous actions, will no doubt drastically abate corruption, grip of poverty and injustice, kidnapping, terrorism etc that are challenging everybody. The authentic existence, freedom, decent living and happiness as the watchword and what every rational being yearns and clamours for in

African and the Nigerian nation. This should not be an exception despite her vast natural mineral resources, much are being wasted daily due to boundary and politico-religious conflicts, egoism, corruption and lasting Islamic-Muslims terror-networks of those Boko Haram, Talibans, Al-Quaida, and other war-mongers. To be advised to conform always to the protection of human life and to stop killing in the name of religion or politics or whatever that stopping these sinful scandalous behaviour is an urgent necessity.

The work of Dr.JoeBarth's philosophical inquiry and knowledge opines that justice, objectively speaking is all about living well and treating others as one would like to be treated. Thus, in its true meaning, it buttresses impartiality, integrity, righteousness and avoidance of the abuse of human life as an urgent necessity in any African cultural milieu. However, be this as one observes, certain difficulties and anomalies and the contemporary African, cultural conflicting problems are for many Africans and Nigerians inclusive. The Pan-Africanism is the epitome of African Forum and African Union, progressiveness, peace-march for better future and the advancement of African nations as a panacea for quicker resolution for the chaotic backwardness and suffering countries coupled with the promotion of Negritude as worthy action packed ventures.

Uprightness could yield more fruits when their leaders embark on right reason (*recta ratio*), the touch stone of what Thomas Aquinas philosophy delved more into. Avoidance of vain glories and such issues of utopia imbued with emotional intelligence, narcism and Machiavellian way of livelihood will not help matters regarding the invitation of discursive dialogues and orientations, living and observing daily the maxim of Live and Let Others Live; and Happily). The resolution for African and Nigerian populace will come true equally by the African leaders of today if they have a re-think on the *status quo* excellence regarding the international community, having a listening ear for the truisms to their problems, and endeavouring to imitate more, the good aspects of the Western world's *modus operandi* and objective norms. On this realm, the motivational formation and all youth rights to the basic education as moral virtues alone in today's world are inadequate for an ideal man, instead of living and dwelling and swimming through the shackles of mundane policies of bad governments through ignorance or naivety. The author, Dr. Joebarth Abba, emphasized more on the pro-active operative remedy for easier resolution through dynamic spirit, harmonious understanding, and togetherness to eradicate the high rate of corruption constant wars by terrorists, racial justice and leading to the African nations to having an ideal Philosopher King or political Messiah This will by so doing be erasing the African notoriety which would lead to the new African liberation the zeal for an inspired resolution for the refreshment and standardization of the African's Human Rights Charta of 1981. Such clandestine problems of those who respect human life and anti-peace personality or groups might cry to God for real change of heart. Nevertheless, the Church's and the State's credibility should prove more competence in the human rights, human dignity and abuse of human life and conflicts.

Prof. Dr. Wilhelm Vossenkuhl,
Dept. Phil., University of Munich Germany

PREFACE

The debate on the theme of Justice has always been a source of controversy. This work, The Philosophy of Thomas Aquinas on "Justice and Human Rights: A Paradigm for Afro-Cultural Conflict Resolution: A Nigerian Perspective" addresses the thorny issues surrounding this controversy.

Whatever may be the nature of these controversies, we must appreciate that in reality, humanity has been debating essentially about the same issues despite the separation of history, geography and civilization experiences. As we have seen, with time, humanity has found consensus around the issues after a very difficult journey focusing on building new knowledge bases for appreciating these issues.

Over time, the notion of Justice has become coded within the framework of national and international law. Since the formulation of the 1948 UN Human Rights Declaration, we have seen issues of Justice and human rights taking centre stage. There are of course here and there, countries where these rights are not respected, especially in most of the Middle East and other countries in Africa and Asia. However, these are the exceptions rather than the rule.

This work has taken on these issues by adopting both the hermeneutical and pedagogical methodologies by making this work an opportunity for readers to both learn and identify areas of activism. The work looks at early philosophers both in groups and as individuals and looks at the Sophists, Aristotle and Plato.

The work also draws attention the fact to the multidimensional nature of Justice and calls for a more serious understanding. For example, in providing these dimensions, it examines forms of Justice such as Commutative, legal and social justice. The author then goes on to address these issues as they have been manifested over time, then narrows the work to the Nigerian situation.

The author later on uses the teaching of Thomas Aquinas to address the issues of the foundation of both human rights and justice.

The culture of human rights has still not emerged in Africa for many reasons. First, today, many African leaders and their own people still see Human Rights as something that a benevolent state confers on its citizens. The climate of dictatorship and the limited experience with Democracy has predisposed Africa to these distortions.

However, to the extent that the Church's duty is to create the necessary condition for the emergence of the kingdom of God here on earth, we must remain relentless in our work for human rights.

To this end, we commend Dr. JoeBarth Abba for this tremendous contribution and addition to knowledge in this book. I highly recommend the book to both church and state leaders along with students of both theology and law.

Bishop Matthew Hassan KUKAH
Sokoto Diocese, West Africa, Nigeria

ACKNOWLEDGEMENTS

The tenacity of purpose equanimity and joy urge me again to give my greatest gratitude to Almighty God for the inspiration on the accomplishment to get through to the end of this scientific work (Is.26:12). God's grace and blessings helped me to round-up yet another Doctoral Dissertation in Medieval Philosophy and Early Modern Theorist, the Angelic Doctor Thomas Aquinas. My humble regards to his Eminence Francis Cardinal Arinze for his concerns and fatherly motivation. In the same vein my special gratitude to my Archbishop, Most Rev. Dr. Valerian M. Okeke and his Auxiliary Bishop Denis Chidi Isizoh, for their motivation and encouragements and my teaching apostolate. My Hearty thank you goes to the Nuncio-Dominican Republic Archbishop Chukwukelo M.T. Okolo for his steady prayerful support, and paternal concerns and mentorship. My filial affections cum respectful regards go to all my Professors in Germany, USA, Italy and Nigeria, especially PD.Dr. Hans Otto Seitschek, Prof.Dr.Wilhelm Vossenkuhl and Prof. Dr. Ludwig Mödl. These Germen Academia fatherly and moderated my Dissertation and judged me worthy for the Ph.D title in the philosophical discipline. I should not forget the moral support, prayers and mentorship of Gerhard Ludwig Cardinal Müller whose optimism, foresightedness and hardworking spirit to protect and defend the teachings and deposit of faith of Catholicism inspire many strong faithful Christian believers and all your former students in Germany. My unalloyed gratitude is due to the families of Bernharda and Raymund Brunner, Margaretha und Rudolf Maass for their heart-warming parental cares throughout the cause of my sojourn and study apostolates in Europe; for this selfless generous sacrifices; God bless and reward you evermore. My great appreciation to all my medical practitioner friends in Europe who always freely shows steady concerns for my happiness and welfares like: Drs. Ludwig Sierolawski, Adolf Hiergeist, Thomas Graeve, Gerhard Einhäuser, Herga and Karl Gau. God reward you abundantly for your sacrifices and generosity. My fraternal thanks go to Prof. Drs.Wilhelm Vossenkuhl, those who wrote the foreword and prefaces, Most Rev. Dr. Matthew H. Kukah, the english lecturers proof readers: Dr. Chike Okoye, Sr. Dr. Thelma Anubalu and Anastasia Ify Ezeh respectively proof read this work for onward direction to its production. A flash point of lovely appreciation goes to these many more close friends and academic colleagues who made my progress ever-green as I pedal to and fro the University my strivings for this valuable achievement for the good of the Church and humanity; Prof. Drs. Sigmund Bonk, Walter Schweidler, Joseph Bonnici, Dhawan Nikita,

Assoc.Prof. Jude Dozie Nnaji, Rev.Fr.Drs: Anthony Ejeziem, Eugene Odoh, Matthew Ezea, Others are Rev. Frs: Theophilus Odukwe, Hyginus Ekeh, Fabian Ekeh, Col. Egnr and Dr. Mrs. Caroline Ogbonna, Navy Commodore Engr John Bosco C.Eze.

A Chunk of great thanks to Pan-Africanism Peace Pacts, UN Secretary General Anthonio Guterres and his predecessor Ban Ki Moon, High Commissioner for Human Rights, Zeid Ra'ad Al Hussein and Amnesty International, cordial regards to Margareth Huang Sali Shetty, Monica Pinto, UN Special Rapporteur on the Independent of Judges and Lawyers for their good works to usher in happiness, and to protect human life and rights for the common good of all. Equally, deserving significant thanks are, Prof. Dr. Kandala N.Bakwin, Drs. Dietmar Müller, Cyril Emeka Nnadi, Engr. Samson Odeh, the family of; Sir and Lady Raph and Agatha Offoukwuka, Aloy and Edith Muodum, Michael und Mary Rose Okonkwo.

I remain ever grateful and indepted to my parents and relations, James and Agnes Abba, and I lovely salute the youths of Great Iheaka Town- Iheakachukwu, City of God, Nsukka; the robust efforts of GREAT IHEAKA UNITY FORUM for their unity and peaceful co-existence and progressiveness. My affections and esteemed regards go to all my net work of friends and well-wishers nationally and internationally for our happy moments and goodness to each other, but for want of time and space I might have unintentionally not mentioned you.

I greatly appreciate you all as we remain happily and prayerfully united evermore.

– Author

LIST OF ABBREVATIONS

AAS	*Acta Apostolicae Sedis*
Art	Article
B.C.	Before Christ
Bk	Book
CAN	Christian Association of Nigeria
CIDJAP	Catholic Institute of Development, Justice and Peace
CDC	Constitution Drafting Committee
Cf.	Confrere
CLSA	Canon Law Association of Nigeria
CNN	Cable News Network
Co.	Company
Ed.	Editor
EU	European Union
Gen.	Genesis
GS	Gaudium Et Spes
ICESCR	International Covenant on Economic, Social and Cultural Rights
ICCPR	International Covenant on Civil and Political Rights
IFP	Initiative for Peace building
Inc	Incorporation
ILO	International Labour Organisation
ICCPR	International Covenant on Civil and Political Rights
1CESCR	International Covenant on Economic, Social and Cultural Rights.
IPOB	Indegineous People of Biafra
Lawsa	Law Student Association
Lk.	Luke
MDG	Millennium Development Goals
MEND	Movement for the Emancipation of the Niger Delta
MOSOP	Movement for the Survival of the Ogoni People

NGO	Non Governmental Organisation
NIREC	Nigeria Inter Religious Council
NASW	National Association of Social Workers
NSCIA	Nigeria Supreme Council for Islamic Affairs
OAU	Organisation of African Union
OIC	Organization of Islamic Conference
Pg.	Page
Publ.	Publish
Qtn.	Question
Quest.	Question
SAP	Structural Adjustment Program
SECAM	Symposium of Episcopal Conference of Africa and Madagascar
Vat.	Vatican
Vol.	Volume
UN	United Nation
UPN	Universal Periodic Review
UNDR	Universal Declaration of Human Rights
UNHCR	United Nations High Commissions for Refugees
USA	United States of America

GENERAL INTRODUCTION

This Dissertation focuses on Justice and Human Rights in Thomism Philosophy. Thomas Aquinas really moved into the quest for a panacea or a desiring solution to the problems of co-existence, justice, fairness, common good, coupled with expected livelihood as regards the Nigerian continent.

This scientific research creates more awareness on the panacea for an urgent and possible conflict resolution in order to curb this incessant or constant cultural confliction, creating fear and panicky situations in the various states of the country. He emphasized more on man's behavior and interaction towards his fellow man as contrary and arbitrary injustice, which stems from deprivation of justice, rights and fair-play. Pathetically, in the Nigerian nation, there are the denial of justice and fair-play. A real think-tank for the peoples' rights and freedom strengthens the focal-points of ethico-moral dimensions for the pedagogical, theological, psychological and spiritual reasoning that are very much needed today in this society.

This work was first written in English language so that the wider world will grasp faster the crux and the meaning of what African continents and some continents of the world are experiencing for a possible remedy for the common good of mankind. Thomas Aquinas is vast in his treatment of what justice and rights of mankind meant and he as well, elucidated and showed his grounds in clear-texts for the present day society, especially, to the African-Nigerian cultural situation.

In Aquinas enlightening thoughts, the object of justice is right. His doctrine on people's quest and craving for justice and egalitarianism, freedom and equity occupied him mainly both in the global levels of ethical and political spheres. Justice as in this perspective is firm and constant disposition, a habit rendering to each person what his right is. In the world of today, man's inhumanity to man is not praise-worthy. He emphasized more on man's behaviour and interaction towards his fellow man as contrary to arbitrary injustice, which stems from deprivation of rights and fair-play. Justice and happiness is more of harmony among all the various components of the community or state yearning for stability.

Corruption and violence or unnecessary silence and non-challance attitude are some of the causes of poverty, poor policies and wastages in different countries of the world. Africa and the Nigeria the populace are not exception to these problematic issues. In consequence also, the denial of fairness, the necessary human freedom which clarifies the focal-points of morality (ethics), and pedagogical direction are lacking in our society today.

The aim of this scientific search in the light of Aquinas' knowledge and doctrinal relevance is to seek the reason and a solution to the problems of the Nigerian suffering masses and injustices in the state with the subsistence of the human person.

How the Aquinas doctrine should address these problems of her cultural milieu in the face of certain anomalies and difficulties in her country's cultural conflicting situation is a major concern of this work. Actually, the contemporary man and the question of Justice and Human rights are not unknown phenomena. To be in a sound; healthy mind and body and acting well too as supp with the virtue of justice have

been perennial problem of man. Our target here also is to make every effort to link the rift between perfect reality of human rights practices in our country that keeps going the wrong way, while the two indubitably remain as separate as the fingers of the hand.

Authentic existence, freedom and happiness life is what a rational being yearns for. How can one exist and live authentically, peacefully and orderly without constituting any danger or problem to another's happiness and progress in the society? Both philosophers and men of jury today and of different epochs has been trying to bring to lime light the explications cum proper meaning of these concepts of justice and human rights and a better standardized life. The necessity of a good life for man and the acceptance and belief that God is truth and goodness in himself and that God is neither evil nor did he create evil in his creations. This is the nucleus and the whole gamut of Aquinas formidable synthesis of classical philosophy and Christian theology.

The primary objective of this scientific work is shared into four parts. This research work is a topical issue with the connotations of not only the philosophical inquiries but also the juridical and theological dimensions. The work is comparably analytical and expository in nature.

The first chapter of this work is an exposé showing the general overview on the definition and meaning of justice and human rights. The foregoing chapters delved into the classification and conceptual aspects of justice and common good of all. In the chapter two of this work, violation of human

rights, by the Nigerian citizens and the havocs caused are treated, and then, the issue of the rule of law cum Human Rights and a look at equal rights problems in Nigeria follows, and how we can apply the Aquinas thought in the nation's ethno-cultural systems of her government takes the later part.

Justice in the state and the rule of law coupled with the relationship with the government of the present day society was looked into. We looked at the state (society) where chastisement, corruption, intimidation, fraud, sectionalism, discrimination, kidnapping, robbery and other ill-treatments and practices persist and through which people have the rare hope of progress in life. This is also exemplified in the spate of deliberate political assassinations, unending political misrules, cases of police brutality and tortures, illegal detentions, extra-judicial killings and torts of false imprisonment by some police officers, mosaic religious violence, and "gender based" violence among others. How can the Nigerian government in the state levels, re-administer and maintain justice for injustice for instance, in a country where justice is least practiced, or where justice is delayed and denied without qualms? How can man continue to live in such State of state of chaos and lawlessness? This is the role, which Christianity and moral theology have in the life of man; generally to address and clarify; this should spur them on to strive for the best quality of life *(summum bonum),* for all people of God in this earthly hemisphere.

As Aquinas puts it, man is to follow the ordinance of reason and seriously brush aside various types of injustices and malicious acts for the good of others. The issue of equality of right before the law, justice and human rights in Nigeria, man as subject of rights and obligations in the State whereby a reasonable man could be seen as if he is an enigma of complexity in his 'natural ego so to say.'At this juncture, Aquinas categorically argued thoroughly and vehemently, thereby explaining that man has no right to dominate his neighbour whether on the ground of ethnicity, personality creed, race, colour, age or status. The third chapter is on Aquinas' profiles, his doctrine on human rights and justice; Thomas Aquinas and his work coupled with his views and expectations on justice and human rights, man as subject of rights and obligations and the justification of common good in giving one his deserved right. The neglect of justice and peoples rights has been as a thorn and a cankerworm in our flesh and this has eaten deep into the fabric of our society. The freedom of right and human acts then, comes to the fore. The researcher also delved into human interactions, as an exchange or inter-play of personalities of man.

The chapter four and chapter five with chapter six focuses on the observations and synthesis, suggestions and synthetic evaluation and conclusion touching uprightness and rightfulness and equity, after which I brought this research work to a reasonable conclusion.

The evaluative conclusion points are for the strength of any progressive nation like Nigeria. It is the strong will of its inhabitants to live more godly, dedicated and focused lives; and to always be conscious of her problems and strive daily on how to abate her problems. There is every hope that the Nigerian nation will still blossom and be great peaceful and progressively stable. There is need for all the citizens to value democracy and advocate the dignity of peoples as manifested both in the right to choose their leaders painlessly and in a peaceful condition. Justice remains the greatest of all the virtues as this regulates man's will, while human rights undoubtedly is that inalienable rights of any human person given by nature solely for the reason for being a rational and for human being created in the likeness and image of God,-*imago Dei*, (Gen.1.26f), as a rational being.

Chapter One: Notion of Justice and Human Rights

1.1

Contemporary Notion of Justice and Human Rights

Before we go into details about the above topic, let us give the background meaning of what the contemporary notion and exposé of Justice and Human Rights are all about. It means the present-day or up-to-date idea and opinions of the understanding of Justice and Human Rights in our society.

A conception of justice is a set of principleS for choosing between the social arrangements which determine this division and for underwriting a consensus as to proper distributive shares. The concept of Human Rights is especially well suited to take into account of what is necessary according to how social institutions relate to basic-good for all men and women.

Such differentiations are already being made with regard to some constitutional rights. The word justice is dependent on the shorter latin word "*iustus – (a-um)*" and for some authors, it means justice or right, for others legitimacy, welfare, sympathy, fairness, giving every one his due. Justice is equally "*Suum cuique*" meaning to each one, his due.[1] There is no unified understanding of justice as people define it based on their own background, nomenclature, culture, level of enlightenment etc. Justice can be defined as a concept of moral rightness based on ethics, rationality, law, (natural law), religion, equity along with the punishments of the branch of ethics. Then as far as Human Rights are concerned, they are those rights that are attached to every human person.

This is taken as a generic name for a group of rights recognized under the law. These rights are inherent to all human beings; whatever their nationality, ethnic origin, colour, religion, sex, language, residence or other status. It has been delivered as rights "derived from natural or fundamental, or constitutional law. More so, there is also the ethical concept of Justice.

---

1 C. Schwarz., / G. Davison et al., Chambers 20th Century, Dictionary, New Edition, Clay Ltd,. London Press, England 1993, p. 909.

The meaning is derived from the Latin word *iustitia,* from *iustus*, meaning just. Hence, justice as a noun refers to the quality of being just. However, the adjective "just" contains different meanings that are relevant to the present study. It can mean: honourable and fair in one's dealing and actions (e.g., a just cause), properly due or merited (e.g just deserts), and so forth.

The adjective just generally expresses conformity with what is legally or ethically proper.

In this context the opposite adjective, ' unjust'means 'violating principles of justice or fairness. That is being unfair. Already, one can identify in the adjective 'just'the close functional relation of fairness to justice as ethical principles. In its ethical sense, the noun 'justice'expresses the idea of fair-mindedness, objectivity, lack of bias, disinterestedness, detachment, impartiality, equity, equality, equitableness, reasonableness, fairness, fair deal, fair treatment, fair-play, no discrimination, equal opportunity, and the likes. We could also see the basic demand of justice in its general sense as contained in the classical principle, which *requires that each person can be given what is due to him by law*[2] or simply that *each person receives what is due to him.*[3] This is the basic law of general justice. Law in this context refers to in the Socratic usage as "the original form of the good (*agathon*), on the basis of which all things pertaining to social actions are measured.[4] In reality and essentially speaking, the person who practices justice lays legitimate claim to his or her own right by giving and letting the other have his or her right.

Justice in its general sense represents one of the many virtues of social institutions, as already explained. It has also been explained that fundamental to justice as a basic principle of institutional practices is the concept of fairness which relates to right dealing between persons who are cooperating with or competing against one another.[5]

In this view, the question of fairness arises in the context of justice, "when free persons who have no authority over one another, are engaging in a joint activity and among themselves settling or acknowledging the rules

2 Cf. T. Aquinas., Summa Theologiae, II-II, Q. 58, 1, Rome 1952.

3 Cf. T.D. Campbell., Justice, in: Outhwaite W., and Bottome, T. (eds.), BDTCST, p. 304.

4 S.N., Okechukwu., The Right*to Life* and the Right to Live. Ethics of International Solidarity. Peter Lang Publisher, Frankfurt 1990, p. 298.

5 Cf. S. Freeman., (ed.) /John Rawls, on Justice and Reciprocity, Justice as Fairness, Distributive Justice and Fairness to Goodness, Cambridge Press, London, 1989, p. 59.

which define it and which determine the perspective shares in its benefits and burdens."[6] Fairness therefore, plays a considerable role in the formation of any just society or any nation. A certain reflection on the nature of justice also considers the term justice as having three basic dimensions-an anthropological, an ethical, and a political dimension.[7]

The search for justice, like the search for the truth and the good belongs to the anthropological condition of human existence. However, due to the specific condition of human knowledge, the different approach or hermeneutical interpretation of the problem of justice lead to different views about the concept of justice. The ethical dimension of justice portrays the tension between the juridical and moral senses of justice.

As social facts, morals and laws are sources affording roots for the idea of justice. Hence, justice is subjected to the condominium of moral philosophy and legal philosophy.

Very pertinent here, however, is the traditional ethical idea of justice as a cardinal virtue. As political issue, justice is related with the issues of political community, namely enabling a good life for man, through which it also gets its standard. One says here that justice is seen as an essential principle of political activities.[8]

Justice and Human Rights in our contemporary world have multifaceted meanings but all gear objectively towards the same expected goals as regards giving to each person his due or deserved right. Traditional conception of justice commonly agree on the value of justice as a basic human virtue and therefore a fundamental ethical concept. Aquinas identifies the virtue of justice in its subjective sense with the rectitude of the mind.[9] Much earlier on, in his idealistic mind, Plato refers to the ideal condition of justice [10] as the condition under which the just man lives the fullest and the best life and he is simultaneously happy and good.[11] He identifies justice not with the external actions of man, rather with his inner self-the harmony

---

6 Loc. Cit.

7 Cf. Hollerbach, A., Reflexion über Gerechtigkeit, in: Brieskorn, N. Müller, J., (eds), Gerechtigkeit und soziale Ordnung: Für Walter Kerber, Freiburg, Basel, Wien 1996, p. 43.

8 Hollerbach, A., Reflection, pp. 43-46.

9 Aquinas, T. Summa Theologiae, II-II, Q. 58, Rome 1952.

10 Guthrie, W.K.C., The Greek Philosophers, London 1950, p. 109.

11 Cf. Gopalan, S., Social Justice, An Axiological Analysis, Madras 1972, p. 220.

of the spirit of man with the orders of his reason. However, as an ethical virtue justice is not only a spiritual quality of the human mind; it equally demands a specific behaviour.

It is therefore not just a mere (theoretical) concept it is a principle governing human behaviour, which has its root primarily in the human will. Thus, justice is described as the first virtue of human activities.

Justice must be concretised and determined through human action. Aristotle defines justice in this light as the state of character that disposes people to perform just; acts to behave in a just manner, and wish for what is just. The opposite of this state of character leads to injustice and unjust acts. According to him, an unjust act implies either one that breaks the law or one that is unfair (through advantage of another). Hence, both the law-abiding man in a general sense and the fair man are considered to be just people in the minds of Aristotle (1129a3-21).[12] Moreover, the Holy Scripture identifies the just man by his habitual good and right thinking and uprightness of conduct towards one's neighbour or fellow man.[13] From this, it becomes clear that in its ethical dimension justice does not just appeal to our good will, good intentions and good conscience; rather, it demands a practical realisation.

Man must accept the duty of achieving justice as a responsibility. Justice is seen from light as an essential component in the ethics of responsibility. Hollerbach even talked in this relation, about the justice of responsibility. This is distinctly and explicitly based on reasonable quality of equity and fairness; being just and impartial in the administration of justice.[14]

To do justice or to justify an act righteously is to be just, and to be righteous which humanly speaking means, giving full advantage for the people to be reasonable, to vindicate mildly and to treat fairly the situational problem that is being handled. This entails showing adequate reasons or grounds for one's action and to absolve certain things accordingly.

The contemporary notion of justice is governed by reason.[15]

Justice is the standard by which the benefits and penalties of living in society are distributed. The basic means of justice is found throughout the

---

12 Aristotle, Ethics, p, 171.

13 Cf. M,O. Eboh., Right to Authentic Human Development in the Light of the Social Teachings of the Church, Rome 1995, p. 107.

14 Verantwortungsgerechtigkeit, vom A. Hollerbach Reflexion, p. 45.

15 Plato, The Republic, Pt V-Bk. IV, p.p. 160/161.

different books and types of writing of politics, law, and medicine as well as its ethical understanding and other differing spheres to which it is applied. The original terms most approximating justice have been frequently translated in English as 'righteousness' and 'judgement.'

A rule of thumb can be that when these terms appear in a context of social distribution or social conflict, justice would be a better translation.

When we look into the foundation of justice, we notice that justice is founded in the being of God, for whom it is a chief attribute. Actually, God is the sure defender of the poor and the oppressed (Jer 9:23, Ps. 10:17).

The demands of God's justice, thus extends beyond the nation of Israel and indeed, the whole world. Considering the industrial value of justice in this idealistic mind, Plato sees justice as referring to the ideal social relationship(s) and its resultant just society as an ideal form of a perfect society.

However, as mentioned above, justice as principle at work regulating human relations cannot just be an ideal concept in the mind, as Plato supposes. According to Gopalan… justice certainly emanates in the human mind as value but it has necessarily to be expressive of man's dormant wish for ideal constructions and realization through the institution.[16] Hence, whereas for Plato justice is seen more as an ideal virtue; for Aristotlem, it rightly become the *norm* of social relations in the society, involving the participant actors in true human institutional life and activities, in the actualities of its virtuous act's shortcomings.

It is a principle of social behaviour and activity aimed at the good life of the individual and the general welfare of the society as a whole. This also goes to highlight the significant function of institutions in general in the development of the objective work of justice. As a relevant institutional concept, justice is described as the "fundamental… measure for the political social world, the social institutions of marriage and family, the economic system, education and the state. It is the criterion by which these social areas are measured with the idea of the good.[17]

Actually, Aristotle maintains that among the cardinal virtues, prudence,

---

[16] S. Gopalan., Social Justice, p. 230.

[17] P.Scmitz., Gerechtigkeit, in Theologie and Philosophie 62 (1987), p. 564, cited in Okechukwu S. N., The Right, p. 297.

justice, fortitude and temperance, only justice is clearly focused on the good of others in its own merit.[18]

A specific component of the ethical dimension comes into focus here when the concept of fairness is brought into institutional set-up of justice.

The Scripture condemns the partial treatment of the poor in social life (Lev.19, 15), and exhorts masters to treat their subjects justly and fairly (Col. 4, 1). In this case, the ethical fitness not only concerns subjective behaviours, rather as already can be seen, it is a principle with an objective-institutional relevance.

Fairness plays a crucial role in the concrete realisation of the general objects of justice, which include rights and obligations, benefits and burdens, which men both claim and owe to one another in society.

The norms and basic justice state the minimum requirements for these objective claims and obligations, which for instance include the requirements for mutual love, care and respect by individuals and communities.

The justice of God is characterized by special regard for the poor and the weak; a corresponding quality is demanded from God's people (Deut10:18). When they properly carry out justice, they are agents of divine will (Isa59:15). St. Paul presents God's justice as Grace of God flowing into and through the believers to the needy for righteousness (2Cor9:8-10).

The demand of God for justice is so central that other responses to God are empty or diminished if they exist without it. (Mt 23:23, Amos 5:21). Regarding its focus, we realize that justice is closely related to love and grace (Deut.10:18-19; Hos10:12), rather than being a contrasting principle.

It thus provides vindication, deliverance, and creation of the community in addition to retribution.

Need is the criterion for distribution of benefits although, the provisions do not exclude ability as a criterion once this priority is met. Thus, the focus is upon the oppressed with particular attention given to specific groups, such as the poor, widows, the fatherless, slaves, resident aliens, wage earners, and those with physical infirmities, (Job:12-17, P.S 146:7-9; Mal 3:5). Justice is demanded of all the people, but practically of the political authority. Justice is associated with the basic requirements of life in community. Basic needs are basic rights.

---

[18] Cf. T. H. Irwin., Aristotle, in: Becker, L. C., (ed.), E., EE, Vol. 1, p. 58.

Thus literally, justice belonging to the needy'is properly translated as the rights of the needy,(Jer 5: 28).

The context for the carrying out of justice is the justification of community and the considerationof the people in it (Job 24:5, Lk7:29). Justice is deliverance, rectifying the gross social inequalities of the disadvantaged, (Ps.76:9). It puts an end to the conditions that produce the injustice. Sometimes such redress will not be to the advantage of everyone in the community.

The oppressed are raised, the oppressed are judged (Lk1: 51-53). Paul uses the language and meaning of justice to describe God's work of salvation in his theme of righteousness of God. It occurs primarily in Romans, where he treats the inclusion of the Gentiles in the new order of redemption. By Justice, God brings into community of the Gentiles, who previously had no rights in the commonwealth of Israel. It then stands clear for that natural equality of men which cements their fellowship because human beings is basically the same everywhere as they are sharing in the same natural sense of justice.

Another concrete example of Justice and manifestation of humane spirit and goodness on the theory of justice is also seen in the New Testament-(Matt 20. 1-16), where Jesus almost reasonably, showed and applied justice and mercy, generosity and consideration pertaining to a just reward as explicated in the parable of the labourers in the vineyard.

The Lord Jesus showed us the practical meaning of the equality and sameness of human beings and the importance to treat all in the society with and goodness and prudence in spectacular situational problems at every point in time.[19] Justice then, means, to show one's abilities and good wills to the best advantage. Justice and human right equally, have macrocosmic (state) and microcosmic (an individual) perspectives. Considering it microcosmically, justice and human rights exists when each person works

[19] Cf. Matt. 20, 1-16, – "Das Gleichnis von den Arbeiten im Wienberg", (Parable of the Labourers in the Vineyard), Justice and Generosity of God… " Justiz- Gerecht und Gütig an allen Menschen" Also, Cf. (Rom 9, 14-29 " Die Freiheit und das Erbarmen Gottes", – God is not Unjust. Parable of the Labourers in the Vineyard, Justice and Generousity of God… This is a coherent notions of the treatment of the equality of human being s , irrespective of their personalities; be it either a male or female, rich or poor, status or ethncity.

at the craft (as the only and exclusively system) for which nature best fits an individual.

Be that as it may, each in his own areas of specialization and talent where one should be performing brightly well enough is required. That means, each minding his own 'business' or (talent) without encroaching into or interfering with other people's things or rights. That is the meaning of the topic in question and thereby avoiding harm, envy or constituting a barrier or being a stumbling block in another person's own field or freedom. That is the more reason why justice is the virtue between two extremes of gain and loss. So, the contemporary notion of justice could also mean the will of man's power to choose the good in which the sense desires are concerned.[20] Aquinas in his own ideology described justice not only as a virtue but sees this as a habit and as the principles of a good act which needs to be defined by the means of a good act, clearly seen as a matter proper to the virtue of justice. The proper matter of justice and human rights in Aquinas consists in the things that have to do with relationship with fellow human beings.

In his convictions he conclusively believes that justice or right means "rendering to each one his rights."and according to St. Isidore's notion.

It means is that a man is said to be just because he respects the rights *(Jus)* of others.[21] This is to say that 'Justice' unequivocally is the recognition of the dignity of every person.

One can also, *inter-alia,* say that justice and human rights take into account, man's social nature and makes sure that in our choice of goods, we will serve the reasonable good of the other human beings.

We should conceive human rights primarily as claims on coercive social institutions and secondary as claims against those who uphold such institutions. Such institutional understanding contrast with an interactional one, which presents Human Rights as placing the treatment of human beings under certain constraints that do not presuppose the existence of social institutions.

The German Constitution, for instance always buttresses the fact that everyone shall have the right to life and to peaceful atmosphere for all the

---

[20] Cf. H. Achten Meier., Harpers Bible Dictionary, Theological Publication in India, St. Peter's Semiary, Malleswaran, West Bangalore, India, pp. 519-520

[21] Cf. T. Aquinas., Summa Theologiae, IIa IIae, Quest 57 Art. 1ff.

citizens. Human rights can certainly be violated by governments and their agencies and officials, by the general staff of an army at war, and probably also by the leaders of guerrilla government or of a large cooperation with others. We can capture this idea by conceiving it to be implicit in the concept of human rights by which human rights postulates are addressed, in the first instance at least, to those who occupy positions of authority within a society (or such a comparable social system).

The civil rights postulated in the Universal Declaration of Human Rights make clear and specific demands on governments, while the rights postulated in article 25 seem merely to assert that it would be a good thing if any society were so organised and that all had enough to eat and to be at peace. But this contrast seems deceptive if the realization of even the Human Right is not to be subjected to cruel, inhuman, or degrading treatment (Article 5). It requires that such treatment by private agents, too, must be effectively discouraged and presupposes certain commitments and dispositions on the part of the citizenry.

John Rawls in his own view presents the contemporary meaning of human rights, justice and fairness as analytic construction when he said that Justice and fairness are, indeed, different concepts, but they share a fundamental element in common, which could be called reciprocity.[22]

Actually, for Rawls, a human right is and should remain a moral claim on any coercive social institution imposed upon oneself and therefore a moral claim against anyone involved in their imposition.

Human Right requires its own jurisdiction only when it is empirically true, as this may be for some civil and political rights that secure access to its objective presupposes the inclusion of a corresponding legal rights in the law or constitution.[23]

Indeed the concept of justice is often misunderstood; even in practice, it is sometimes neglected. Human society had for ages become increasingly alienated and divided which ideologies-religious and otherwise-have multiplied. Philosophical schools have differently constructed the concept of justice in terms of utility, rules, regulations, laws and equality of rights etc.

---

22 Cf. J., Rawls., / S.Freeman., (ed.), Collected Pappers, quoting Cicero – On Justice and Reciprocity, Justice as Fairness, Distributive Justice, Justice and Fairness to Goodness, Cambridge, London 1999, p. 10.

23 Cf. Rawls. J., / Freeman, S., (ed.), Collected Pappers, On Justice and Reciprocity, p. 9.

In our times, the differences have not narrowed, rather we notice through the various modern means of communication that injustice has increased in a world where people are becoming more aware of their 'rights'and are prepared to die for them.[24]

On the ethical principles, Bourke itemized it all in his own notion by saying that the general concept of justice is quite at home in the mind of intellectuals and non-intellectuals alike.[25] Justice is not to be confused with an all-inclusive vision of a good society, or thought as being identical with the concept of right. It is only one part of any such notion or conception; and it is but one species of right. Roman law in the recent past regards justice as a sense of positive law and a Roman personnel holds that: "Justice is affixed and biding in which one is given his own due."[26]

The emphasis here is stressed more on something that is really one's own belonging or right. It is the practical recognition of the other person as person and possessors of right. When we compare what justice and fairness are, indeed, their differences and concepts, we see that they share a fundamental element in common, which we may call the concept of reciprocity.

The principles of justice are those required once the constraints of having a morality are applied to what can be mutually acknowledged on those occasions when questions of justice arise. Sometimes; we may think of a human society as a more or less of self-sufficient association regulated by common conception of justice and aimed at advancing the good of its members. However, as a cooperative venture for mutual advantage, it is characterized by a conflict as well as an identity of interests.

There is an identity of interest since social cooperation makes possible a better life for all human beings than any body would have if everyone were to try to live by his own efforts, yet at the same time, men are not

24 Cf. Ike.O.F.,/Edozien.N. N., Understanding Africa, Traditional Legal Reasoning Juiris Prudence and Justice in Igboland, As a Basis for Cultural Rooted and Sustained Development. CIDJAP publications, Enugu- Nigeria 2001, p. 47.

25 Cf. Bourke, U.J., Ethics: A Text Book in Moral Philosophy, Mac Millian Co., New York 1986, p. 304.

26 G. Sabine., History of Political Theory, (4th ed.) Illinois, 1973, p. 167. See also the "Black Ausrtralia's Fight for Rights", One World (Geneva, 69, 1981, p. 12ff, cited by J.S.Mbiti., "Contemporary on 'Sacred Sites' in R.A. Evans., and A.F. Evans., Human Rights: A Dialogue Between the First and Third World's. Maryknoll: Orbis Press, 1983, p. 119ff.

indifferent as to how the greater benefits produced by their joints labours are to be distributed in equity. Also in Rawls own ideology is that we think of human society as more or less sufficient association regulated by a common conception of justice and aimed at advancing the good of its members.

As a cooperative venture of mutual adventure, it is characterized by a conflict as well as an identity of interests. There is an identity of interests since social cooperation makes possible a better life for all human beings than any one would have it; if anyone were to try to live freely by his own efforts yet at the same time, being not indifferent as to how the greater benefits produced by their joint labours are distributed, in order to further their own aims which each prefers on greater things to a lesser share. Justice as it has been in the modern or contemporary era as out-spoken, because of its grandiose affiliations to mankind. The principles of justice and its contemporary meaning serve to specify the application of "arbitrary"and "proper,"and they do this by formulating restrictions as to how certain practices may define positions and offices, and assign them powers and liabilities, rights and duties. These principles are those required once the constraints of having a morality are applied on what can be mutually acknowledged on those occasions when questions of justice and egalitarianism arise.

The major problem in the analysis of the concept of justice is how these principles are derived and connected with this moral concept, and their logical basis, and further, what principles if any, have a special place, which might properly called the principle of justice?

At this juncture, let us peruse the issues of Human Rights in general as a well founded claim; and when given as a claim, is then recognised by civil law. It becomes, therefore an acknowledged claim or legal right enforceable by the power of the State.

Right, here therefore, could as well be understood to mean a recognised claim which legally empowers one or confers a right of ownership of something on someone. This is a recognised claim that is sanctioned by the civil law and it is enforceable and so demands respect.

Right ipso facto, then, is that which is straight, true, good and just. It is opposed to wrong; and that which does not conform to a given standard is termed as evil. When a law points to the right directions to be followed, it could achieve the ends of a state and for the good of all. How then could we conceive Human Rights?

The obvious reason remains that whoever keeps the law of a state does right and whoever violates it does wrong. Right, referring to things designates both material and immaterial possessions which explicitly and exclusively belong to a person or is mine. If it belongs to me or my neighbour; and when it is his or mine, it could appertain to us by a subjective element called right. Nevertheless, in our explications and other analysis of 'Human Rights', it means that it is A human being that is being referred to directly.

The expression 'Human Rights' seems commonly used especially most often by persons in distress or under threat of deprivations or wrongs. Though human right is a kind of shield being used against a group with individual idiosyncrasies and vicissitude psychologically, but this is a fact!

The expression of these terminologies are often misused either deliberately or ignorantly or being used to achieve desired impact of evoking sympathy.

Human right is more often than not, confused with other legal rights terms that have their origin in the constitutions and in nature as being fundamental for the non-debased existence of man. Human rightS is often interchanged with Fundamental Rights or civil liberties.

A society devoid of right and order could also be devoid of reasonable progress. Every human right is fundamental to man, human rights therefore means the same thing as fundamental rights and they include rights under the rules of natural justice. This shows that human rights have been construed as being natural, inherent and inalienable. Most of the human rights writers have always highlighted the meaning that human rights represent demand which individuals or groups make on society, some of which are protected by law while others remain to be attained in future. A clarification on why the addition of 'Human'to 'Right'is what R.J.Vincent here explains that this goes to mean that everybody should have them. The subjects of human rights are not members of this or that society, but of the community of human kind as a whole. There are some doubts as to whether groups can be counted as members in the sense of themselves being subjects of human rights.

But the basic qualification for holding human rights is to belong to the human race.[27]

It could be rightly assessed that the object of human rights are like in comparison with all other plain rights which are of great importance.

The human aspect here on this issue, means, things fundamentally being linked up with the theme of Human Rights.

But Human Rights properly speaking here is to be referred to as absolute rights indefeasibles or things not to be done away with. On the importance of human rights, R. J. Vincent as well said:

> the idea that human beings have rights as humans is a staple of Contemporary world politics. Internal conventions global, regional and State are at length and in relation to a large number of rights. People speaking for states assert it in its collective form and non-governmental organisations that make its observance their raison d'etre. Individual extremes appeal to it as reporters presumed, and scholars try to make more sense out of it in what they seek to understand.[28]

In fact, the conception and objectives of Human Rights are basically on the fundamental elements of the rights of man.

Human Rights are in fact, the totality of all rights which an individual inherits merely because he is human with life, blood, soul and spirit. Some of these natural rights are often selected, and protected in the constitutions of the various states as fundamental or constitutional rights which the state must none infringe upon, but enhance. Fundamental Rights are better known as "Fundamental Human Rights" are in many countries, seen as common features in constitutions that hardly need to be explained.

And for T. Aguda, Fundamental Human Rights were not created by the state but are eternal and universal institutions, common to all mankind and antedating the state and founded upon natural law.[29]

Another question one could ask is based on the diversity and multiplicity of meaning as regards to the way the society looks at the concept of justice.

---

27 R. J.Vincent., Human Rights and International Relations, New York Press, USA 1986, p. 9.

28 R. J., Vincent., Human Rights and International Relations, New York Press, USA., 1986, p. 7.

29 Cf. Aguda, T.A., The Judiciary in the Government of Nigeria, Nigeria 1983, p. 41.

The reality of these diverse meanings of justice and fairness comes then to the fore. Justice, like other virtues needs to be practised and considered by means of the good act bearing on the matter proper to the virtue of justice in our contemporary society.

The nucleus point here is that each version of a particular notion or concept of Human Rights and justice finds its natural home in different ways of looking at our today's society; and because there are several of such perspectives, it is understandable that our philosophical concepts should display such diversity.[30] This touches the issue of religion on justice as it has for ages been a powerful factor in human life and history.

In establishing ethics and morals, religion has also played some significant roles in this aspect; for it was primarily so, that moral codes were formulated and enforced in most ancient society which is completely dependent on its inception and practice. The defining character of the contemporary notions of Human Rights has been shaped by the reformist impulse of the late nineteenth century.

The abolition of slave trade, the development of factory legislation; and the beginnings of mass education, trade unionism, and universal suffrage all served to broaden the dimensions of individual rights and stimulate an increasing international interest in the protection.[31]

That was a serious spectacular mistake made by those involved in those early periods or era because certain actions are wrong humanly speaking no matter the social or political context and certain rights are inalienable no matter the social or political exigencies. On the issue of human rights per se, in the past few decades, many scholars on this area and regional studies

including Africans have become fully engaged in the thriving interdisciplinary discussion about the philosophical and historical antecedents of the contemporary notions of universal human rights.

The central concern here can be posed in the form of simple questions: What is the origin of human rights? Are the human rights Western Concepts, or are they truly universal? If they are universal, what normative contributions have it to the continent of the world? Also important is the

30 Cf. Miller, D., Social Justice, Clarendon Press, Oxford 1976, p. 7.

31 Patterson, Freedom, slavery, and the Modern Constructions of Rights, London 1987, p. 176ff.

debate about the historical development of Universal Human Rights that dominated the thoughts of the contemporary Human Rights Supporters.

Also, within the past two decades, human rights scholarships have produced many engaging theories and conceptual frameworks for the understanding, interpreting and promotion of human rights.

To strengthen this view, Van der Ven opined that one cannot and need not deny that Human Rights are of Western origin. It cannot be denied, because they are morally based on the Judaeco-Christian tradition and Graeco-Roman philosophy; they were codified in the West over many

centuries, they have secured an established position in the national declarations of Western democracies; and they have been enshrined in the constitutions of these democracies.[32]

The Idealists, Marxists Philosophers, on their part described the rights of man as the highest and ultimate value. While many other scholars trace the philosophical foundation of Human Rights to natural law and Western liberal traditions, others argue for a more broad understanding of the term, focusing on differing notions of rights within both Western and no-Western societies.

Even more contentious is the debate over the meaning of "Human Rights"and the appropriateness of employing the concept within the context of the history of colonial societies. The recent discourse on the origins and philosophical foundations of rights will focused mainly on natural law theory. Many writers equally, have traced contemporary conceptions of rights and liberties from natural law and ancient Greek stoicism through the Medieval period and the Enlightenment. Natural law philosophy as characterized by a belief that laws and rules of conduct are embedded and derivable from the nature of man as fundamental to the inalienable character of human rights.

Since the nature of man is the same in the world over, the laws derived from that nature are seen as universal and true to all persons, at all times and places, in so far they are objective and eternal and are neither changeable nor alterable.[33] Some suggested that this philosophy underlies the concept

---

32 J.A.Van der Van.,/ D. S. J.Dreyer., Is there A God of Human Rights? The Complex Relationship between Human Rights and Religion: A South African Case, Boston, 2004, p. 29.

33 Cf. M. Macdonald.," Natural Rights"in Theories of Rights, JeremyWaldron (ed.) London 1984, p. 27ff.

of rights as expressed in the socio-political developments during the period of the fifteen and sixteenth century in Europe. The renaissance and the decline of feudalism inaugurated a long period of transition to the liberal notions of freedom, justice and equality, particularly; in the use and ownership of property.

The issue of fairness and justice is of paramount importance. Duties or obligations to others are generally thought to include a wide range of duties of justice. Moreover, duties we owe to others as our social responsibilities involve a high degree of moral sense of fairness in the consideration of the interests and feelings of others in our social activities. From this basic point of view, the relation of fairness with justice as a fundamental ethical value is seen as a very essential one.

John Rawls expresses this idea clearly in strong conception of fairness in connection with justice. Rawls strongly claims that the fundamental idea in the concept of justice is fairness. Obviously, Rawls claims seemingly equation of fairness with justice, but he quite rightly argues that fairness is the most important idea in the concept of justice.[34]

By such claims he sees justice as virtue of social institutions[35] or what he simply calls social "practices."This Rawlsian view is really held as the first really major attempt at fully exploiting Aristotle's much earlier idea in his claim that 'partial' or 'particular justice'[36] that is, the justice concerned with distribution of honours and money (i.e. socio-economic benefits), can best be understood in terms of 'the fair.'[37] Thus, fairness is strongly considered in this light as an indispensable condition for achieving a just society in the different modes of its social organisations and activities.

This created an unprecedented commitment to individual expression and world experience that was subsequently reflected in diverse writings from the teachings of Thomas Aquinas and Hugo Grotius to the Magna Carta, the Petition of Rights of 1628 and the English Bill of Rights of 1689.[38]

---

34 Cf. A.J. Simmons., Fairness, p. 29.

35 S. Freeman., (ed), John Rawls: Collected Papers, Cambridge, Massachusetts, London, 1999, p. 47.

36 Aristotle, Ethics, J. A. K. Thomson., (trans.), London 1976, p. 139f.

37 Cf. Simons, A. J., Fairness, p. 356.

38 Weston. B., "Human Rights,' 'Human Rights Quarterly 6, 3, London 1984, p. 259. Also in "african Values and the Human Rights, Cobbah. J. A. M., Debate: African Perspec-

The fact of the Universal Declaration of Human Rights of 1948 was that by virtually all countries in the world including non-Western countries, does not distract from this reality, since some thought that the initiative for Universal Declaration of Human Rights was mainly Western.

Nor do we need the Western origin of Human Rights to be denied, since the origin of institutions-in this case human rights, says nothing about their validity; the context of discovery should be separated from the context of justification to avoid the logical fallacy of a categorical error.[39]

The dreams and efforts were to create more stable and peaceful world order culminated in 1948 with the Universal Declaration of Human Rights.

The Universal Declaration was nothing short of a revolution in thought: instead of each nation being the master of its own domain, incumbent universal principles or rules now appeared.

A higher authority-in this case, the United Nations- issued a set of guidelines which, at least in theory, was meant to inhibit its member nations from violating these agreed-upon Ruman Rights. No longer could a nation treat her it's own citizens or those of other nations simply as it wanted. The Universal Declaration set minimum standards of conduct for governments all over the world.[40] In spite of efforts before the Universal Declaration to establish a model standard of conduct applicable to every individual and government, no prior document could match the Universal Declaration in scope or participation.

The development and eventual fruition of the Universal Declaration exemplifies how individuals and groups from diverse backgrounds mutually produced an extraordinary document that transcends customary borders. Governments or individuals who ignore or violate Human Rights, often face diminished reputation, scorn, or harsh criticism.[41] Even with its shortcomings, the Universal Declaration of human rights must rank as one of the most esteemed accomplishments in political, social, economic, and cultural history.

---

tive, Human Rights Quarterly 9, London 1987 p. 314.

39 Cf. Van der Ven. J. A., Jaco, S., et al., Is There A God of Human Rights? The Complex Relationship between Human Rights and Religion: A South African Case, Niederland 2004, p. 11.

40 Cf. The Economist, Human Rights Law, December 15, 2001, pp. 4-16.

41 Cf. The Economist, Special Report on Human Rights: Righting Wrongs August 18-24,, pp. 18-20.

On the Universality of the Human Rights, Dugard said:

> The Declaration is universal not only because it was adopted by the General Assembly of the United Nations on 10th December 1948- two years later but that 10th December was proclaimed Human Rights Day- but more especially because its basic principles was derive from (customary international law, which it turned as witness for the International Covenant and Civil Political Rights of 1966 and the International Covenant on Economic, Social, and Cultural Rights of 1966.[42]

Some writers have argued for a precise and historically specific definition of Human Rights that is distinct from general notions of rights that may include customary moral and legal notions of rights.

Such advocates of Conceptual specificity contend that the notion of Human Rights is relatively recent idea founded on Post-Second World War developments and, specifically, the adoption of the Universal Declaration of Human Rights (UNDR) by the United Nations in 1948.[43]

The first Universal Declaration that has enjoyed wide acceptance and enforcement is the Universal Declaration of Human Rights made during World War II. The Organisation of Africa Unity (OAU) now Africa Union followed with the African Charter on Human and People Rights.

The African Charter has been incorporated into the laws of Nigeria and has an expanded version of the rights stipulated in the constitution. These declarations are aimed at securing peace, justice and freedom for all mankind. The rights cognizable under the constitution include: the right to life, personal dignity, personal liberty, fair hearing, compensation for compulsorily acquired property, family life, thought, conscience and religion, freedom of expression, movement of expression, movement and assembly and freedom from discrimination ... These rights under chapter IV are known as fundamental rights. They are fundamental because they are recognized, entrenched and guaranteed by the constitution. "Human Rights", Fundamental Rights" can be used interchangeably.

Notwithstanding, the constitution recognized "fundamental rights concretely." However, Fagothey argues that "a right involves a system of rela-

---

42 J. Dugard., International Law, A South Perspective, London 2001.

43 Even this point is subject to dispute. At the signing of the UNDR in 1948, many countries in Africa and Asia were still under colonial rule and were not members of the United Nations. They were, therefore, not part to the drafting of the original document, although most of these nations subsequently ratified the decalaration.

tions in which there are three terms and a basis or foundation on which the relations are grounded." He illustrates this with the example of a workman having a right to his wages. We may separate four elements, or components, the workman who has earned the wages, the employer who is bound to pay the wages, the wages the workman has earned, and the work done whereby the workman has earned the wages.

Accordingly, there are identified four basic components of a right, namely, subject, term, matter, and title. For Fagothey, the subject of a right can only be a person. Rights exist for that person because he is obliged to guard the moral value of his being and fulfil himself by voluntary observance of the moral law and thus reach his last end.

Surely, for this kind of action, rights are essential, because one must guide oneself by the use of one's inner freedom. That means one must be guaranteed immunity from hindrance in one choice of the necessary means. The subject of right as a person is not limited to physical or natural person but extends to juridical person.

The term is thus the person or persons morally obliged to respect or fulfil the rights of another. Emphatically, however, it is noted that the matter of a right can never be another person "since in the exercise of any right the subject always subordinates the matter to himself or herself and uses it as a means to his or her own end." Hence, a person cannot be subordinated to the interest of another to be used and consumed as a mere means for another's benefit. While this view is in accord with Kant theory in which man is always an end and can never be used as a means, it is in conflict with Marxist theory which places the interest of the state as paramount; even while trampling on the rights of individuals. Fagothey is however quick to assert that this position "does not mean that for one to work for us, we buy their labor not their persons, and labour can be the matter of right". Fagothey finally refers to the title of a right as the reason for which a particular concrete right exists. According to him, title of a right is the reason for which a particular concrete right exists. According to him, title establishes a connection between the subject and the matter of a right is seen. Fagothey illustrated this saying that a person has a right to own property in general, but this right is abstract, not specifying any particular piece of property.[44]

---

[44] A. Fagothey., Right and Reason: Ethics in Theory and Practice , Ohio, Meril Publ. Co, 1989, p. 230.

Something is necessary to give this particular person rather than someone else the right to give this particular piece of property to change the abstract into a concrete right. These are however limited to political and civil rights.

Nevertheless, in contrast, others argue for a more flexible definition of human rights that focuses not so much on the restricted context of post-war usage as on the continuing idea that have historically been central to the concept of human and social justice in various societies.

These differing conceptions are central to the definition human rights. The foundation of contemporary concept of human rights and that of its adoption by the United Nations in 1948 marked the beginning of the Human Rights that has redefined our understanding of ethics and justice.

However, questions over the impact of the UNDR on the status of colonized people arose even while the declaration of purporting it to be a "Magna Charta for Humanity" which was being drawn up at a time when half of the world's population was still under colonial domination as inescapable.

Perhaps to address this odd reality and remove any ambiguity over whether the provisions of the Declaration applied to colonized people, the drafters of the Declaration included a clause that stated quite categorically thus: "The rights set fort in this Declaration apply equally to all inhabitants and non-self governing territories."[45]

However, on the public discussion over the contemporary notions of Human Rights and the Charter centred on the affirmation concerning the "rights of all peoples to choose the form of government under which they will live. This statement excited the hopes of colonial nationalists everywhere, who saw it as an unequivocal recognition of their right to self-determination and independence. In any case, they cautiously welcome the charter, fearing that its ideals would turn out to be mere platitudes. The Charter has been indeed useful since its adoption and has remained useful human instrument nobly conceived for the application of justice and Human Rights purposes.

As part of this Charter, participants agreed to establish a commission on Human Rights but before the creation of this commission in 1946, the term Human Rights, as previously noted, had not been a commonly used expression, while the development of Human Rights principles had been

[45] Doc. A/777, United Nations Year Book, London Press, England 1948, p. 465.

occurring for centuries. A universal declaration of rights ranked high on the agenda of this new organization known as the United Nations. However, many governments were reluctant to accept detailed provisions concerning Human Rights.

The commitment to the promotion of Human Rights expressed in the United Nations' Charter was followed by the UNDR in 1948 and the international Human Rights conventions that have come to be collectively known as the International Bill of Rights.[46] The Declaration of independence held certain rights-notably, life, liberty, and pursuit of happiness, as being" self-evident" And a key part of the U.S. Constitution, placed immediately after the articles defining the mechanical functioning of the newly formed U.S government, became known as the bill of Rights.

The Bill of Rights consist of the first ten amendments to the body of the Constitution which specifies certain civil and political rights.

For instance, in the First Amendment, government shall make no law respecting an establishment of religion or prohibiting the free exercise of religion. Government may not abridge the freedom of speech, or the press, or the right of the people peaceably to assemble. The people also have the right to petition the government for a redress of grievances. These conventions, which were subsequently complemented at regional levels in Europe, America, and Africa, today constitute the core indicators of contemporary international Human Rights standards. In the early twentieth century, World War I and its aftermath brought greater attention to humankind's interdependence. A shared desire to condemn warfare and develop institutional frameworks for international cooperation took form. Establishment of the League of Nations and the International Labour Organisation and the inception of social welfare organisations such as the International Conference of Social Welfare reflected this new mood of international, regional, and national collaboration.

Among social workers, the establishment of intergovernmental organisations such as the International Committee of Schools of Social Work

---

[46] These Include the International Covenants on Civil and Political Rights and the International Covenant on Social and Cultural Rights, which came into effect in 1976. The regional Conventions include the American Declaration on the Rights and Duties of Man; the European Convention on the Protection of Human Rights and Fundamental Freedoms; and the African Charter for Human and people's Rghts, also known as the Banjul Charter.

and the International Permanent Secretariat of Social Workers his parallel to collaboration. This international promotion of social work formed a key concept that social work values could transcend borders; a notion that would manifest itself in the drafting of the Universal Declaration a few years later. However, while concepts of Human Rights issues occurred, despite recognizing the dangers of war, especially after the immense destruction caused by World War I, Europe became almost immediately embroiled once again in armed battle. Budding international organizations faltered owing to limited support and no real enforcement powers. For instance, the League of the Nations which are owing to the limited support and real enforcement power is there to act wisely.

While construction of the Declaration might appear to have been primarily a project of Europe and United States, this was not the case.

Other regions of the world had developed their own laws, principles, and religions that in many ways had much in common with concepts eventually included in the Universal Declaration. In spite of disagreements over the precise origins of the idea of Human Rights, what is evident is that the contemporary meaning of Human Rights had evolved over the years. The naturalist philosophies of the sixteenth century, the bourgeois revolutions of the seventeenth and eighteenth centuries, the socialist and Marxist revolutions of the twentieth century and the anti colonialist revolutions that began after the Second World War have all combined to broadly define the modern concept of Human Rights.

Concerning the contemporary idea of human rights Ibhawoh Bonny said:

> It stems from a universalization of rights defined through a political process by international agreements. Indeed, most contemporary studies on rights refer specifically to " Human Rights"and define them as those embodied in the UNDR and its subsequent conventions.[47]

These ideas of the rights of man played a key role in the late eighteenth and nineteenth-century struggles against political absolutism in Europe.

They also deeply influenced the Western world from the seventeenth to nineteenth centuries, provoking a wave of revolutionary agitation that swept across America and Europe. They inspired documents such as the English

[47] B. Ibhawoh., Imperialisms and Human Rights, Colonial Discourses of Rights and Liberties in African History. New York 2007, p. 13.

Petition of Rights, the United States Declaration of Independence, and the French Declaration of Independence, and equally the French Declaration of the Rights of man and citizens. These three documents were based on the image of autonomous man endowed with certain inalienable rights.

However, this idea of universal inalienable rights as actually enshrined in the UNDR did not emerge as a bolt out of the blue or develop in a vacuum; rather, it was an expansion and re-articulation of earlier traditions of rights.

Human rights for P. Nherere those claims and entitlements that one has, as one of the rights, against society as represented by government and its officials, and which rights inhere in the holder by virtue, simply and purely of his or her being a human being, and which override all other claims and rights that do not have the same status of Human Rights.[48]

Human Rights, therefore, contemporarily speaking, is so to say, the right each human being has to personal freedom or integrity. "Rights"sometimes occupy the same semantic field with the nearly synonymous terms," " freedom"and liberties.' 'What seems to have confused the definition of rights are the attempts by philosophers, political theorists, and practitioners to theorize, specify, and justify a special category of fundamental or essential rights that pertain to individuals simply by virtue of their humanity.

This confusion poses significant conceptual challenges regarding the meaning of rights. The word 'right' is derived from Latin word *rectus* which in the noun form means that to which a person has just valid claim, be it land, a thing, or the privilege of doing something or saying something. We have what is called a legal right which is either the liberty (protected by law) or acting or abstaining from acting in a specific manner, or the power (enforced by law) of compelling a specific person to do or abstain from doing a particular thing.

A legal right is thus the capacity residing in one man or group of men, to control a thing with the assent and assistance of the state, the actions of the other.[49]

---

48 Cf. P. Nherere., 'The Philosophical, Moral and Historical Basis of Human Rights'in Saiwa L.A., (eds) (1997) Human Theories and Practices: Summaries of Lectures delivered at the African Human Rights Camp, 1996 in Zimbabwe, p. 3.

49 C.A. Oputa., Human Rights in the Political and Legal Culture of Nigeria, 2nd Idigbe Memorial Lectures, Lagos, 1988, pp. 38-39. see Nwabueze., B.O., Constitutionalism in

That word "Human" has been defined as pertaining to, characteristic of, or having the nature of mankind, moral and rational creatures.

Human Rights are therefore rights which all persons everywhere and at all times equally have by virtue of being moral and rational creatures.

They are inherent in any human being simply because of his humanity-the birth-right of all mankind. The expression"Ruman Rights" in its widest connotation embraces those civil, political, economic, social, cultural, group, solidarity, and development rights which are considered, indispens-able to a meaningful human existence.[50]

For Eze on Human Rights in Africa, "Right" in this scenario is used in a composite sense and it includes both moral and legal rights. Legal human rights are those Human Rights that are guaranteed by positive law *(Lex lata),* while moral human rights are claims which ought to be in the positive law (Lex feranda). Thus Human Rights have been defined as representing demands or claims which individuals or groups make on society, some of which are protected by law and have become part of *lex lata* which remain as aspirations to be attained in future.[51]

Constitutions and other codes do not create Human Rights but declare and preserve existing rights. Perhaps, this is why statutory positions for the first generation Human Rights are couched in negative terms.

For instance, to say that no person shall be deprived of his personal lieberty presupposes that personal liberty is an existing right. In this meaning, Ezeagu C. said:

> Human Rights, are inherent rights to be enjoyed by all human beings of the global village and gifts to be withdrawn, withheld or granted at someone's whim or will. That means, in this sense they are said to be inalienable or imprescriptible. When they are removed from any human being, he will become less than human. They are part of the very nature of a human being, and attach to all human beings every-where in all societies, just as much as do his arms and legs.[52]

---

the Emergent States (London: C., hurst and Co. Ltd), 1973.

50 Cf. O. N. Ogbu., Rights Law and Practise, Nigeria, (Enugu, CIDJAP, Publishers, 1999, p. 2.

51 Cf.O.C. Eze., Human Rights in Africa: Some Selected Problems (Lagos, 1984, Chap. 2.

52 C. Ezeagu., Law and Human Rights, Deliberated on the issue of 'Understanding Human Rights Law in Nigeria' Vanguard News Paper, Oct., 2012, p. 35.

It is note worthy to remember that the end of the Second World War 1939-1945 marked the dawn of a new age rights.

Since the adoption of the United Nations Universal Declaration of Human Rights (UNDR) soon after the war in 1948, the subject of rights has become a theme of dominant language for many people around the globe as well as the language of choice for making and contesting entitlement claims. We could also ascertain that UNDR was a groundbreaking document. The was because the idea that underlined it is that all human beings are entitled to some basic inalienable rights by virtue of their humanity which marked a shift from earlier notions of rights, because, at least in theory, it was applicable to everyone irrespective of gender, race, and social status. Many atrocities being committed by people led to a growing acknowledgement that all human beings are entitled to a basic level of rights and that states and societies have a duty to protect and promote these rights.[53] That means, the protection of right and human dignity should always be upheld and cherished at any point in time in each individual's life. The new post war international consciousness of the need to protect the basic rights of all peoples by means of some universally acceptable parameters partly influenced the 1945 Charter of the United Nations; which reaffirmed a faith in fundamental human rights, in the dignity and worth of the human person, in the equal rights of men and women of every nation.

It is also stated that the United Nations' commitment to fostering the development of friendly relations among nations is based on the respect for the principle of equal rights and self-determination for all people and promotion of human rights and fundamental freedoms for all without distinction as to status, sex, language or religion.[54] However, the concept or notion of human rights, is one juristic concept that evades an apt definition.

In 1945, the nations of the world realized and expressed in the Charter of the United Nations, that future peace of the world depended on guaranteeing to every man, woman and child certain fundamental human rights, liberties and freedoms.

---

53 Cf. B.Ihhawoh., Imperialism and human Rights op.cit., p. 12.

54 Cf. Article 1 of the Charter of the United Nations. The main significance of the UNDR is that it took the unprecedented step of identifying a core set of rights to which every person is entitled by virtue of being human and acknowledging that the protection of these rights is a global responsibility.

In a succession of Declarations and Charters, continent upon the globe, those rights and freedoms have been enshrined as among the most precious aspirations of the people on almost every continent of the world.

Civil and political rights are essentially conceptualized as checks on the abuse of state power, and include the rights to privacy, free movement, personal liberty, free association, freedom of the thought, conscience and religion, and equality before the law.

Human rights have been described by naturalist School of jurisprudence as inalienable and proceeding from the laws of nature and not as gift of any civil authority. The philosophical foundations of human rights are traceable to the Natural Law theories of the early times. In their view, nature endowed man with certain rights that protect and preserve the sacredness of the human person as inviolable, equal to his fellow man, free and independent.

The Natural Law Theory emphasises the universal nature of the right of man. As Niall Mc Dermot said:

> Human rights are part of the common heritage of all mankind without discrimination on grounds of race, status, religion or certain differences. These rights, common to all mankind, have a long history, many of them finding their origin in religious teachings. But now, in our lifetime, they have been formulated more fully than ever before and agreed on by all people from all parts of the world.[55]

The Natural Law Theory of Human Rights has been sometimes severely criticized by the authoritarians as a threat to religious and spiritual authority due to its mishandlings.

We can also say that Fundamental Human Rights are those rights which stands above the ordinary laws of the land and which is antecedent to the political society.

It is precondition to civilized existence.

They are Fundamental Rights because, not only as the very term "fundamental" suggests, are they primary conditions to civilized existence, but unlike ordinary laws of the land which can be freely or changed by the legislature (in the ordinary process of legislations), they cannot be easily altered by the legislature. Their alteration involved especially in cases where they have been written, the same process, which is necessary for alteration of

---

[55] N. Mc Demmott., Opening Address to the International Conference on the Human Rights Education in Rural Enviroments, Lagos- Nigeria, 1985, p. 10.

the constitution itself.[56] The Fundamental Human Rights are primary conditions to any civilized existence.

In societies governed under a written constitution, these rights are not only protected, but are also guaranteed by that constitution.

In the case of fundamental Human Rights, they can neither be suspended, nor even curtailed, except in the manner laid down by the constitution; this again applies to those cases where these rights have been written into the constitution. Since these rights derived their guarantee from the constitution, it follows, therefore, that provisions of the ordinary laws of the land which conflict with, or are repugnant to them, must at least reflect the extent of the conflict or repugnancy; otherwise that could be void.

It follows necessarily also, that since these rights are guaranteed under the constitution, no government functionary, be it legislative, executive or judicial, can act in contravention of such rights, and this, of course, underlies the well known legal and quasi political axiom that the constitution of any democratic state or nation is, indeed, its supreme law.[57]

The Universal Declaration of Human Rights did not arise from a vacuum. Early civilizations produced religious codes that established standards of conduct for fairly homogeneous groups within limited territorial jurisdictions. By requiring people to treat fellow humans with dignity, help and provide for by one another's needs, many religions are precursors to Human Rights.[58]

Nevertheless, comptemporarily, rights, like laws, are viewed not as a body of immutable rules, institutions, and procedures but seen as dynamic historical formations that are shaped by economic, political, and social processes. It is clearly known that ever since the ancient times, philosophers have written about equality and justice.

---

56 Cf. C. Ndibe., Justice, Fundamental Rights Provisions to the Constitutions, All Nigeria Judges Conference Papers, London1982. In our world, official agents are paradigmically exemplified by governments and their agents and agencies. A paradigmatic instance of official disrespect of human rights is, then, their violation by a government. Governments may do so by issuing or maintaining unjust laws or orders that authorize or require human-rights violations or they may do so " under color of law,"that is, by perversely construing existing legislation as licensing human-rights violating policies.

57 Cf. J. A.Van der Van., S. J. Dreyer., et al, Is There A God of Human Rights? Pretoria, p. 36.

58 National Coordinating Committee for UNHR 50 1998 Franklin and Eleanor Roosevelt Institute home page (0nline). See www.udhr50.org/historyimeline.htm

These great thinkers, including Plato and Socrates, more than two thousand years ago explored the realm of basic inalienable rights of man, which in those times, literally meant "man"[59]

The Greek philosopher, Aristotle, wrote that unjust man is a man who is not content to have an equal share with others. Since unjust thing is the unequal thing, it is obvious that there must be a mean between greater and less inequality; if then the unjust is the unequal, the just is the equal.

In the year 1215, a cornerstone of Human Rights came into existence when English nobles, Bishops, and Archbishops forced the then reigning King John to end the abuses against his subjects. The subjects drafted a document known as the Magna Carta, which King John signed. The Magna Carta, prohibited a sovereign from taking property without due process and the detaining of his subjects without legal judgment by their peers-the forerunner of trial by jury. The document also highlighted the importance of family and provided for safety from abusive treatment. Another concept behind the development of Human Rights is natural law, which holds that a certain order in nature provides norms for human conduct, Saint Thomas Aquinas, wrote that natural law was humanity's "participation", in the comprehensive eternal law.[60] People could grasp certain self-evident principles of practical reason, which corresponded to the various goods toward which human nature inclined. Natural law was a standard for human laws: unjust laws in principle did not bind in conscience.

During the seventeenth century, European philosophers advocated for what they viewed as the natural rights of its citizens-the idea that people by their certain basic rights precede the establishment of any government. It is the contention here that rights generally, and Human Rights in particular are best defined and understood within the linguistic and social context of popular usage by the historical actors who employed the language.

On this terrain Rawls said:

---

59 Wronka, J. Human Rights and Social Policy in the 21st Century: A History of the Idea of Human Rights and Comparison of the United Nations Universal Declaration of Human Rights which United States Federal and State Constitutions, Rev. ed. Lanham, Md.: University Press of America, 1998, p. 43.

60 Cf. Hall, K. ed, The Oxford Companion of the Supreme Court of the United States Oxford and New York: Oxford University Press, 1992, p. 581

This concept of natural rights went beyond theoretical views of man and society and aimed at establishing actual rules of conduct. Initially, these natural rights focused on freedom of the press, with subsequent attention to freedom of thought in politics and religion. abolition of slavery and more human treatment of criminals also formed part of the natural rights movement and royalty.[61]

The uprising in the eighteenth century against government and royalty in France and the American colonies engendered considerable discussion as to how nations should treat its citizens.[62]

There is non-interference by the state in areas affected by contemporary Human Rights notions such as freedom of speech, freedom of the press, freedom of lifestyle, freedom of religion and the right to own property.[63] In all of the primitive idea of divine justice, one discerns the supernatural envisaged as eternal power with man as the buffeted recipient which favours punishment. Seeing religion as it is justice in the ancient Greece, it is crystal clear as the idea of reason that came from Heraclitus about 501-504 B.C showing the religious conviction to mean the most real thing of all, as the soul's most distinctive and important attribute for wisdom or thought.

Based on this conviction, God is reason and since God is the one permeating all things, Heraclitus believes that God is the Universal which holds all things in unity and orders all things to move and change in accordance with thought or principle.

And these thoughts constitute the essence of law as Stumpf remarked that God as reason, is therefore, the universal law insofar as they possess God of fire in their own natures and thereby possess the capacity for thought.[64]

On the Stoics' ideology and the theory of natural law, Stumpf also explicatively opined that this concept provided the basis for the stoics' idea

---

61 Rawls. J.,\ S. Freeman., (ed.), Collected Pappers, quoting Cicero – On Justice and Reciprocity, Political Liberalism , Justice as Fairness, Distributive Justice, Justice and Fairness to Goodness, Cambridge Press, London, 1999. p. 11f.

62 Cf. Reichert. E., Social Work and Human Rights, A Foundation for Policy and Practice, Columbia University Press- New York,2003, pp. 20-26.

63 Cf. R. Alexy., Theorie der Grundrechte, Baden-Baden 2001, in Van der Ven, Is There a God of Human Rights? , 2001 p. 98.

64 E.S., Stumpf Philosophy, History and Problems, McGraw Hill Book Company, New York Press, USA, 1971, p. 13.

of cosmopolitanism, the idea that all men are equally citizens of the world and precisely because they all share in the one God's reason.

It was this concept too which formed the foundation for the classic theory of natural law, which are with some variations, which had a continuous impact upon western thought and political practices. It was preached by the Stoics and adapted by early and medieval Christian theologians who became a dynamic force in the American revolution, and is even in modern times a vital theory of the nature of law.

A. SOPHISTS

They actually emerged a century later, compared different customs and civilizations and also questioned whether the gods were really sacred and inviolable.

They later concluded that these were the creatures of man and like gods and his conventions, therefore capable of change. Consequently, they oriented Greek thought and ideas to a form of humanism and challenged the thinking of their time by posing such questions as: are the distinctions between Greeks and barbarians, between slaves and masters, based upon evidence or simply upon prejudice?

Protagoras of Abdera was the oldest and, in many ways, the most influential of the Sophists who taught in Athens.

He brought the ideas of justice into a humanistic frame work by saying that man is the measure of all things, of the things that are, that they are, and of the things that are not; they are not.[65]

Knowledge for Pythagoras, is limited to our various perceptions and these perceptions differ from one another.

He then contended that change was an illusion and not a fact (illustrated by the paradoxes of Parmenides and Zeno Elas). This resulted in the ultimate reduction and absurdum by Zeno's pupil Gorgias; that if the being is infinite and eternal, it cannot be located in a particular space and time and therefore cannot exist, that is being and nothing would then be the same.

The argument, of course, made the point that justice could vary in different places and times. For this Pythagoras school of thought is of the

[65] Cf. Protagoras in "Theaetetusl", 152a (refer to Plato's dialogue).

opinion that the idea of justice was relative and permanently changing, and this point of view led them to the following conclusions:

> That the rules for moral conducts are fashioned deliberately by each community and have relevance and authority only for the people in that community. That moral conduct is unnatural and that humanity abides by such rules only because of "peer pressures' 'and "public opinion." Thus if all actions could be kept private, even the "good"would not act morally."[66]

That the essence of justice is power, or that "might is right;"thus the Sophist's response to the question 'what is the good life?'would have to be 'the life of pleasure.

Around the fifth century B.C., Herodotus in his history and Aeschylus in his plays, depicted man as a puppet but with some minor degree of choice while Zeus was presented as the punisher of overwhelming ambition so that justice now acquires a pattern of man's free will.

B. PYTHAGORIANS

The ancient Pythagoreans accepted that justice was to be found in equality, a notion which has remained a very important component of the ideal of justice. Equality here designates the ability to share or to distribute properly. Where there are burdens to be borne, they should be laid on those everyone, or on those capable of bearing them, or at least on the relatively many shoulders on those best to be able to bear them. The problem, however, was to determine what ought to be actually adopted in a given circumstance. Where could one draw the equality line?

QUANTITATIVELY OR QUALITATIVELY?

In the attempt to solve this all too common applications, the notion of reciprocity, interpreted to mean "an eye for an eye", standard of retaliation evolved.

The Nigeria scenario, might be interesting to observe that the traditional Igbo society had resolved this dilemma through its communal reverence to *Ala (earth,)* and the concept of social responsibility.

---

[66] Cf. Protagoras in " Theaetetusl", 152a (refer to Plato's dialogue).

C. PLATO

For him justice is only one of those things that receive the honour of a treasure of ten books. In the Republic, the first book constitutes a dialogue which starts with a moral and political question like what is Jusitce? Can it be defined? From these questions, clear answers were given but the argument ends in the manner of the other ethical dialogues. But the dilemma this time must be solved. Justice, the supreme virtue, must be defined in and for itself.

He placed justice within the soul, a virtue in which case is being balanced against a definition of the corresponding vice.[67]

Plato marks a profound difference in his attempt to systematically organise the meaning of justice, in distinction to Hesoid and other ancient poets in pre-literary Greek history that exploited the symbol of the word for dramatic purposes. In this case, it then becomes clear to the question being asked in relation to what justice is all about. What actually is the basis of social and moral obligations? Why should it be law-abiding or morally inclined?

How is it in certain things if one is not interested on the moral codes? And this could simply be put as so to say, why should one be good or be doing good?

One notices that there are paradoxes in Plato's justice, perhaps no philosophical attempt to formulate such a conception can never escape them. They illuminate the intermediary nature of his role in Greek cultural history and the mediating quality of his genius, poised between an oral past fast disappearing and a literate consciousness now coming to its own.

This is especially true of his political justice which asserts one "to do one's own thing."But what is that one's own thing?"No operative answer seems possible and the formula does not seem explicable except in its own terms.

It merely insist that the citizen do properly what is in fact, right and it is expected of one, we might say, one's assigned role. Who or what could have assigned it, unless it be the existing life-style of the social dimensions, within which he is living? Equally for Havelock, one would prefer a society where the need for adjustments required to preserve or restore propriety which does not exist. His justice becomes the symbol of unchanging sta-

67 Plato, the Republic, Bk, 4, 43, 432b ff (Penguim Classics, 1974, p. 202ff.

bility.[68] Whenever Plato processes to implant justice in the human soul, he leaves a definition which is clinched in the following paragraph thus:

> In reality, justice pertains not to the outward action (performed) upon one (concern), but to the inner, that which really pertains to oneself and to the self's concern; the individual avoids allowing the elements (gene) in the soul to mind each other's businness and get involved with each other; he actually makes a proper disposition of what is personal to him (oikeia); he personally assumes command of and organizes himself and becomes friends to himself; becoming in all respects one out of many.[69]

In another aspects, there is a difference between acting on deliberate choice, acting from a generous impulse, and acting on animal appetite.

However, Plato's answer to the question "what is justice?" is that in the individual it consists in keeping a proper balance between three elements namely, intellect, ambition and physical desire. These must all have their due and proper fulfilment, and find their proper place in the good life.

This means Plato's solution to the problem is individual morality.

True morality consists, in giving due satisfaction to the different elements in us and preventing any of them from dominating at the expense of others. If justice does not apply to outward action, it becomes an inner and private condition and morality of the self but not society.

In a way, the conception of justice as the symbol of a purely personal morality gives room for varied interpretations.

Havelock maintains that Plato's moral philosophy cannot shake off paradox. Plato's description of political justice was conservative and in many respects avoided a sharp break with traditional notions. The Platonic ideal of justice was the concrete harmony of the State.

Plato's just state was that in which every man does the job to which he was best fitted under the direction of the wisest.

The just man is he, who performed the task or function proper to him in accordance to his place in the society.[70] But following the hierarchical order, Plato understands the meaning of justice through its application to the three classes of people in early Greek society, (philosopher- rulers, soldiers, and workers); each minding their "own business", ultimately in order

---

[68] Cf. A. E., Havelock. The Greek Concept of Justice , p. 320.

[69] Plato, Republic, Bk. 4, 443, C9 ff.

[70] Plato, Republic, Bk.4, 10, 433a

to find out how each person could order his own life, by respecting the functions and needs of each component as part of one's nature (reason, will and emotion)." ... and further we have often heard it said and even so often said to ourselves that justice consists in minding our own business and not interfering with other people."[71] This does not always follow in certain circumstances and occasions in a lively community.

D. ARISTOTLE

His theory of morality revolves around his belief that man, as everything in nature had a distinctive "end"to achieve or has a function to fulfil. He then began his Nichomachean Ethics by asserting that: "every art and every investigation, and similarly every action and pursuits considered to aim at some good. Hence, the Good has been rightly defined as that act which all things aim at"[72]

Regarding this type of postulation, we are led to ask the question, "what is the good at which human behaviour aims? "

Plato answered this question in his "Doctrine of Ideas,"where he said and maintained that this supreme principle of good was separated from the world of experience and from individual man and was to be arrived at by the mind's ascent from the visible world to the intelligible world.

Aristotle, on the other way round maintains that the principle of good and right was embedded within each man.

Moreover this principle could be discovered by studying the essential nature of man and could be attained through one's actual behaviour in daily life.[73]

He distinguishes himself in the realm of ethics by bringing it down to practical life. But there cannot be a universal good such as Plato held to be the culmination of his Theory of Forms.[74] On this very point, Aristotle's theory of justice differs from that of Plato which has to be seen and understood.

---

[71] Plato, Republic, Bk4, 433a, b (p. 204, Penguin Classics, 1974).

[72] Aristotle, Nichomachean Ethics, Penguin Classics, 1976, (Ed., J.A.K. Thomson); Bk. 1, I, 1094ai.

[73] Aristotle , Nichomachean Ethics, Bk. 1. 1094a1-22.

[74] Cf. Aristotle, Bk. 1, vi.

In his Metaphysics, he sharply criticized Plato's "Doctrine of Ideas."[75] Although he does not give much time or space to the idea of justice as Plato does, but he Aristotle makes it known in several places in his

writings that all men cling to justice of some kind, and states clearly in the "Ethics" that "there is more than one kind of justice."[76] For example, that involving "the rightly framed law"which is a complete virtue, but not absolutely, but in relation to our neighbour. In *Rhetorics*, he gives it some content by saying what justice is: "The virtue which assigns to each man his due in confirmity with the law, while injustice is a vice whereby "man claims what belongs to others in opposition to law."[77] Aristotle believes that man is a political and social animal, who "alone has the sense of just and unjust,"and he sought to reconcile justice with the conflicts he observes about him. Differently from Plato, he makes justice a human concern. Aristotle, however concedes that a common element runs through all these, which he characterizes a proper proportion or relationship between individuals. Elsewhere, he considers it as "treating equals, equally and unequal unequally but in proportion to their relevant differences." Aristotle's view is that retributive justice employs geometrical proportion.

A just act necessarily involves at least focus terms, two persons for whom it is meant to be a fact, and two shares in justice is exhibited. And there will be in the same ratio to one another as the persons, for if the persons are not equal, they will not have equal shares; and it is when equals have or are assigned unequal shares, or people who are not equal in equal shares, that quarrels and complaints break out.

So, justice is a sort of proportion, and injustice is the opposite.

The man who acts unjustly gets too much and the victim of injustice gets too little of what is good. It is then the duty of the law to:

consider the difference caused by the injury of injustice; and it treats the parties as equals, only as king where one has committed and the other suffered an injustice, or whether one has inflicted and the other suffered a hurt. Accordingly, the judge tries to equalize the in- equality of this injustice."[78]

---

[75] Aristotle, Bk, Vbii, 110b.

[76] Aristotle, Rhetoric, 1366b.

[77] Aristotle, Nichomechean Ethics, Bk. V, ii, (1130a18-b8).

[78] Aristotle, Ethics Bk. V. ii, 1130b.

This is the more reason why in the case of dispute, people have recourse to judge who acts as a divider or an intermediary between the two parties to secure a mean.

As such, the just must be a mean, equal and relative.

In 'Ethics', Aristotle initially divides 'the just into the lawful and equal or fair. These are, respectively, his universal or general (legislative), and a particular (judge- made decisions in individuals case).

The legislative type of justice requires obedience to the law, and therefore comprehends a civic virtue. Judicial decions are distinguished from morality and are divided into distributive and corrective, that is' 'the distribution of honour, wealth, and the other divisible assets of the community, and that which supplies a corrective principle in private transactions. This corrective principle is still further subdivided into those acts and relations which are voluntary and those which are involuntary. The examples of this he gave as referring respectively to commercial dealings, and then to personal crimes or upon one or the involuntary made for a particular incident. Aristotle's main concern is with the particular and corrective or remedial type of justice in which the judge's task is to redress and not to punish. He further regards justice as embracing, many if not all the other virtues, including a relation to persons as well as to things; involving a just distribution of the latter, and a fair meting out of punishment.

Further, equal reciprocity since this does not apply to either distributive or retributive justice in this meaning. The Pythagoreans had held justice "simply as having done to one what one has done to another. Aristole also reasonably remarked: "if an official strikes someone, it is wrong for him to be struck in return, and if someone strikes an official it is right for him not only to be struck in return but to be punished as well. Again, it makes a difference whether the act was voluntary or involuntary, (from the stand point of the injured party).

It is proportional requital that holds the state together.

Aristotle also maintains in his "Politics" that equals should be treated alike but unequals proportionally to their relevant differences and all with impartiality whereby justice would be understood and served.

It is the view of Bodenheimer that Aristotle's tying of justice to diverse human situations may be termed the most distinguishing feature of his disagreement with Plato's central idea of justice as harmony.[79] Concerning Human Right for Thomas Aquinas, the subject of justice is nothing but right.

This is to say that 'justice'unequivocally is the recognition of the worth, dignity and humanity of the other. However it could be noticed from all these clarifications that justice and human right have been used to designate many other things different from these ontological meanings.

The dictionary of philosophy gives more lights of what justice and injustice is all about thus:

justice and human injustice are normative concepts of morality which play a great part in socio-political consciousness. It is a combination of several phenomena considered from the point of view of how good and evil are 'distributed' from and among people.[80]

This shows that the misinterpretation of what justice means leads to its misuse. Moreover, justice as the name implies, is making sure that the unequal is treated equally; that is egalitarianism of which the inverse is injustice. Justice undoubtedly does pertain to man's righteousness not only to do the just thing but also to be just as well. Justice and Human Rights have macrocosmic (state) and microcosmic (individual) perspectives. Considering it microcosmically, justice and human rights exists when each one works at the craft (as the only and exclusively) for which nature best fits an individual. Be this as it may, each in his own areas of specialization should be performing well enough.

This means each minding his own 'business'and (talent) without encroaching into or interfering with other people's things or rights.

That is the meaning, the question of avoiding harm, envy or constituting or being a stumbling block in another persons own field. That is the more reason why justice is the virtue between two extremes gain and loss. Let us peruse succinctly too into the pre-Thomistic meaning and definition of justice in the western tradition and some other kinds of definitions in our contemporary era.

In the pre-Thomistic period and the meaning of justice, the Greeks have it as political term when it concerns life in the state. Justice for Greeks could be said to mean harmony or square number and proportionality.

---

79 E. Bodenheimer., Jurisprudence, New York, Press, USA1940, p. 47.

80 I. Frolor., (ed.), Dictionary of Philosophy, Moscow 1967, p. 208.

Also, earlier before, Plato especially with some philosophers in Greece have different meanings of justice. Some of these prominent philosophers are Callicle and Thrasmachus. They observed that natural justice is the right of the strong man and legal justice is merely a barrier which multitude of weaklings put up to save themselves. Nevertheless, Thrasymachus argued justice as only the interest of the stronger.

Plato's own conception of justice is linked with the theory of state. He sees its function like a wheel-hob that holds spokes of a bicycle together.

Justice is regarded here as a dual-virtue where the highest good, the state with its members are conserved. Aristotle's notion of justice is a state of mind of what is just. For the Epicureans justice is regarded as only a consent which is supposed to take place in mutual intercourse from time to time. Roman law regards justice as a sense of positive law.

A Roman personal holds that: "Justice is affixed and biding in which one is given his own due."[81] The emphasis here is stressed more on something that is really on one's own belonging. It is the practical recognition of the other person as person and possessors of right.

In comparism with Augustine's own theory and conviction, the virtue of justice is spoken in many different ways and a particular lustre is also attached to the following formulation when he said that, justice'as the ordering of souls by virtue of which it comes to pass that we are no man's servant but servants of God.

This is true of the already quoted above statement; that the most sober and factual of all and which says 'justice'is the virtue which enables man to give each one what is his due.[82]

But, what is each man's due? How does anything come to belong to a person at all? And factually speaking, how could a thing so truly belong to a person that every man and every human authority has to grant it to him and allow him to keep it?

---

81 G. Sabine., History of Political Theory, (4th ed.) Illinois, 1973, p. 167. See also the " Black Ausrtralia's Fight for Rights' ', One World (Geneva, 69, 1981, p. 12ff, cited by J.S.Mbiti, "Contemporary on 'Sacred Sites'in R.A. Evans., and A.F. Evans., Human Rights: Adialogue Between the First and Thrid World's. Maryknoll: Orbis Press, 1983, pp. 119ff. Orbis, 1983, pp. 119ff. cited by J.S.Mbiti, "Contemporary on 'Sacred Sites'in R.A. Evans., and A.F. Evans., Human Rights.

82 Cf. St. Augustine, Concerning the City of God against the Pagans, by Hery Bettenson,; ed. by D. Knowles, Middlesex. Pequim Books, Bk. X1X, 1972, p. 881.

In Augustine's theory, therefore, the state should render every one his due. And as Cicero has it, justice has its origin in law in natural force, the mind and reason with which the intelligent man measures justice and injustice. He further explained that justice has its root in nature; and nature; itself is governed by reason of the mortal gods.

It then stands clear as that natural equality of men which cements their fellowship because men are basically the same; sharing the same natural sense of justice everywhere. So, justice is the will of man's power to choose the good which the sense desires are concerned.

John Rawls in his own view presents justice and fairness as analytic construction when he said that Justice and fairness are, indeed, different concepts, but they share a fundamental element in common, which could be called reciprocity.[83]

One can also, *inter-alia,* say that justice takes into account man's social nature and makes sure that in our choice of goods, we will serve the reasonable good of other human beings. Thomas Aquinas cleverly derived most of his philosophical tenets from the nature of man and followed the political theory of Aristotle that man is by nature a social animal who need justice and fair-play among other necessities. He therefore described justice like other virtues and as a habit; that is, the principles of a good acts which needs to be defined by the means of good act clearly seen as a matter proper to the virtue of justice.

The proper matter of justice consists in the things that have to do with other relationship with other men. In his conviction, he conclusively believes that justice means, "rendering to each one his right."regarding the different kinds of justice namely, legal, distributive, commutative, moral, commutative, organisational, retributive, social, spatial justice will be treated in the foregoing chapters. Aquinas specially pointed out that justice is a moral virtue which induces man to recognise the good of his own neighbour.[84]

The common good of all virtues whether in relation to ourselves or in their relation to others is always referable to common good. Therefore, all acts of virtue directs one to the common good. Aquinas' main view is that

---

83 Cf. J. Rawls.,/ S. Freeman., (ed.), Collected Pappers, quoting Cicero – On Justice and Reciprocity, Justice as Fairness, Distributive Justice, Justice and Fairness to Goodness, Cambridge Press, London, 1999. p. 10.

84 78. Aquinas, T., Summa Theologiae, IIa- Iiae Qtn. 58 Art. 1.

justice is actually the primary virtue in relation to the other virtues. But since law directs to the common good, justice directs this generally to legal justice. It is the legal justice which directs man to the common good that immediately mediates between the goods of the individuals.

Human agents also therefore are not to collaborate in upholding a coercive institutional order that avoidably restricts the freedom of some issues so as to render their access to basic necessities insecure without compensating for their collaboration by protecting its victims or by working for its reform.

These rights are from the original core of the Universal Declaration of Human Rights of 1948 of which a fundamental article reads: "Everyone has the right to life, liberty and security of persons."[85]

Having seen the contemporary notion of human rights and justice respectively, let us then have a look at classification of justice and human rights.

85 United Nations Universal Declaration of Human Rights Fundamental Art. 3.

1.2

Classifications of Justice and Human Rights

In our focus here, we will elucidate first and foremost, the classifications of justice and equally its subdivisions by Thomas Aquinas and succinctly, to be included with Aristotle's theory of ethics pertaining to justice after which we come over to the issue of the classification of Human Rights. Justice for Aquinas remains a virtue and a principle of good act, as we have seen in the early chapters of this work.

Aquinas classified justice into these three major divisions:

a) when it refers to private individuals collectively as members of the State.
b) when it is legal, it moves from the collectivity to the individual members concerned;
c) when these are connected with private persons and the justifications connecting private persons, it is therefore termed variance.

Aquinas also made us to know and to understand the other different classes or kinds of justice in these various forms.

A. Commutative Justice

Commutative justice is a kind of justice relating to the exchange of something in a mutual, interchangeable or reciprocal order.

This inclines people to respect and have a good regard to everything which does not belong to them. So, here in Aquinas' meanings of justice, one realises that justice like law, is no respecter of persons but something to be done in all righteous manner, in equity and fair-play. It takes an accurate account of our persons and behavioural factors and ethical problems.

Descriptively, The term "commutative" (justice) is derived from the Latin word, '*commutatio*", meaning "exchange."

In other words, it is that justice that regulates the relations between individuals, or groups, it demands respect for the rights of others, and the exchange of things of equal value.

Hence, cheating, fraud, theft, and destruction of other people's properties are violations of commutative justice. "Positively, commutative justice is convened with transactions involving property values, contracts, buying and selling, and the exchange of goods and services. Here, the emphasis is on the due respects of the property values (goods), of the individual, and not primarily the common good. Negatively, commutative justice concerns itself with damages done to the person or property of another through negligence or malice." When St. Thomas Aquinas gives a definition of justice as rendering to everyone what is his due, he is implicitly referring to commutative justice.

In other words, if a person collects goods worth one thousand Naira (N1,000.00) on credit from a business store, he is obliged by commutative justice to return the equivalence of those goods in capital within the time specified. He has broken (commutative) justice, if he were, on returning, insist on paying less than one thousand naira (1,000.00), Then, he is in addition, obliged by commutative justice, in term of promise (credit), and engagements based on mutual agreements. The transferred right produces corresponding obligation of returning the payment on the appointed time; and under the pain of flouting commutative justice done. Here, there is also a relationship between commutative justice and distributive justice. This relationship is better illustrated using a labour contract. In the first place, the labour contract seems to involve an agreement between individuals.

Thus, the employer being obliged by commutative justice to his employee to pay a just wage corresponding to his work. If the former fails to do so by taking advantage of his superior bargaining power, he is violating the principles of commutative justice. On the other hand, it may well happen that due to uncontrolled forces of inflations, and poor market conditions, the employer though willing, would be unable to pay the earlier stipulated just or living wage to his workers. In this peculiar case, the employer by allocating a fair share of the profits to his workers would be conforming to commutative justice, even though he was forced to pay substandard salaries in order to remain in business".

It is here that the society, under its legitimate government should do everything possible under distributive justice to bring down the inflation, as to enable the individuals employer to meet up with a living wage.

As we mentioned earlier, the provision of the enabling economic environment in the society, is a veritable aspect of distributive justice. When such favourable atmosphere is restored, the individuals' employer can then meet up with its own part of commutative justice. Here seems to create a meeting point between commutative justice and a distributive justice.

This again re-instates the import of concerted efforts of the individual, on the one hand, and the community, on the other.

This relationship which is essentially communal is built on the principles of "I am" because "we are", and since we are, therefore, "am" , it is also easy to see why laisser-faire individualism can not be subscribed to, for a just society to emerge.

In other words, there is an extent individual effort can go in the overall management of life. For instance, there is no guarantee that under justice-individualism, the problem of limitations and inequalities of human existence can be addressed, since everybody will be on his own, and none, to-co-ordinate their efforts.

And if the situation is allowed to stay, there is no doubt that its ugly efforts will affect almost everybody; ultimately but especially, the least advantaged. How then is the less-privileged of the society to be guaranteed certain amount of rights? Or, are the benefits accruing to them merely from benevolence? In other words, does any right, in form of "justice" belong to the less privileged of the society? Has man any claim to "right" independent of external factor or ascription? We shall examine these and more under "moral justice." It is therefore, unjust for an individual or person to do away with another's belonging either by taking or reaping where one did not sow or a person taking by force whatever that does not specifically belong to him. As justice then inclines one to respect the belongings and property of others, commutative justice considers and regulates these actions of each member of the society in regard to what others consider as mere parts. Commutative justice also regulates and guides the actions and duties of one another and so in his regard to that of others. It is also based on men and their duties and relationships towards the others and their final ends.

Man as man is bound to attain his personal and private natural ends out of the ground of commutative justice. This he does by aiming at his own perfection, a duty and obligation to respect that of the others in order to enable them too to reach their own natural respective ends.

B. LEGAL JUSTICE

Legal justice means according to law or the lawfulness of an act to be justified from the point of view of law.

This legal justice concerns also the punishment of the wrong doings and the redress or justification of injury and right through the creation and enforcement of a public set of rules. Legal justice stipulates the condition under which penalty may be inflicted and making the scale of punishment to be equal to fit the nature of different crimes being committed against the people.

As to the sphere of civil law, it regulates the amount of principles for applying the law. Also, this legal aspect of justice makes these statements into common good. Legal justice is sometimes referred to as "general legal justice"; it could be confused with the term "general justice."

Making further explanation in a distinct manner, we have two categories of this legal justice the first is the equity while the other is the common legal justice, the front of the stand point of equity should be taking into account, the special circumstances which qualify the literal precepts of justice.

Judicial decisions are distinguished from morality and are divided into distributive and corrective, that is"the distribution of honour, wealth, and the other divisible assets of the community, and that which supplies a corrective principle in private transactions.

This corrective principle is still further subdivided into:"those acts and relations which are voluntary and those which are involuntary."[86]

The examples of this could be referred respectively to commercial dealings and then to personal crimes or upon one or the involuntary made for a particular incident.

That of common legal justice refers to the exact carrying out of law for the sake of justice within the community.

[86] United Nations Universal Declaration of Human Rights Fundamental Art.3.

And the strict letter of the law that have to be qualified as the demands of equity ought to be examined. Thus, the whole idea of justice unequivocally points to its legality for the good of the other. Another aspect of justice is concerned with the individual's obligation towards the state (community).

Here, the community is pictured as an organic whole, where the individual is merely a part, meant "to contribute his due share towards the welfare of the community, and the promotion of the common good."

Although, this obligation consists primarily in the observance of laws of the state, aimed at the common good, it also binds the individual "to perform acts over and above those prescribed by positive legislation". In other words, legal justice still obliges the individual to perform such "un-legislated" civil duties as casting one's votes, readiness to be voted for, and to accept public offices. It also includes the disposition to accept certain service, and duties considered to be for the public interests.

Legal justice also enjoins one to pay his legitimates taxes, on, and when due. Since "the common good takes precedence over the private interests, legal justice demands that the common good should not be sacrificed for the private interest of the individual, or for his convenience."

The concept of legal justice as enunciated, can easily be used to evaluate certain expressions of justice, (as utilitarianism) that seem to arrogate to a section of community what belongs really to the whole. Legal justice implies that the "whole" is greater than any of its "parts".

C. DISTRIBUTIVE JUSTICE

Distributive justice means the several individuals of a number taken separately, referring individually to all members of a group, what applies to all concerned, it divides or shares and giving to each his own reward or merit. This distributive justice, conceptually speaking, is equally a sharing or a set of principles for choosing between the social arrangements which determine this division and for the underwriting a consensus as to the proper distributive shares in the society. This concerns the distribution of the benefits or burden of a society's matters. It is the regulation of wages and profits, protection of person's rights through the legal system and allocation of welfare benefits.

On certain reasonable grounds, distributive justice applies in a sense of equal proportionality in the distribution of the natural advantages and burdens in the State. What can be the criteria of relevance in the rules to be applied? Since certain ways of distributing things affect the total sum of satisfactions, this fact must be taken into account in arranging social institutions, but according to this principle of distribution, the explanation of common-sense precepts of justice and their seemingly stringent character is that, they are those rules whose experience shows must be strictly respected and not to be departed from, but only under exceptional circumstances if the sum of advantages is to be maximized. In the mind of J. Rawls, the precepts of justice are derivative from the one end of attaining the greatest net balance of satisfactions to the other. There is no reason in principle why the greater gains of some should not compensate for the lesser losses of others; or why the violation of the liberty of a new law 'might'not be made right by the greater part shared by many.[87]

So, distributive justice (or "social justice", as it is often called) is "the counterpart of legal justice". In other words, as the individual is obligated to the society (community); in the same way, the society is obligated to the "individual." Understood in the context of "communication" or "relationship" (already introduced), justice becomes "a two-way traffic", a "contract".

Here, distributive justice implies the way and manner the goods, the privileges, works, and duties are fairly and equitably allocated to all the members of the society. Therefore, it obliges the society, under its government "to allocate equitably the benefits and burdens of the society among the members, not wholly on the basis of a quantitative equality but according to the needs, merits and abilities of its "human components." Hence, the unfair allocation of goods, and service to its member's by the society is a direct violation of distributive justice.

Of course, the principles of distributive justice may be denied by the laissez-faire individualist who claims that the duty of government is to be restricted to defending the subjects against violence, and enforcing the claims of commutative justice. Distributive justice is a society's recognition of the impact of the individuals towards its existence.

---

[87] Cf. J. Rawls., / S. Freeman., On Justice and Reciprocity, "Distributive Justice" Camebridge Press, London p. 3.

It implies that "we-are", because "I am", and therefore, a fair and equitable attention ought to be given to every component of the whole, just because they belong to the whole, and explicitly or implicitly contribute to its very existence. However, the pattern of distribution that ought to be adopted by the community must differ from that obtainable in commercial corporations, towards its shareholders. In commercial corporations the advantages or profits are shared in proportion to each one's contributions to the company's capital and work.

But the ideal communal arrangement based on distributive justice must be public welfare as determined by the relative capacity and the normal needs of its members. Again, each individual has a claim to his just portion of advantages, estimated in some degree at least by the need he has for assistance, and protection of the society.

Distributive justice also imposes certain obligations on the government to see that the enabling economic environment is created as to help the average individuals to realize their highest potentials and happiness. This implies the provision of needed amenities, like rural electrification projects, efficient telephone facilities, good network of road, subsidized system of education and other welfare services.

These are some example of distributive justice, or the society's obligations towards the individuals. In traditional setting, collective efforts are put together to build road, and bridges to clear the paths leading to farms, and the markets. There is also a collective effort in creating (mud and thatch) houses for the individuals; a practice that is often carried out in turns. In this perspective, distributive justice can be rightly called "administrative justice based on a balanced organizational management.

In this context, the individuals' limited efforts are pulled together to achieve a common goal, based on the welfare of each of the members. It is therefore, a system of collaboration of efforts to solve individual problems, based on needs. It is to be emphasized here that the distributive justice is not aimed at establishing "equity" of distribution among the members of the community. Rather, its aspiration is to give "a fair, and equitable distribution of resources within a given social set up. Although "justice" as such, is rooted in "the fundamental equality of all men, demanding equal treatment, equal distribution of goods, rewards, punishment, under normal circumstances", such equality, in actual fact is better considered as "the equality of proportion.

In other words, due to discrepancies, inequalities and varied needs found in every social set up, it is more appropriate to talk of the equitable distribution of resources (based on equality of proportion), than "equal distributions."

In fact, if a segment of the society is in a greater need due to over-marginalisation, and equal allocation is used in the sharing of resources, it will amount to unjust distribution (or injustice). Because of its closer emphasis on the component parts of the society, distributive justice is often considered as "social justice".

Of all the known types of justice, "social justice" bears much resemblance with justice-in-communalism. But the emphasis on "co-existence", and the "belongingness" of man as a pre-condition of proper distribution and sharing of resources seems to distinguish the latter from the former.

Distribution for example of the tax revenues, social services benefits, income etc., might be organised equitably on any aspects; at least on three principles of justice, mathematical equality, merit and need.

Aristotle's view is also that distributive justice should employ geometrical proportion. It is then the duty of the law to: "consider the difference caused by the injury of injustice; and it treats the parties as equals. Accordingly, a good judge tries to equalize the inequality of this injustice."[88]

This is the more reason why in the case of quarrels or disputes of any kind, people have recourse to a judge who acts as a divider or an intermediary between the two parties to secure a mean. As such, the just must be a mean: equal and relative.

The protection of the basic rights which assures human dignity is of utmost importance especially in the world of today where human rights and human dignity are sometimes abused with wanton impunity and non-challancy in the society. The edict of United Nations and International legal Instrument has it that every individual is entitled to respect for the freedom, liberty, dignity of person and accordingly, no person shall be subjected to torture or to inhuman or degrading treatment. This law provides, that all persons under any form of maltreatment, detention or imprisonment shall be treated in humane manner and with respect for the inherent dignity of

---

[88] Aristotle, Ethics Bk. V. ii, 1130b.

the human person. Respect for human dignity is a critical issue in many countries of the world.[89]

Any human community, including political society is held together by bonds of trust and respect which are made visible and effective in the exercise of responsibility for another.

P. C. Anton upholds the tenets in the basic writings of Thomas Aquinas said thus said that it is this ultimate value that led Aquinas to this clear description of Human Rights although man is of the same genus as other animals, man is of a different species.[90]

On this ground, if no good ground can be shown for treating people differently, they clearly ought to be treated alike. Precisely, this is one of the procedural presuppositions of justice. So, the distribution of common good among individuals in the state could follow these very principles. As a community the distributive justice which is directing the relation of the community to the individual person assures that common good is shared proportionately. Modern psychologists are of the opinion that treating people maliciously or unjustly like beasts might lead them to become beasts in the process. The Aquinas and Aristotle philosophical thoughts on the meaning of justice here retained their unequivocal signification namely, 'giving each his or her due'and if we refer to Aquinas directly, it is giving each man his due rights. Actually, man is by nature a social being, and this is a maxim that everyday experiences seem to buttress.

With breathtaking advances in the field of information technologies, with the ever increasing popularity of social networks like Facebook and Twitter, the boundaries of our global village are receding as the hours grow

---

89 Cf. United Nations Body of Principles for the Protection of All Person under any Form of Maltreatment, Detention or Imprisonment, Principle 1-unioted nations Document A/43/49(1988). Principle 6 further declares that "cruel, inhuman or degrading treatment should be interpreted so as to extend the widest possible protection against abuses, whether physical or mental, including the holding of detained or impriosoned person in conditions which deprive him, temporarily or permanently of the use of any of his natural senses 'such as sight or hearing, or his awareness of place and the passing of time"And Article 1, Convention against Torture amd Other Cruel, inhuman or degrading Treatment or Punishement adopted and opened for signature, ratification and accession by General Assembly Resolution 39/46 of 10th December 1984. Entered into force on the 26th June 1987 in accordance with Article 27(1).

90 Cf. Anton. P. C., On Justice: Basic writing of St Thomas, New York Press, USA 1975, p. 687.

long. Thus, these are the increasing need to delineate certain principles that will guide the operation of our commonwealth.

What are the core values or virtues that are to be enshrined in the perfect society of our dreams? For when we talk of man's sociability, when we talk of man as society, we tend to prescribe or describe the teleological order found in nature, where everything has and knows its place, where there is law and order, cause and effect, action and reaction, if it is devoid of harmony, then we would be back to the Contractarians nightmare of the Hobbesian State of nature, where life is short, nasty, brutish, and revolt and disorder are the high points of the day.

We live in a world steep in strife: this is not a phrase from some dooms day prophesy, but the sad reality of human existence.

Today, man flourishes but in fear, war, skirmishes, violence, political and civil unrest, thus it is impertinent to ask ourselves some reflective questions, what is the way out of the quagmire? If the social theories are to be believed then society did not evolve by blind chance or evolution, it was deliberately engineered; and thus society needs to live up to it at the end of the bargain, to provide an enabling social condition for individual; no matter the race gender, physical and mental abilities or lack of to actualize their capabilities.

There exists, therefore some fundamental assumptions, ethos or creed that any society, State or government not only needs to ascribe to but must strive to attain in order to be legitimate.

There are the man divisions of justices and these are; distributive, retributive and corrective justice. Distributive justice otherwise known as the benefits and burdens in a society are shared in a fair and equitable way. Retributive justice is concerned with the rectification of justice by punishing offenders, and these punishments should be just and fair.

In the third division, corrective justice, we are concerned that people are adequately and fairly compensated for whatever loss they may have suffered by those who have violated their civic rights.

Justice here demands that compensation should be proportionate to the rights infringed or the loss suffered. Utmost care should be taken that we do not equate justice with equality as the ancient Greeks did, or perceived it from the standpoint of egalitarianism, which revolves round the notion that all humans have right to equal consideration and respect. In its extreme form, egalitarianism would insist that primary goods be distributed equally. This should not be the case rather we should view justice from the Aristotelian standpoint of proportionality, which insists that like case should be treated in like manner and cases that are different should be treated differently.

This leads us to the idea of equity, the idea that distribution of a society's primary good must be done according to worth, merit, need, talent, etc., for the failure to make valid distinction between persons in certain cases would surely be injustice. In line with the aforementioned, justice has been defined as fairness. In his famous work, "A theory of Justice", John Rawls outlines two principles of justice; the basic liberties of members of a particular society, and the second, the different principle which demands, on one hand fair equality of opportunity for all regardless of gender, race, or social status, and secondly, that inequalities in primary goods could be condoned if it favors the least advantaged ones in a society.

Indeed, the relationship between justice and social order is highlighted in justice's demand that the rights of individuals are not violated either by others or by constituted authority, thus it buttresses the claim that every man should be given his due. The State it tasked to uphold the autonomy of the individual and should strive not to infringe on the rights of its individual members.

So, in a society where the laws and social norms are people-oriented and fair, social order flourishes. But in a society where the society's systems are unjust, citizens are restive and civil disobedience abound. This can tip the dynamics of social order, tilting it towards anarchy. For the stability of any society is a reflection of the sentiments of its members; if they feel that they are being treated unjustly or unfairly, then the stage is set for unrest and grumbling and this in turn rents the fabric of society into bits and parts. There is disunity, distrust and the remnants of order in that society which give way to social unrest and strife.

For justice only makes sense when the rights of citizens are protected and there is a fair distribution of the burdens and benefits of society. Social order is the direct consequence when hard work and merit are rewarded and offenders are fairly and appropriately punished. For without justice or any viable principles of justice, we cannot talk of social order when the state is unjust or permits injustice. Rather, we find moral and rational grounds for civil disobedience or a full-blown revolution as recent happenings in the Middle East have aptly portrayed.

Another point is that society is a *pot-pourri* of strange bed fellows, society is a mishmash of different cultures, a mixture of persons from different religious and social backgrounds, with what then do we resolve issues of conflicts, which if not properly handled would result in social unrest and disorder? Justice serves as the bridge; and we now look at what social justice is all about.

D. SOCIAL JUSTICE

Social justice means justice relating to the welfares of man's life in an organised community for the better growth of their livelihood; and it is characterized by friendly and harmonious association in the community.

Social justice in this sense is a sort of proportion, and injustice is the opposite and this relates too to the distributive justice.

The man who acts unjustly gets too much and the victim of social injustice gets too little of what is good.

A just act socially speaking, necessarily involves at least two persons for whom good relationship it is meant to be a fact, and what the two share in justice being exhibited or the case in point that is being handled.

This should be in the same ratio to one another as the other persons, and if the persons concerned are not equal, they will not have equal shares; and it is when equals have the same or are assigned unequal shares, or people who are not equal in equal shares, that quarrels and complaints break out.

The idea of human flourishing is central not only to our personal and ethical reflections about our own lives and the lives of those around us, but also to our political discourse about our social institutions.

E. JUSTICE AS WELFARE

Dissatisfied with theNmetaphysical, and abstract nature of justice as legitimacy. Jeremy Bentham (the father of utilitarianism) discovered a concrete demonstration of justice in the notion of 'welfare', and in particular human welfare. Human welfare, for him, simply means pleasure, or happiness, though it also came to be regarded as utility. The final conclusion from his discovery is that "one is best which produces the greatest amount of happiness."

In his book, 'Introduction to the Principles of Morals and Legislation" Bentham outlines the following six-steps procedure for assessing the worth of any one person of those whose interests seem most immediately to be affected by it: and take an account? Take an account of the number of persons whose interests appear to be concerned; and repeat the above process with respect to each.

Sum up the numbers expressive of the degrees of good tendency, which the act has, with respect to each individual, in regard to whom the tendency of it is good upon the whole: do this again with respect to each individual, in regard to whom the tendency of it is bad upon the whole.

Take the balance; which, if in the side of pleasure, will give the general good tendency of the act, with respect to the total number or community of the individual. If on the side of pain, calculate the general evil tendency, with respect to the same community.

At that time, especially in nineteenth-century, the hedonistic calculus becomes a dominant force in England, sweeping across the political and ethnical lie of the society. Every action and exigency of man is assessed positively or negatively from the extent it was able to bring pleasure or pain.

The action that generates more pleasure than pain is regarded as right, and just, while the action that brings more pain than pleasure is wrong, and therefore unjust.

This is because according to Bentham "nature has placed mankind under the governance of two sovereign masters, pain and pleasure. They govern us in, all we do, in all we say, in all we think". In other words, man is governed by two basic stimuli; namely, to seek pleasure or happiness, and to avoid pain, or sadness. This is for Bentham, justice for man. And when it is applied to the community, it means that any action that procures the greatest possible happiness for the greatest possible number is right and just. Otherwise, it is wrong and unjust.

There is certainly a certain amount of happiness. That underlines every act of justice. In other words, a well-balanced system ought to bring its own satisfaction and happiness. But there is more to "justice" or "rightness" than more "greatness happiness of the greatest number" can explain. In fact, if "happiness" is like "justice" in so far as they bring certain amount of satisfaction, it is different from it in almost every other respect. Justice is more of harmony among all the various components of the community. It is, as it were, a constant disposition to reconcile the welfare of the privileged and the less-privileged in the society.

Its target is to discover the best way to satisfy the rich and the poor, the "greatest number", and the 'less number using a methodology that is relatively less cumbersome.

Meanwhile, justice as welfare in Bentham's sense, seems to create classes based on dichotomy of 'number', and therefore discriminatory and disharmonious in its implementation of justice apart from being cumbersome.

F. JUSTICE AS SYMPATHY

This is the extension or so to say an expansion of sympathies. It is often presented as justice which provides a means of solving the intractable problem of human limitations. And because human facilities are greatly scarce and limited, there arises the conflicts of interest, which for Hume and Mill are presupposed by the concept of justice. Warnock identified five of such limitations surrounding human life as mentioned earlier. They include, limited resources, limited information, limited intelligence, limited rationality and the most crucial one, the 'limited sympathy.'

The limited resources has to do with the fact that material needs for man are relatively scarce. Of all the material needs of man, three are the most basic and critical; the need for adequate and sufficient procession of food, shelter (housing) and clothing.

It means, for instance, that neither food nor housing has been sufficiently provided for man by nature.

And this necessity seems to create a certain conflict of interest, on how to divide very limited commodities among a greater population. Just as resources are limited, so is the useful information needed to wrestle with, and overcome the adverse forces of nature. Apart from information, there is need for greater rationality and intelligence on the part of man. These factors are highly considered by Warnock as critical to human survival, and flourishes. But of all these factors, Warnock considers "limited sympathies" as the most devastating. In other words, if individual sympathies could be enlarged or expanded, man can better cope with the limitations of other factors. For instance, where enlarged sympathies are guaranteed, "sharing" of limited facilities becomes an alternative option. In other words, the available justice in the midst of acute shortage of human resources is sympathy opened to sharing. As one aptly observes that, "even if there is enough for every body's need, there is no guarantee, and not even much likelihood, that there is enough for everybody's desires".

And therefore, man has to do with what is immediately available, in terms of resources by the expansion of sympathies. This singular disposition (to sympathy) is here presented in this section as "justice", especially needed to ameliorate the crisis of the human limitations, scarcity, powerlessness, and ambivalence.

In fact, "there would be no point talking about justice", according to Hume, "but for the limitations of human benevolence, and the competition for scarce goods". In other words, were the human benevolence (sympathies) is to be sufficiently guaranteed, and resources to be abundantly plentiful, the concept of justice (and its applications) will seem no longer (to be) relevant. Meanwhile, it must be remarked that justice-as-sympathy has much in common (in terms of its ethical foundations) with our main focus "justice-in-communalism". Their meeting-points as well as their areas of divergence will be duly highlighted when the later is studied. But just as we mentioned earlier, "Sympathy", whether enlarged or not is an emotional disposition, good enough to disappear when the journey becomes rough and rugged.

No wonder, it needs the stability, and the enduring features of communalism and belongingness of man, to prop it up. Justice As Fairness-like "sympathies), justice as fairness has been introduced earlier in the chapter this time, as the contributions of Warnock, and Rawls respectively towards (as solutions to) the problem of the human predicament, fraught with limitations, inequalities, and ambivalence.

Our focus in this section however is to find out the specific characterization of justice in Rawls' principles of "fairness" as contained in his theory of justice. In other words, what is "justice" in "fairness". Is "justice" in Rawls' sense synonymous with "fairness; or is "fairness", an aspect of justice? How does the theory reconcile the intractable issue of "rights" as it concerns the individuals, the community (society), and the less privileged?

To satisfy one can result in denying the others. How then, does the theory attempt the needed balancing of the equation? Perhaps, the ultimate question may also be to ascertain how far justice as fairness shares certain ideals in common with the principles of justice-in-communalism, as shall be studied, later.

In the first place, Rawls seems to clear our basic prejudice concerning the term, "justice as fairness."

On other the words the concept does not mean that "justice" is the same thing as "fairness." It is rather applied with a distinctive qualification to stress that the principles of justice ought to be chosen behind "a veil of ignorance", so as to ensure that no one is advantaged, or disadvantaged. In other words, for Rawls, the principles that will eventually emerge as legitimate for guiding the individuals in the society ought to be formulated under a certain condition of fairness and impartiality. It seems therefore that Rawls' use of "fairness" is basically first and foremost, methodological. There is a firm belief here that the principles of justice, which, as it were, ought to bind and regulate the fortunes and destiny of the individuals must be carried out under certain sober and unbiased conditions. Again, this approach shows that certain environmental factors seem to favor justice.

In other words, certain virtues tend to thrive more under certain conditions, and conditioning, than in others.

In Rawl's case, an unbiased principle of justice is presented as an offshoot of planned arrangement, under meticulously fair conditions.

Following these blue prints, it seems there is little or nothing to expect in terms of "justice" and 'freedom' from a radically emerging revolutionary regime, with its blood stained hands, coupled with its non-democratic stance. In other words, there is certainly an element of fairness or fair conditions at the basis of justice; otherwise, it will seem like, erecting a giant edifice without a solid foundation. This foresight with regard to the principles of justice is no doubt a credit to Rawls. And as we shall see, there is an equally strong (moral) justice in terms of "co-existence" and "sharing" underlining the principles of justice-in-communalism just as "fairness" is to Rawls sense of justice. Apart from this ground work of justice, Rawls seems to evolve two moral principles based on fairness to demonstrate his visions of justice.

These principles already highlighted are as follows:-Each person is to have an equal right to the most extensive basic liberty, compatible with a similar liberty for other Social and economic inequalities are arranged so that they are both to the greatest benefits of the least advantaged and attached to offices and positions open to all under conditions of fair equality of opportunity. Considering the foregoing, one can easily perceive "fairness" and "equality" as a common thread underlying Rawls' seems of justice.

In other words, his picture of justice seems an attempt of unbiased distributions of limited amenities among individuals, with a particular emphasis on the least advantaged.

He proposes that each person is to have equal rights to the most extensive equal liberty for others. In practical life, it seems that this principle can achieve only little. It is a fact of experience that everybody does not need the same facility. While some may enjoy the "most extensive liberty", others may never even consider it a value at all. Again, while such a liberty can promote the progress of some individuals, it may constitute an obstacle to the others. In this meaning, it is to be remarked against Rawls that different people do not perform the same way under the same conditions, neither do they prefer the same condition of life at all times for their self-fulfillments, and actualizations. While majority of people may like extensive freedom, and exposures, there are others who may not prefer them for their self-fulfillment. The monks in the monastery under enclosures seem as much fulfilled, and self-actualised as their counterparts in the 'open-world', and sometimes, they may even seem to feel more fulfilled.

Thus, there seems to be more to justice than mere 'fairness" and "equality" of liberty can proffer. In other words, it is not easy to determine the extent of "fairness" an individual needs in terms of 'freedom" and "liberty". All border on the disagreements concerning what "fairness" consists in. That is not to imply that there is no tinge of objectives fairness in any meaningful notion of justice.

G. JUSTICE AS GIVING EACH PERSON HIS DUE

The very use of the "expression" of "justice as a general theme of the section is aimed at stressing that justice means more than just one concept.

It means that a given concept can hardly contain all that it takes to define the over-all meaning of justice in the society. It is perhaps this apparent maze-surrounding the concept that dawned on Plato when he first wanted to define justice, as found in book one of his Republic.

For Plato, justice appears to have been variously presented by his contemporaries as rendering everyone what is his due.

The interest of the strongest harmony (and collaboration) among various parts doing good to one's friends and evil to one's enemies

For a better understanding of Plato, it is important to observe that the issue of "justice" in his Republic arose in the context of his consideration of what "the good life" means for men.

As a follow-up in a form of dialogue, Plato x-rays the various answers that might be offered to the question "what is justice?" it is here that a brief examination of the above listed forms of justice will be rewarding.

After Plato, St.Thomas Aquinas in line with Aristotle has treasured the concept of justice as given every one 'what is, his due. Like Plato and Aristotle, Aquinas considers "justice" itself as the greatest of all virtues. He consider it as that virtues which "regulates man's will, so that he wills for himself what belongs to himself, and wills for others what belongs to them. In other words, the human will is equipped with the capacity to choose, to decide, or to consent. It has a natural tendency to perform these actions on behalf of itself. Man has natural tendency to choose, to decide, or to consent towards what will be beneficial to himself.

But when this natural tendency to oneself is "supplemented by a constant disposition to place the interests of others on par with ones own, one is said to posses the virtue of Justice". Justice is therefore defined from this perspective as a firm and constant disposition, a habit to give (to) each one what is his due.

Here, the emphasis seems to be on the act itself, how it is evaluated as a just act. Again, unlike other forms of justice treated earlier, justice-as-due, seems to focus on the ontological provenance of justice, its interest is more on how the disposition originates, and how it can be applied in a well ordered society, where a certain gradation of ownership is guaranteed for everyone. This notion of justice will no doubt serve a useful purpose in a situation where there is order, and harmony, including a well arranged system of distributions of goods, and services. It will hardly be relevant however, in the same sense, in an extremely difficult setting, or "in systems which have broken down". But every system has indeed broken down, especially when it comes to the question of "ownership", as introduced by the concept of "giving to everyone what is his due (own)". Ownership here can mean "the property system obtaining within any society". It can also mean "what a person in fact controls even when no property system, good or bad is in force." Even in both counts-as a "property", or as "what a person controls", it is important to note that not everyone can always boast of either of them; especially in a system which has broken down. Here, we talk of the highly "marginalized", "the least advantaged", the "poor", the destitute, coupled with extremely handicapped. These are the groups categorized earlier under *"Ogbe-nye" or "Ogbe-enye"meaning (poorest of the poor).*

That is, 'community-gives", or the class of people that are fed entirely by the community. This group is singled out among others, just because of one factor, namely, their apparent negation of, otherwise a universal and set principle of justice. In other words, justice defined as 'due', (meant for "everyone") is exclusive of a section of the community with neither material properties of their own, nor "what is to be controlled."

But the problem is whether this least advantaged segment of the society actually deserved any "due" to be accorded them, more so when they have no "due" of their own? If so, is this "allocation" accruing to them in justice, or in charity? Most people will subscribe to the fact that they (the less privileged deserve such, in justice, not only because of their common "essence" as man, but also, because of the common ownership of the gifts of nature, vegetables, minerals, plants, and gold. These gifts and more which are the mainstay of a modern country's economy are indeed natural endowments of man, as such. So, in all, justice as "due" seems to be restrictive, and does not cover the various considerations of man. There are however more reasons why the fact that they belong to the community as members, of the belongingness of man.

This specific outlook of justice is brought out clearly by "justice-in-communalism" as we shall consider later. "Justice as Might" justice has also been considered as "might", or the "interest of the stronger". Book one of Plato's Republic cited the sophist, Thrasymachus as maintaining that justice is simply "what is advantageous to the stronger." Although Plato totally rejected this view, it has not removed the impression, coming from experience that the stronger are more often seen as the pillars of socio-political powers; and their interests are often equally disguised as "justice" for all. Therefore, Thrasymachus clealy maintains that 'whatever suits the strongest is best". In this perspective "the ruler is always just". Apart from Thrasymachus, some other philosopher have equally conceived political power as following the same trend of 'more power', more claim to justice'. Hobbes holds that "just", and "unjust" presuppose the coercive power capable of enforcing the obligations, and that no complaint of injustice could be made against the sovereign legislator. In other words, compliance to the law presupposes a coercive power, since covenant without a sword in no covenant at all.

No complaint of justice, can be made against a coercive sovereign legislator.

The modern Marxists conceive justice in the society as directly dependent on "the conflicting economic interests in the society and law reflects those of the dominant class." Here, justice becomes the economic interests of the ruling and dominant class. Thus, Thrasymachus is not alone in presenting justice as might, or the interest of the stronger but the problem really is whether justice ought to mean the interest of the stronger? In other words, is it fair to consider justice merely as a "might? This would have been the case if the "stronger' were to be sole constitution of the society. But the fact remains that the society is made up of the "stronger" as well as the weak", the 'rich' and the 'poor', the "enlightened" and the "illiterates."

These are the two faces of a coin on which every society is built. It means that the society reflects diverse compositions which can hardly be overlooked in the sharing of resources without being unjust.

To consider "justice" or "law" merely as the interest of the stronger is to be partial, one-sided, biased, and therefore, unjust. It is this imbalance in the perception of justice, that justice-in-communalism seems to address as its primary objective through its principles of common good, cooperations, sharing and common participations.

Consequently, the inordinate tendency to arrogate to oneself as well as one's interest over others is often checked, and controlled by the community.

This is based on the Igbo principle that "no-one can win judgment against the clan. In fact, the natural tendency to govern too much is equally resisted, in the communal setting with different councils in consultations.

H. JUSTICE AS HARMONY

This is greatly treasured by Plato. It is the concept of justice-as-harmony among various parts of the soul, as well as those of the State. In his Republic, Plato emphasizes that:

"There will be in the city little disease and few law suits. But care must be taken to hold the balance between music and gymnastics, (for instance): excess in the former leads to effeminacy, and excess in the later to harshness ... and the noblest natures ... require a harmonious blend."

Here, justice in the society seems to be likened justice in the soul. Like the human organism, the society is recognized to possess various organs, or major parts, each performing different functions.

For Plato, the issue is not so much the nature of function each organ performs in the society, as the definite contribution it makes to the "political organism" as a whole.

In other words, the emphasis is directed rather to the collaborative effort of the various parts (of the society) towards the attainment of the ideal State.

It means that, if each of the respective human organs performs its role creditably and harmoniously, "there will be little or no disease: in the entire (organism) body". Similarly, only "a few law suits" will be had in the society where its various components and parts work judiciously and harmoniously towards societal goal. Thus, under justice-as-harmony, the individual survival can never be the ultimate end-in-itself but only a means-to-the-end, namely; the survival of the entire society.

It means that the individuals ought to work together in collaboration, and harmony towards the attainment of the end of the larger community. This is because "the society comes into existence because no individual is self-sufficing. We all have many needs".

Like every organization, Plato believes that society exists as a result of segments towards the attainment of society's survival.

Therefore, a just and well-ordered society aims as "not to make one class especially happy, but to secure the greatest possible happiness of the community as a whole ... "here the emphasis lies on each section, or segment of the society performing its distinctive task in such a way as to complement the contribution of other sections, for the over-all good of the society. The ethical ideal of Platonic philosophy lies not in the ability and happiness of the individual, but in the ethnical perfection of the species.

This is really in line with "his (Plato's) doctrine of ideas, that which truly is in the ethical sense not the individual man, but mankind, and the form in which this truly existent humanity appears is the organic union of the individuals in the State. The ethical ideal becomes for Plato the political. From this perspective, Plato considers justice as a virtue whose character or structure is to be found as much in the life of an individual person as in the life of the society itself. Like the three parts of the human soul. Plato also identifies three classes of the State; the harmony of which makes the state stable" Justice in the soul is produced when each of its parts is functioning properly, each playing its role. In the same way, justice in the society is attained when there is a harmony among the three classes of the state: the guardians (the ruling class), the auxiliaries (the soldiers) and the artisans (the masses). Now, having considered justice as found in the soul as well as in the state, it is necessary, to revisit certain basic questions inherent in this position namely: is harmony really justice? Are the two concepts ("harmony" and justice") synonymous, or not? And why? What is in the nature of harmony that makes it to be considered as justice?

In other words, what is justice as harmony? If justice as harmony in a composite entity, (like the soul, and the state), what will it be in a non-composite- types? These questions and more are some of the problems associated with Plato's concept of justice, as contained in the harmony of various existing segments.

That notwithstanding, justice-as-harmony finds its concepts parallel in the economic, and modern organizational principles in terms of "division of labor on the one hand, and collaboration of efforts", on the other.

From this brief highlight, it appears that Plato's concepts of justice regard every human situation, and position, as fulfilling a particular role in the entire "life-play". In such a "play", some are naturally the "chief actors", some are the "prompters", while others are mere "beggars" and pawns, and yet, others could be socially marginalized. From the foregoing citation, it seems there is nothing wrong for Plato concerning the entire arrangement in so far as each is playing his own role in the "life-play".

However, in a sober reflection, the glaring weakness surrounding justice-in-harmony can easily be noticed for a just society. Who will like to be marginalized so as to create the harmonious equilibrium in the "life-play"? in John Rawl's original position under the veil of ignorance, it is most likely that no one can ever volunteer to be a scapegoat in certain circumstances.

Therefore, allowing a certain section of the society to experience privation without considering it squarely as "privation" is grossly unfair in a just society. This is one of the greatest attacks against utilitarianism, on its principle of the "greatest happiness of the greatest number."

It can equally serve as a criticism against "justice-harmony", or "justice-as-mere-collaboration" for the good of his society, but directed at the expense of a given segment of the society. So, justice-as-harmony can only provide a partial outlook of justice.

I. JUSTICE AS COMMUNISM

This justice-as-communism must be distinguished from justice-in-communalism. In his book, the philosophy of communism, Charles Boyer describes communism as 'merely one of nineteenth-century philosophies which tried to explain the universe by a transcendent God.'

In other words, a basic of communism is its utter denial of a transcendent God. Boyer considers this denial as "the foundation. The very soul of the system (communism)" Communism, like Marxian socialism belongs to a wider class of collectivism, which is directly opposed to individualism-as-justice. With the denial of transcendence, communism builds its philosophy upon a materialist and anti-religious stance. Communism is presented as an ethical solution to ceaseless struggles, through its leveling principles.

Here, instead of recognizing the natural foundation of classes, and work towards harmonizing their respective rights, and endowments, communism opts for outright abolition of these classes. Here is a situation where the community ... the community assumes direction and control of all public affairs, and where it absorbs the whole of human life.

In a situation where the individual has to be directed, and controlled by the state, it may be interesting to ask how much freedom and initiatives are left with the individual? Even if the state has to give the individuals all they need for their meaningful existence, the problem still remains on how much initiatives and self affirmation that are left to them under this arrangement.

No doubt, man does not leave on bread alone.

There is more to human fulfillment than mere 'state provisions" can offer. In fact, the irony of a "spoon fed child" arises, not on his being under fed but on his being over fed. In such a case, the child seems to be robbed of those two essential aspects of his being human, the use of "reason" (to fend for himself) and "freedom", to exercise it. Perhaps, the greatest criticism against communist's leveling principles' is on the fact of this un-freedom, and especially its interference with the right of the individuals to dispose as they wish of their possessions.

Very often some western critics seem to confuse these communists' traits with the principles of communalism. But communalism does not promote the 'leveling principles" of communism. It does not propose that 'Peter' should be robbed in order to pay "Paul", or vice versa. Rather, putting into considerations the limitations and inequalities surrounding human existence, justice-in-communalism calls on man to co-exist with one another as to be better able to share their lives, and their destiny together. Before we examine this system in details, let us consider other various classifications of justice.

J. MORAL JUSTICE

Yet to receive as much recognition" as other kinds of justice, is "moral justice"; which as the concept suggests accrues to man on the basis of his "essence", as well as his "moral" qualities as man. In other words, moral justice refers to those rights, or basic rights due to man, just because of what he is, as man. it is justice founded on the principles, of Aristotle's "*man as such*", or "*dasein*" or man as a gateway to understanding other realities (Heidegger). Again, "moral-justice" conveys a sense of justice due to man because of what belongs to every individual, irrespective of what he is, in terms of status, position, and place of birth, time, or circumstances of life. It is a right that belongs equally to the privileged and the less privileged, the rich and the poor, the mighty and the weak, the greatest possible number of, and the least segment of the population.

Moral justice is both a property of a class that has dues: (to be accorded them, in commutative justice), and its counterparts that have none, in terms of objective material rights.

It belongs equally to the physically fit, and the handicapped, to the citizens of advanced countries as well as those of the developing nations. Any meaningful distributive justice must always reflect this synthesis of nature. In fact, in situations as Omoregbe aptly remarks when special circumstances demand otherwise as in the case of great marginalizations, the equal distribution of the goods among all the citizens or all the sections of the country would itself be an unjust distribution."

Here, moral justice demands that the marginalized section of the community should be allocated more of the resources than the already flourishing section. Perhaps, the evolution of the concept of "federal character", and "disadvantaged" in Nigeria is in recognition of basic moral justice.

The philosophical foundation of this pattern of "allocation" based on equitable distribution rather than equal distribution is rooted on the common ownership of the goods of the country (nature).

These goods belong to every member of the country, the privileged, and the less privileged. The goods belongs to man as such. Even in the global scope, there is at present, as Omoregbe observes a flagrant injustice in the distribution of the goods of the earth among its human inhabitants.

Here, a few nations seem to have unjustly appropriated to themselves the natural resources that belong to man who inhabits the earth.

Following the reason advanced so far, it means that when therefore these marginalized (poor) nations ask the rich nations to give them some of the goods they have greedily and unjustly appropriated to themselves, they are not asking for a favor but demanding' their (moral) right . . . in fact, this moral right that is due to the poor and marginalized nations does create the corresponding, reciprocal moral obligations on the rich nations to "share", such resources with the former. In other words, a moral right (justice) of a party seems to create a reciprocal moral obligation on the other party. The excellence of justice-in-communalism (as we shall examine) lies on its unshakable emphasis, on the principles of moral justice, including "sharing" of resources, "common good", common participations and subsidiarity.

We shall consider these in the subsequent chapter. So far, we have examined various ways through which human rights (justice) is expressed. It is necessary now to estimate the extent of their merits in solving the problem of human limitations, inequalities, powerlessness, and ambivalence.

K. REMEDIAL JUSTICE

Remedial justice means that which intends to counteract and repair or cure and remedy the evil and wrong or loss already done to a person or group in the society. This is otherwise called certificatory justice, it deals with remedies and thus, it is called 'remedial.'It rectifies the privation of what is supposed to have been done or given to a person or class but has not been done. Remedial justice deals with fairness in human transactions and dealings both voluntary and involuntary cases. Examples, such as pledge, barter, loan disappointments etc are inclusive. This connotes the spirit of social justice. It guides the conducts of the individuals in their own class of nature and regulates their social interactions and orderings. Aristotle admitted that if a man fails to be just, he has taken more than his share.

Justice, therefore becomes a virtue akin to equality and fairness; while injustice is vice and unjust. He, Aristotle, categorically ensured that justice and fair-play should be given to each individual in the state as members of the civil society. In this meaning the rectificatory or remedial justice tries to reinstate or correct the imbalance or injustice perpetrated despite the personalities that are involved.

On this purpose, for as Aristotle would say, when a person is wronged, he is said to have suffered a loss while the offender had to some extent gained.

Most often through rectificatory justice and the mediation of a judge, the injustice could be corrected or rectified, the situation is put in order regarding the injustice with the help of the punishment or penalty issued to the offender.

Aristotle described it as the mean between loss and gain when he said:

> ... what is meant between the greater and lesser and the gain and loss are greater, and sees loss in contrary sense; that which contains more 'good'and less ' bad'and its contrary loss. The mean between them is the equal which we assert to be just. It follows that what is just in the rectificatory sense will be the mean between loss and gain.[91]

[91] Aristotle., Ethics, Pengium Books, Great Britain, p. 180.

These methods are conducted or said to mean here that goodness or virtue supersedes vice. And so, Aristotle in his ethical principles sees justice as rectificatory thus: "to add to the party which has too little the amount of which one exceeds what to be taken away from the greater of that amount by which the mean is exceeded by what one has."[92]

It is then this connective role that plays an intermediary. It redresses; connects and corrects, and then, rectifies.

Aristotle maintains again, in his politics that equals should be treated alike but unequal proportionally to their relevant differences and all with the sense and good measures of impartiality whereby justice would be understood and served for every person.

It is the view of Bodenheimer that Aristotle's tying of justice to diverse human situations may be termed the most distinguishing feature of his disagreement with Plato's central idea of justice as harmony.[93] For Aristotle the particular and corrective or remedial type of justice is that which the judge's task is to redress and not to punish.

To itemize every aspect of the categories of justice one has to take note of the fact that there are three main divisions of justice and these are; distributive, retributive and corrective justice.

Distributive justice otherwise known as social justice refers to the proper allocation of a nation's resource, where the benefits and burdens in a society are shared in a fair and equitable way. Retributive justice is concerned with the rectification of injustice by punishing offenders, in corrective justice, we are concerned that people are adequately and fairly compensated for whatever loss they may have suffered by those who have violated their civil rights. Justice here demands that compensation should be proportionate to the rights infringed or the losses suffered.

Utmost care should be taken that we do not equate justice with equality as the ancient Greeks did, or perceive it from the standpoint of egalitarianism, which revolves round the notion that all humans have right to equal consideration and respect. In its extreme form, egalitarianism would insist that primary goods be distributed equally. This should not be the case rather we should view justice from the Aristotelian standpoint of proportionality,

---

92 Aristotle, Ethics, ibid, p. 182.

93 E. Bodenheimer., Jurisprudence, New York Press, USA 1940, p. 47.

which insists that like cases should be treated in like manner and cases that are different should be treated differently.

This leads us to the idea of equity, the idea that distribution of a society's primary good must be done according to worth, merit, need, talent, etc. for the failure to make valid distinction between persons in certain cases would surely be injustice.

In line with the aforementioned, justice has been defined as fairness. In his famous work on, "A Theory of Justice", John Rawls outlines two principles, fundamental liberties of members of a particular society, and opportunity, for regardless of gender, race, or social status, and secondly, that inequalities in primary goods could be condoned if it favors the least advantaged ones in the society. The relationship between justice and social order is highlighted in justice's demand that the rights of individuals are not violated either by others or by constituted authority. Thus it buttresses the claim that every man should be given his due. The state is tasked to uphold the autonomy of the individual and should strive not to infringe on the rights of its individual members. So in a society where the laws and social norms are people-oriented and fair, social order flourishes. But in a society where the social systems are unjust, there is citizen's restiveness, civil disobedience abounds; and this can tip the dynamics of social order, tilting it towards anarchy. For the stability of any society is a reflection of the sentiments of its members, if they feel that they are being treated unjustly or unfairly, then the stage is set for unrest and grumbling and this in turn rents the fabric of society into bits and parts. There is disunity, distrust and the remnants of order inherent in the society give way to social unrest and strife: Justice only makes sense when the rights of citizens are protected and there is a fair distributions of the burdens and benefits of society. Social order is a direct consequence when hard work and merit are rewarded and offenders are fairly and appropriately punished.

Without justice or any viable principle of justice, we cannot talk of social order when the state is unjust or permits injustice. Rather what we find as moral and rational grounds for civil disobedience or a full blown revolution as recent happenings in the Middle east have aptly portrayed.

Another point is that a society is a mishmash of different cultures, a mixture of persons from issues of conflicts, which if not properly handled would result in social unrest and disorder. Justice serves as the bridge. The question of the nature and meaning of human rights is a very complex one. It is fraught with a lot of controversies and as such does not present a monolith. Different and often conflicting theories abound as to the essence, content, and foundation of human rights. The diversities of opinion are often engendered by differences in religion, ideology, socio-economic beliefs, philosophical outlook, gender, race, ethical orientation, culture, and levels of international relation and co-operation.

There is no doubt that the global interest in human rights issues has projected Human Rights to be viewed as a form of religion in today's world. Within many nations, political debates rage over the denial or abuse of rights.[94] Again, public discourse is phrased in the rhetoric of rights and Human Rights legal instruments have been proliferated.

Many Human Rights activists adopt the universals theory when the define Human Rights as moral rights which every human being everywhere at all times, ought to have, simply because of the fact that, in contradistinction with other beings, he is rational and moral. Such an argument would no doubt meet with some difficulties when considering whether or not infants, the unborn, the moribund and the lunatics have Human Rights since the rational or moral germ is either not developed or is completely lacking in them. Be that as it may, one can also see Human Rights as that specie of rights which are recognized as appertaining to man by the very nature of his humanity as a person.

Certainly, the above Universalist understanding of human right stems from the naturalistic perception of ancient and medieval humanism. The earliest direct precursor to Human Rights is found in the notions of 'natural right' developed by classical Greek philosophers such as Aristotle. This concept was nonetheless more fully developed by Aquinas in his *summa Theologia.*

For several centuries Aquinas' conception held sway: there were

goods or behaviors that were naturally right (or wrong) because God ordained them so. What is naturally right could be ascertained by humans by 'right reason', that is, thinking properly.[95]

---

94 O. Ibidapo "Human Rights and State Security": The Nigerian Experience" in Journal of Human Rights Law and Practice, Vol. 5, No. 1. Orbis Press, Nigeria1995.

95 T. Hobbes., Leviathan. London: Penguin Books, London Press, England 1968.

As the reformation caught on and ecclesiastical authority was shaken and challenged by rationalism, political philosophers argued for new bases of natural right. Hobbes posed the first major assault in 1651 on the divine basis of natural right by describing a State of nature in which God did not seem to play any role. Perhaps more importantly, however, Hobbes also made a crucial leap from 'natural right' to 'a natural right.'

In other words, there was no longer just a list of behavior that was naturally right or wrong: Hobbes added that there could be some claim or entitlement which was derived from nature. In Hobbes' view, this natural right was one of self-preservation.

Further reinforcement of natural rights came with Immanuel Kant's writings later in the 17th century that reacted to Hobbes' work in his view, the congregation of humans into a State-structured society resulted from a rational need for protection from each other's violence that would be found in a State of nature. However, the fundamental requirements of political doctrine was derived from his moral philosophy, and as such be argued that a state had to be organized through the imposition of and obedience to, laws that applied universally; nevertheless, these laws should respect the equality, freedom, and autonomy of the citizens. In this way, Kant prescribed that basic rights were necessary for civil society:

A true system of politics cannot therefore take a single step without first paying tribute to morality… The rights of man must be held sacred, however great the sacrifice the ruling power must make.[96]

Aquinas in line with Aristotle's knowledge, regards justice as embracing, many if not all the other virtues, including a relation to all persons as well as to things, involving a just distribution of the latter, and a fair meting out of punishment. This has also equal reciprocity since this does not apply to either distributive or retributive justice. Seemingly wise, it is self-evident that man ought to act well in order to produce the greatest good that is to make the world much more better than it is.

We should now go into the enumerations of the kinds of Human Rights in the various ways as we can see below.

---

96 Kant, I. "Groundwork of the Metaphysics of Morals" in Feinberg (ed) Reason and Responsibility. Woodworks Publ.co. California 1985.

L. CIVIL AND POLITICAL RIGHTS

These are the rights of the community pertaining to ordinary individual citizens coupled with the political rights which a person has the right to exercise. This concerns the right to life, liberty, security of persons, privacy and property, the right to marry and have a family, the right to a fair trial, freedom from slavery, forced labour, torture and arbitrary arrest, freedom of movement and to seek asylum, the right to a nationality, freedom of thought, conscience and religion, freedom of opinion and expression, freedom of assembly and association, and the right which includes participation in public affairs etc.

M. ECONOMIC AND SOCIAL RIGHTS

Economic and social rights is the type of right relating or referring to economy or economics, business or industry.

This means the right to work for a just reward; the right to form and to join trade unions, the right to rest and leisure, and to periodic holidays with pay, the right to a standard of living adequate to health and well-being the right to education and right to participate in the cultural life of a community.

N. COLLECTIVE RIGHTS

Collective rights here means the common rights which denotes a number or groups of people for their expected mutual benefits of everybody in the community.

These are the rights that protect nations from other nations, races, to freedom from discrimination and racism, and of classes to freedom from neo-colonialism.

Therefore, justifying a particular case in sight is praiseworthy in order to secure political equality required; otherwise some necessary adjustments would be a necessity.

O. SUBJECTIVE RIGHTS

The subjective right is that which relates to the subject, a right which is existing as personal or individual but should be lacking impartiality in order to achieve its necessary goal. This is a legitimate right and an inviolable power whereby one vindicates 'his something'as his very own only.

It is a power or the capacity on the virtue of which person ought to do something in contra-distinction to a duty in virtue of a person ready who ought to do something or owe something responsibly. Where duty constricts human freedom, rights conform or enlarge it.

This right is a legitimate power, on this meaning Higgins said:"Right supposes something to be already mine or allows that something is to become mine. Its function then, is to protect me in what is mine"[97]

The right of mankind and even natural right- *"jus naturale,"* also, is on the liberty or freedom that each man ought to use his own power, as he will for himself, for the preservation of his own nature and his own life.

This is because eternal life represents fulfilment of the whole being in God.

One does one's best to be careful and not to frustrate other people's right in regard to their personality, dignity and in accordance of respect which one needs from one person or one another.

An instance of this is the right to food, shelter, life, work, political liberty, family life and the education of children by parents and especially the rights to truth remains a fundamental necessity. As it is, these are basic rights and the needs of a man which are not forgettable. We now move to the next chapter regarding Human Dignity and Rights per se.

[97] Higgins. J., Man as Man, England Press, Baltimore 1948, p. 225.

1.3

RESPECTING HUMAN DIGNITY AND RIGHTS

Having seen what justice and Human Rights are all about in the foregoing chapters, one notices that justice and peace are essential elements and medicinal ointments to a viable democracy in the society. It is also a known fact that Human Rights abuse is a matter of grave concern in a nation today. The crusaders of peace, freedom fighters, Human Rights activists are still finding it hard in checkmating the political excesses which tend to infringe on Human Rights.

The theoretical perspective on the meaning and nature of Human Rights as a concept becomes available to us only through the works of philosophers. Certain laws and legal scholarship are merely dependent on these works. According to Fagothey, 'right' generally is a moral power over what is one's own or more expressly moral power or inner freedom to do, omit or exact something of virtue. In philosophical parlance, there are four components of right, namely, subject (the person possessing a right), term (those persons bound to respect or fulfil a right), matter (that to which one has a right), and title (the reason why the subject has a right to this matter). Thus, according to this postulate, human beings are the subjects of human rights that are to be respected by other persons (human and juristic).

Human rights are those inalienable rights of a person given by nature for the sole reason of being a human being.[98]

Fundamental Human Rights are attached to every human being by virtue of that every fact. They are rights inherent in the essence of man.

Cranston has it as "something of which no one may be deprived without a great affront to justice. For Dowrick, Human Rights are "those claims made by men, for themselves or on behalf of other men, on man as a human

98 A. Fagothey., Right and Reason: Ethics in Theory and Practice, Ohio 1989, p. 230.

being, a member of human kind . . . "[99] Hence, Human Rights are rights and freedom to which all humans are entitled merely by reason of being human.

The argument is that the core of human rights discourse is that it is a right to which only human beings are entitled, which gives meaning to the essence of humanity, and without which humanity necessarily looses (sic) those special attributes that makes (sic) it human. Ajomo had earlier defined human rights in similar terms.[100]

In the same vein, Human Rights can be said to be those liberties, immunities and benefits which, by accepted contemporary values, all human beings should be able to claim as of right in the society in which they live.

Eze notes that "Human Rights represent demands or claims which individuals or groups make on society, some of which are protected by law and have become part of Lex lata while others remain aspirations to be attained in the future.[101]

The above views are unanimous in holding that human rights are inherent rights to be enjoyed by all human beings of the global village and not gifts to be withdrawn, withheld or granted at someone's whim or will. No wonder Nickel observes that Human Rights are conceived in a Universalist and egalitarian fashion. It is in this sense that human rights are said to be inalienable or imprescriptible. In this connection, Macdonald writes of human rights.

If you remove them from any human being, he will become less than human. They are part of the very nature of a human being, and attach to all human beings everywhere in all societies, just as much as do his arms and legs.

Observing righteousness and decent living could be very challenging to every child of God, youth and adults inclusive.

[99] F. E.Dowrick., Human Rights, Problems, Perpspective and Texts: Saxon House United Kingdom 1979, p. 8-9.

[100] M.A.Ajomo., " The Development of Individual Right in Nigeria's Constitutional History in Ajomo, M.A., and Owasanonye, B. (eds.), B. (eds.) Individual Rights under the 1989 Constitution, NLALS Conference Series No.4 Lagos: No.4 Lagos: Nigerian Institute of advanced Legal Studies, 1993, p. 1.

[101] O. C. Eze., Human Rights in Africa: Some Selected Problems. Lagos, Macmillan, 1984, p. 5.

Respect for human dignity and Rights are summed up that man should have a good and strong knowledge of God, his Creator, protector and sustainer.

Then, it is for man to go through his instructions- and exercise that obedient capacity of God's teaching; in his Decalogue as given to Moses on Mountain Sinai. Humanism is a system of thought that considers solution to human problems; as a doctrine that underlines the importance of common human needs or as a devotion to the interest of human race lingered along man's historical development.

Although Human Rights were principally defined and codified in the twentieth century, Human Rights values are rooted in the wisdom literature, traditional values, and religious teaching of almost every culture: the Hindu Vedas, the Babylonian Code of Hammurabi, the Bible, the Qur'an (Koran), the Analects of Confucius, the Inca and Aztec codes of conduct and justice, and African Traditional Religious Beliefs. All these address question of people's duties, right and responsibilities.

In 1948, the General Assembly of the United Nations proclaimed the Universal Declaration of Human Rights as a common standard of achievement for all people and all nations.The foundations documents of Human Rights law are the Universal Declaration of Human Rights of 1948, the International Covenant on Civil and Political Rights (ICCPR) of 1966 and its optional protocol, and the International Covenant on Economic, Social and Cultural Rights, (1CESCR) which is known collectively as the International Bill of Human Rights.

The duty to protect these rights is an obligation both to refrain from violating the dignity of others and to positively come to the aid of others when failure to do would result in the destruction of their dignity. Looking at the Universality of Human Rights, with a world comprising of almost two hundred nations and countless cultural and social divisions, how can human rights be ever be universal? To respond to this issue of universality, social workers must focus on the underlying reasons behind the Universal Declaration. Understanding universality and culture is crucial to the study of Human Rights.

In other words, appreciation of the universality concept requires an understanding of what lies behind the Human Rights.

By studying the purpose of a particular Human Right, social workers can better understand the concept of universality, even when encountering diverse backgrounds and work conditions.

The point of Universal Declaration was to provide basic guidelines for all individuals and nations on how they act and interact with each other.

The declaration establishes a code of conduct, much like a code of ethics for professional organisations. Social workers must subscribe to a code of ethics in how they act with clients, colleagues, and the public.

While opinions of social workers may differ over the meaning of a particular statement of ethics, this disagreement does not prevent the existence of a code of ethics. Respect for human dignity in concrete, historical, natural and social relationships call for definite forms of action and social organisation.

The Universal Declaration of Human Rights resembles a code of conduct for a professional group, such as social workers. The obvious difference is that the declaration aims at including every individual and nation within its umbrella. The concept may initially appear grandiose but not when viewed in the context of a professional organisation.

If a code of conduct can exist for a professional organisation that itself includes vast differences in cultural, economic, and political backgrounds, then a code of conduct can also exist for individuals and nations of the world.

Differences in carrying out the code of conduct may always exist, but a general agreement on the necessity and principles within the code can be established. No wonder, Rawls equally affirms that "human rights ... are those moral rights that individuals have in front of the state, and which they share with one another by means of institutions"Thus, human rights are regarded as products of human and cultural efforts. The basic problem with this view is that as public relations are given absolute priority, the single individuals and the various forms of private relations are excluded as addresses of human rights.

Furthermore, in his attempt to delineate the features of a just society, Rawls conceives of rights as belonging to citizens rather than to human beings. This is because he regards his theory of justice as constructed "for a body of people who form a political society rather than for the human society that forms a moral community.[102]

This does not fail to raise some problems with regard to the relations between human rights and the hypothetical contractive rights that are antecedent to the contract, an in accordance to the veil of ignorance, they should be thought of as entirely formal categories which have yet to be given content by the contracting parties. If rights are included in the list of primary goods, they are not grounded on the contract, they do not issue from the original position, as Rawls maintains."

On the better appreciation of the concept of human rights, it may be apt to review the different ways by which rights have been classified by scholars.

There is no doubt that several schemes of classifications have emerged. According to Nweze Human rights have been classified into personal rights, political and moral rights, proprietary, procedural rights and equality rights.

Personal rights include rights to life, to dignity of the human person, the right to personal liberty and right to freedom of movement. Political and moral rights include the rights to freedom of expression, freedom of association and assembly, freedom of conscience and religion, proprietary rights include the right to fair hearing and to have one's cause heard. Equality rights include the right to freedom from discrimination.[103]

Again, human rights have been categorized according to the period of stages in which they were recognized. Ikpeze observes that the classification into generation "was not predicated on any formula; rather it followed its origin and time of coming into force". The study of the stages was carried out by Vasak who referred to the stages as "generations". The first generation rights often called "Liberty-oriented rights" consists of the civil and political rights and freedoms that are pertinent to safeguarding the persons and citizens basic liberties vis-à-vis governmental authority and requiring of the state to permit or endure those entitlements.

These rights are meant to secure the liberty of the individual from the arbitrary actions of the state.

---

[102] J. Rawls., Justice as Fairness, in Bioethics, Refugees-Magazine on Human Rights Declaration, England 1989, p. 89.

[103] Nweze. C. C., Human Rights and Sustainable Development in the African Charter, A paper Presented at a Workshop on Human Rigths Organized by Nigerian Bar Association, Enugu Branch on 17th September, 1997.

They are enshrined in articles 2-21 of the UDAR 1948 and guaranteed under chapter IV of the constitution of the Federal Republic of Nigeria 1999 as amended. The first generation rights are severally called negative rights because they entail negative obligations on governments not to interfere with the exercise of these rights by individuals.

However, Ogbu observes that not all these rights are wholly "negative" as rights to life and freedom of association for instance, require some positive actions from government to ensure their realization.

For instance, scholars who emphasize the contents of the so-called first generations rights do not include the second and the third generation rights in their definitional periscope of human rights. They regard them to be at best aspirations. Accordingly, the proponents of the primary and the negative rights contend that man is first and foremost a human being and only secondarily a social being."

Nwabueze seems to belong to this school of thought when he writes that Human Rights constitute the intrinsic attributes of the human being, the essence of human personality; hence they are called natural rights.

On this reason, they are more basic and fundamental to human existence than food, shelter, clothing, etc the latter are also basic and fundamental; indeed indispensable for a decent human existence, but they are only extrinsic support, serving to sustain the intrinsic attributes of body, mind and soul, and to enable them to be fully realized and developed.

Some other scholars however maintain a different view by drawing a line of distinction between human rights and fundamental rights.

Human Rights is derived from natural rights. Those rights have been adopted and given positive force of Law by the constitution in form of fundamental rights. Human rights can be regarded as the genus, while fundamental rights are the specie. While human rights attain to the individual at birth, fundamental rights are those recognized and supported by the State. Human rights span the range of human history to modern times. On the other hand, fundamental rights are of recent development and are normally associated with written constitutions.

Nevertheless, Ogbu disagrees with the above opinions, contending that they constitute "A case of distinction without a difference."[104]

[104] O. N. Ogbu., Human Rights Law and Practice in Nigeria: An Introduction, Enugu. CD-JAP Publishers, Enugu 1999, p. 2.

He succinctly puts it: Human rights remain so, whether they occur in the international plane or within municipal confines, and whether they are called "human rights" or "fundamental rights".

It should be noted that the International Bills of Rights, the universal declaration of Human Rights, the International covenant on Economic, Social and Cultural Rights, and the International Covenant on Civil and Political Rights – use the expression "fundamental Human Rights". So also the UN Charter.

Conscious of the fact that fundamental Human Rights encompass and signify the existence of core human values in what could be seen as the basic socio-economic, political and moral principles of just and fair treatment of the individual person or group, generally arrived at by experience, common sense and some consensus, and confirmable by law and/or international treaties and conventions, all of which are influenced by the stage of human development, diverse interest and ideologies.

It was the experience of non-uniform treatment of individuals and groups around the world, typified by the unspeakable atrocities against the Jews during the second World War of (1939-1945), that prompted the then 48-member. United Nations General Assembly to promulgate the much quoted Universal Declaration of Human Rights on December 10,1948.

The Declaration was regarded as a common standard of achievement for all peoples and all nations, to the end that every individual and every organ of society, keeping this Declaration constantly in mind, shall strive by teaching and education, to promote respect for these rights and freedoms, and by progressive measures, national and international, to secure their universal and effective recognition and observance.

By viewing the Universal Declaration as a universal professional code of conduct, social workers can more readily grasp the significance and importance of the declaration. Social workers can also, more readily understand that, many codes of conduct, violations of the Universal Declaration do occur with many alleged violations falling within a noticed area.

However, by viewing alleged violations as a learning exercise and opportunity to better understand Human Rights, social workers can meet the challenge of universality. The seemingly impossible task of relating the Universal Declaration to all individuals and countries becomes manageable. Such particularised demands of human dignity are called Human Rights.

To leave nobody in doubt, the Declaration went into specifics in a number of key dimensions of fundamental Human Rights. It specifies, for instance, that civil and political rights prohibit slavery, inhuman treatment, arbitrary arrest and arbitrary interference with privacy, together with discrimination on grounds of race, colour, sex, language, religion, political or other opinion, national or social origin, property, birth or other status.

Also listed are the rights to fair trial, freedom of movement and residence, the right to political asylum, the right to have and change nationality, the right to marry, the right to own property, freedom of belief and worship, freedom of opinion and expression, freedom of peaceful assembly and associations, free elections and equal opportunities for access to public positions. Under economic, social and cultural rights, the Declaration demands the right to security, to full employment and fair conditions of work, to an adequate standard of living, to education and to participation in the cultural life of the community. The 1948 Declaration is therefore a landmark declaration that no enlightened nation or person in authority can afford to overlook.

Unfortunately, however, nations have reflected the contents of the Declaration's selectivity and applied the various rights to suit their fancies. As a result, the Second World War atrocities and violations which led to the declarations in the first instance are still being perpetrated in many countries of the world, including Nigeria.

The issue of enforcements of Human Rights leads naturally to the issue of enforcement. It is taken for granted, that every individual and nation is subject to Human Rights and freedoms within the Universal Declaration. One may ask with what mechanism existing do they wish to enforce violations of these rights and freedoms? And who actually determines when a violation occurs?

Obviously, without enforcement of Human Rights, the declaration has no worth beyond the paper used to produce its many rights and freedoms. Enforcements of Human Rights generally depend upon the good will or interest of the individual countries. If an individual country has not enacted laws that incorporate Human Rights contained in the declaration, then countries and individuals can circumvent the declaration.

However, in recent years, countries have grown more sensitive to accusations of violating Human Rights and do take steps to recognise Human Rights.

More so, having maximum maturity for self-discipline and self mastery is in every way and daily a salient necessity for one to have that respect for human dignity and to know more about those rights he ought to accord to his fellow human beings. And having this as ground basis will prepare us for a better livelihood through various practices of living a pious and decent life. When we have and cherish this respect for human Dignity and Rights of man and equally the grandeur of endurance, excellence and the rights of human beings, we could have a unified world, the world of justice, the world of peace and a new lovely world; in accordance with what is true, fitting, commendable and genuine in a human world.

We all know and agree that human life and human dignity are inviolable. Yet another strong opposition to the natural theory is presented by Marx. Marx criticized the Declaration of the Rights of Man and of the citizen as bourgeois ideology:

Thus, in his critique, Marx does not identify any difference between the rights of man as man and the rights of the citizen. He therefore argues that it is the state and the law rather than nature that endows man with the rights. He disagrees with the idea of the universality and inalienability of human rights. Furthermore, Marx maintains that liberal rights and ideas of justice are premised on the notion that each of us needs protection from other human beings.

Therefore liberal rights are rights designed to protect us from such perceived threats. Freedom on such a view is freedom to protect us from such perceived threats. Freedom on such a view is freedom from interference. But according to Marx, the above view denies the possibility that real freedom is to be found positively in our relations with other people.

It is to be found in human community, not in isolation, so that insisting on a regime of rights encourages men to view each other in ways which undermine the possibility of the real freedom that is found in human participation. No wonder, Wellmann affirms that human rights ... are those moral rights that individuals have in front of the State, and which they share with one another by means of institutions.[105] Thus, human rights are regarded as product of human and cultural efforts. The basic problem with this view is that as public relations are given absolute priority, the single individuals and the various forms of private relations are excluded as addresses of human rights.

Furthermore, in his attempt to delineate the features of a just society, Rawls conceives of rights as belonging to citizens rather than to human beings. This is because he regards his theory of justice as constructed for a body of people who form a political society rather than for the human society that forms a moral community.[106] This does not fail to raise some problems with regard to the relations between human rights and the hypothetical contract.

If rights are antecedent to the contract in accordance to the veil of ignorance they should be thought of as entirely formal categories which have yet to be given content by the contracting parties; if rights are included in the list of primary goods, they are not grounded on the contract, they do not issue from the original position, as Rawls maintains.

Bayerzt here addresses the issue:

> Man is but a reed, the feeblest thing in nature, but he is a thinking reed. The entire universe need not arm itself to crush him. A vapor, a drop of water suffices to kill him. But, if the universe were to crush him, man would still be nobler than that which killed him, because he knows that he dies and the advantage which the universe has over him; the universe knows nothing of this.[107]

All our dignity for Bayerzt consists then in thoughts.

Bayerzt again said, "The nation's youths are to be instructed to be aware that human dignity is based on the fact that the human being does not just exist unconsciously, but is conscious of its existence; the human being thinks hardly anybody doubts that human life is worthy of protection or human dignity of respect, it is difficult to contradict what this means.

---

105 C. Wellman., "A New Conception of Human Rigths" in Kameka, E& Tay, A. E. (eds.) Human Rights . . . , London Press, England 1978, p. 48.

106 J. Rawls., A Theory of Justice, Cambridge: Harvard University Press, USA. 1971, p. 505-506.

107 K . . . Bayerzt., (ed.), Sanctity of Life and Human Dignity, Kluwer Academic Publishers, London 1976, p. 73.

Bayerzt here is more of Cartesian in his thoughts, he forgot in this his assertion that those who are insane or mal-developed mentally or otherwise have equally their rights to human dignity.

Respect for human dignity and rights of human being and the preservation of his basic human rights require that, even though a right is not conceptually identical with duty, there exists a normative relationship

between the basic right of human person and the imperative or necessary duty of a morally responsible rational agent.

Hence, there necessarily exists both a human subject of basic rights and a human agent of moral duties. This goes then to imply that the subject of human dignity and basic right can neither be the isolated windowless monad of Leibniz, nor the idealistic colossus of rational humanism, exiled from the world of concrete realities into the utopian lonely Island of egoistic subjectivism.[108]

The subject of human dignity and basic rights is therefore a rational social being; this means that he is capable of meaningfully relating with one another and knowing one's rights. Any killing that is not sanctioned by law is unlawful.

In truism, it is very indubitable, that every human being has right to life- not be molested, rusticated or killed by another and no one shall be deprived intentionally, of his life except in the execution of sentences of a court in respect of a criminal offence for which the person has been found guilty of in Nigeria. Where death results from the use of reasonable force in the defense of a person from unlawful violation or property, to affect lawful arrest or prevent escape of a person from lawful detention or for suppressing a riot, insurrection or mutiny, such is not an unlawful deprivation of life.

There has been reports of many unlawful killings in some African countries, such as Congo, Nigeria, etc, many of which security agencies are responsible for. There are also, numerous ethno-religious cum politically-motivated murders for which no one has been held responsible.

This issue touches the issues regarding the rights to dignity of human person. Every individual is entitled to respect the dignity of his person.

This section forbids torture, inhuman or degrading treatment, slavery or servitude, forced or compulsory labor etc. That means, every person or citizen is entitled to freedom of thought, conscience and religion, freedom

[108] Cf. J. Höffner., The Christian Society, Kevelaer 1997, p. 35.

to change his religion or belief and to propagate such religion or belief in worship, teaching, practice or observance.

No one can be forced to belong to a religious group, or change his religion or to practice the tenets of a religious order.

The principal violation of the right to dignity of the human person is the use of torture especially during the investigation of crimes. A person who is arrested and detained on reasonable suspicions of him having committed a criminal offence cannot claim to be entitled to sleep on bed while in detention. Equally inclusive are the issues concerning fair hearing, right to family life, right to freedom of thought, conscience and religion, freedom of expression and press, right to freedom of movement, right to freedom from discrimination, right to acquire and own property cum right to compensation on compulsory acquisition of property, and the infringement on Human Right violation and the problem oft the right to personal liberty, which states that every person is entitled to his personal liberty unless in the execution of a court sentence in respect of a criminal offence for which the person has been tried and convicted.

A person who is arrested on reasonable suspicion of his having committed an offence has the right to remain silent until he consults his lawyer, be informed in writing of his alleged offence within 24 hours of arrest, and be brought to trial within a reasonable time. A child who is of school age may have his liberty restricted for the purposes of his education while those suffering from contagious diseases, persons of unsound mind or persons addicted to drugs may have their liberty rightly curtailed for purposes of treatment. The right to personal liberty is however not absolute. A party cannot shield himself from criminal investigation by invoking the right to personal liberty nor can one hide under the canopy of section 35 of the Federal constitution to escape from lawful custody since that would not augur well the peace, prosperity and tranquility of the society.

The United States National Conference of Catholic Bishops said that the human dignity of all is realized when people, youth and adult gain the power to work together, to improve their lives, strengthen their families and to contribute to the society.[109]

---

[109] U.S.A, National Conference of Catholic Bishops, Economic Justice For All, no. 91.

Among the elements that dehumanize the world are the mechanisms, which happen to be imbued not with authentic humanism but with materialism, and such transient elements.

On this , Pope John Paul II maintained equally that youth ab initio should realise that equality in dignity among all human persons is important.

The Church has always taught and maintained this equality in dignity among all human persons and communities.[110]

As Pope John XXIII affirmed that is not true that some human beings are by nature superior and others inferior in life. All men are equal in their natural dignity.[111]

It entails, therefore, that all have a right to that which enhances their dignity or where authentic human development belongs to. If we have equal dignity, we have equal rights to equal development.[112]

So, the authentic or integral, human development is the dignity of man, the image of God as a person and as a community.

The greatest idea of man is of no value unless it becomes part of life, part of our attitude, our choices, part of our daily routine to protect human dignity. Otherwise, we give a mere rational assent and exclude the dynamic

---

[110] John Paul II, Address to Representatives of all the Latin American Bishops at the third General Conference of the Latin-America Episcopate, 28 January 1979, p. 277.

[111] John XXIII, Message for the World day of Peace on the Theme Development and Solidarity, 8, December 1986, Pacem in Terris, no. 89, Insegnamenti, vol. 9, no. 2, 1982 p. 1886., cf. also Joseph M. deTorre, Informal Talks on Family and Society, p. 89. Solidarity, 8, December 1986, Pacem in Terris, no. 89, Insegnamenti, vol. 9, no. 2, 1982 p. 1886., cf. also Joseph M. deTorre, Informal Talks on Family and Society, op. cit., 89. Solidarity, 8, December 1986, Pacem in Terris, no. 89, Insegnamenti, vol. 9, no. 2, 1982 p. 1886., cf. also Joseph M. deTorre, Informal Talks on Family and Society, p. 89. Insegnamenti, vol. 9, no. 2, 1982 p. 1886., cf. also Joseph M. deTorre, Informal Talks on Family and Society, p. 89. Solidarity, 8, December 1986, Pacem in Terris, no. 89, Insegnamenti, vol. 9, no 2, 1982 p. 1886., cf. also Joseph M. deTorre, Informal Talks on Family and Society, op. cit., 89. no 2, 1982 p. 1886., cf. also Joseph M. deTorre, Informal Talks on Family and Society, p. 89. Insegnamenti, vol. 9, no2, 1982 p. 1886., cf. also Joseph M. deTorre, Informal Talks on Family and Society, p. 89. Solidarity, 8, December 1986, Pacem in Terris, no. 89, Insegnamenti, vol. 9, no. 2, 1982 p. 1886., cf. also Joseph M. deTorre, Informa Talks on Family and Society, 89. 2, 1982 p. 1886., cf. also Joseph M deTorre, Informal Talks on Family and Society, op. cit., 89.

[112] Cf. Paul VI, Populorum Progressio, no. 47.

force of ideas which may concern the dignity of another man or another group.

The North-Eastern Bishops in Africa pointed out clearly, "If a man is not given the priority, development is impossible."[113] What can give man that priority if not respect and the protection of his inalienable dignity?

Man is inseparable from his dignity; for one cannot speak of human dignity without man. Therefore the pontiff underlines the recovering and healing of the degraded human dignity as the duty of the Church.

To rediscover and make others rediscover the inviolable dignity as the duty of every human person makes up an essential task, in a certain sense, the central and unifying task of the service which the Church, the clergy and the lay faithful, are called to render to the human family.[114]

This is an essential and central task because this dignity belongs to man and man is the end of the Church and evangelization.

The dignity of the human person is the most precious possession of an individual. The youths cannot but have and even need greater respect for dignity and rights of human beings in our present day society.

A reasonable nation should avoid whatever thing or things that could be threats to humanity, and threats to human rights and human dignity.

When we violate human rights we are violating human dignity since the inalienable rights of man, have their foundations in human dignity, a dignity that is based on man's being created in the image and likeness of God. (cf. Gen.1:26).Though, man is seen as the centre of God's creation, his inalienable rights, his dignity are being violated daily at random.

In reaffirming the centrality of man in creation in this world, youths should observe and have to vehemently denounce all forms in which human rights are being violated.

On this, Pope John Paul II said: "We are firmly convinced that there is no programme in today's world in which man is not inevitably brought to the fore, even the platforms of the programmes are made up of conflicting ideologies concerning the way of conceiving this world.

If in spite of these premises, Human Rights are being violated in various ways if in practice we see before us concentration camps, violence, torture, terrorism and discrimination in many forms, this must then be the

[113] North-East Bishops, Joint Declaration, 14 July 1966, in: CAMARAH; op. cit., p. 172.
[114] Cf. John Paul II, Christifideles Laici, no. 37.

consequence of other premises, undermining and often almost annihilating the effectiveness of humanistic premises of these modern programmes and systems."[115] Fundamental Rights and freedoms are not in the power of government to give and take as it pleases. They are not *'gratis''* but they inhere in man by the very fact of his being. The major international declarations, treaties and constitutions in conjunction with applicable principles of customary International Law in turn were inspired by nature to recognise and support this view. Human life is unique and the highest value in our world.

The creator of mankind allows man by virtue of his being human some inalienable rights which are metaphysical and ontological. Basic Human Rights are not negotiable or disposable by government take-over of schools no matter under what pretext. We are not entitled to fundamental freedoms at the discretion of government. Is this not good news for many African-Nigerian youths and adults who have lived under all sorts of deprivations?

Human Rights so to say, do cover domestic, as well as international circumstances. Unless individuals, communities, corporations, governments, and other groups recognize Human Rigths at home, the promotion of Human Rights on a broader level appears meaningless or, at best, superficial.

The most appropriate place to really begin the study and application of Human Rights, lies within a person's own environment or domicile.

This Human Rights requires countries to hold free and democratic elections which shall determine the desires of the people. Any individual has the right to run for government position or support candidates running for office. Government may not discriminate against individuals in its provision of public services.

Obviously, abuses of these Human Rights occur in many countries, including those with a strong democratic tradition, such as the United States. Where everyone may have the right to take part in government, lack of financial resources can hinder this participation.

Without adequate funding, an individual has little chance of being elected, particularly in state or federal elections. Regarding the Human Right's laws are the laws which include that it can be used to promote or protect Human Rights. It is primarily found in three forms and is constantly evolving; in State Constitutions (particularly their Bills of Rights), in treaties between States (found in Human Rights convention and covenants),

[115] John Paul II, Redemptor Hominis, no. 17.

and in international customary law (e.g certain provisions of the Universal Declaration of Human Rights).

To be sincere, government can do no more than to always guarantee the rights of peoples as ordained by natural law.

One way to do this will be to respect our Bill of Rights set out in chapter four of the Nigerian 1979 Constitution and incorporate international human rights norms in municipal legislation.

If not, it will be the clear duty of our courts to be always alert and judicially active in the protection and enforcement of fundamental rights and freedoms. Whether this language is palatable or not, God, not man is the right owner, and origin and source of life. The youths are to respect and protect human life wherever they are. The discipline of Theology and the prophetic role of Catholic Priest have been called to intervene.

One of the outspoken Catholic bishops of Nigeria, John Onaiyekan said: "For Africa and the Third World, human rights issues are matters of life and death and this appears to be the conviction of the Symposium of Episcopal Conferences of Africa and Madagascar (SECAM).

Human life should be saved not to be destroyed.[116] Following the initiative of Vatican II, Pope John XIII and Paul VI, SECAM has since its inception in 1969, made declarations relevant to development, human promotion and Human Rights, all intimately linked with evangelization. SECAM sees its vocation to preach the good news as deep identification with the poor, the captive, and the blind, those oppressed as seen in (Lk.4:18-19), and the under privileged of our society.

Indeed, all categories of persons ought to enjoy fully the right to all authentic human development, and as the Holy Father Pope Paul VI tells us in the above quotations; we are all brothers and sisters in common humanity for we have a common heavenly Father.[117]

What gives each person his rights to development is this equality in dignity among all human persons. This one I would say, is from nature. The Church advises us to maintain this equality or egalitarianism among all human persons and communities. Furthermore on the rights of children

[116] J. Onaiyekan., Evangerlizaion and Human Rights Issues in Africa Today, Some Pastoral Reflections, Paper presented at the Pan-African Missionary Encounter of Claretians Working in Africa, Nekede (Owerri), 17th to 23rd August, 1990.

[117] Cf. Paul VI, Populorum Progressio, no. 47.

and youths, the endorsement of the United Nations Declarations of Human Rights and the Vatican Council II affirms that children and young people have the right to be stimulated, to make sound moral judgements based on a well-formed conscience and to put them into practice with a sense of personal commitment, more perfectly.[118]

The Council insists that all those who are incharge of civil administration or in control of education make it their care to ensure that young people are never deprived of this sacred right.[119]

The respect for Human Dignity and Rights of human beings should be greatly promoted. The government should make the world a more serious place where all human rights, including reproductive rights are fully respected, and where every young person, like everybody else, is both free and responsible.

At the look of things in today's society, the monitoring of human rights violation and the fighting and prevention of terrorist attacks should give any wise nation sleepless nights and spur them into having continual working modalities and policies and usage of covert action in response to terrorism, national and global security. For example, there should be a serious focus on studies on conflict and terrorism because of challenges posed by terror and political violence for international peace and security.

The government should always sincerely hunt terror and terrorists with their tactical intelligence to prevent any terrorist threats to international peace and security. More often than not, terrorists strike with weapons of mass destruction. Nigeria ought to and should have a fair share of human good, Human Rights records but today it is vice –versa.

The societal problems are made and could be corrected. Human Rights, as a terminology, were quite popular in Nigeria in spite of it having been ruled by many military regimes.

The regimes were said to be dictorial and repressive or to abuse the rule of law, until General Babangida employed it as an instrument to rationalise his overthrow of the Buhari/ Idiagbon regime in August 1985.

The nascent regime expressed commitment to uphold the fundamental Human Rights of Nigrians. Human Rights soon became serious with the cold-blooded murder of Dele Giwa, the founding editor-in-Chief of

[118] Cf. U. N., Human Development Report , 1993, p.v.

[119] Cf. GE art.1c.

Newswath magazine. Although its declaration to uphold human rights was laudable, there was an embedded signal of limitation to the regime's commitment in this regard, which did not catch the attention of many analysts in the euphoria of regime change and action.

The General had indeed noted with a caveat in his maiden broadcast that fundamental Human Rights and civil liberties will be respected but their exercise must not degenerate into irrational expression nor border on subversion. The civil society in Nigeria, which had been galvanized with the political bureau debate on Nigeria's future which had earlier suffered a miscarriage became mobilized and agitated for a regime change through the transition process which the regime itself had initiated.

At this point, the international community began to express an incipient concern about growing violation of rights and the several doctoring of the transition programmed, called "hidden agenda" by the emergent Human Rights community. The fate of that transition programmed is now a history. It engendered one of the costliest political crises, seconded only to the civil War of 1967-1970 in the Nigeria's annals.

More often than not, we feel insecure, and unfree, as almost like slaves in a free country or nation. Some people are manipulated, some are marginalized, exploited and even mowed down liked pigs subjected to any unjust command and butchered by some ungruntled elements, the undedicated security agents.

There has been confusion concerning internal and external problems and the yearning are both from ruler and ruled. Why does our society often slide into disaster and various mayhem. Restoration of sanity, modesty and the removal or minimization for hatred of a falsehood and prejudice of extremes both of ignorancy and arrogancy coupled with pride is necessity.

Decent living is worthwhile for every generation of any epoch. Knowing more about human dignity and human rights could help the society grow in the desired manner and progression.

For human dignity to be upheld, it needs a grandeur of endurance, excellence and the very right of human beings to have a unified world;

the world of justice, peace and new lovely world which is in accordance with what is true, fitting, commendable and genuine. This means categorically that human life and human dignity are inviolable.

As Bayert once said, all our dignity consists, in thoughts. And he then instructed us to be aware that human dignity is based on the fact that a human being does not exist unconsciously, but is conscious of its existence.

What can give man that priority if not respect and the protection of his inalienable dignity?

Man is inseparable from his dignity for one cannot speak of human dignity or human rights without man. Therefore the pontiff underlines the recovering and healing of the degraded human dignity as the duty of the Church and the State. To rediscover and make others rediscover the inviolable dignity as the duty of every human person, makes up an essential task, in a certain sense; the central and unifying task of the service which the Church, the clergy and the lay faithful, are called to render to human family.[120] This is an essential and central task because this dignity belongs to man and man is the end of the Church and evangelization. The dignity of the human person is the most precious possession of an individual. If in spite of these premises, human rights are being violated in various ways, if in practice we see before us concentration camps, violence, torture, terrorism and discrimination in many forms, this must then be the consequence of other premises, undermining and often almost annihilating the effectiveness of humanistic premises of these modern programmes and systems."[121]

Fundamental Rights and freedoms are not in the power of government to give and take as it pleases. They are not *'gratis''* but they inhere in man by the very fact of his being.

Our nation's youths should not at any time forget that violence is an integral part of the attitudes of terrorists and with its adverse effects to human right and dignity. To promote human dignity and eliminate certain threats in today's society, the government should assist combating terrorism by being prepared to act and to respond to terrorism, so as not to allow their activities to rise on daily bases. Christianity is the meeting point of earth and heaven. It lays claim to whole man, body and soul, intellect and will, inducing him to raise his mind above the changing conditions of this earthly existence and reach upwards for good life."[122]

---

[120] Cf. John Paul II, Christifideles Laici, no. 37.

[121] John Paul II, Redemptor Hominis, no. 17.

[122] John XXIII, Mater et Magistra, 1961, nos. 1-2.

This entails the Church involving herself with the exigencies of man's daily life, with his livelihood and education, and his general earthly welfare and progress.

The African experience of person takes in one of the full swoop of the community (human and spiritual), and the individual.

Anton in the Basic Writings of Thomas Aquinas said that we should therefore work for the respect and protection of the fundamental rights of the human person, for the realization of the common good rightly understood, and this will motivate the youths towards the elimination of all trace of racial discrimination. The Church has great concern for the development of the whole man and all people; for it is man who is always at the centre and at the focus.[123]

123 Cf. P. C. Anton., (ed.), Basic Writings of St.Thomas Aquinas, (New York Random House Inc. 1945), p. 687.

Chapter Two: Nigeria-African Predicaments and Human Rights Violation

2.1

Conflicts Dialogue Resolution and Human Rights Violation in Africa-Nigerian Nation

Conflict and Dialogue Resolution especially of Human Rights Violation in Nigeria is a very sensitive and challenging topic in the Nigeria-African scenario and this concerns majorly, the peaceful co-existence, unfair treatment of minority groups and social injustice, ethnic or religious intolerance and other pertinent kinds of boundary disputes in our present nation numbering over 170 million persons. Conflict, actually means a serious disagreement or argument, typically, a protracted one to come into collision or disagreement; be contradictory, clash at variance, or in opposition and negation.

On the matters of dialogue; dialogue simply means a conversation between two people. Dialogue is a means towards a quicker resolution of conflict, quarrel or problem. It also means a discussion of positions or beliefs, especially between two or more people or groups, especially one directed towards exploration of a particular subject or resolution of a disagreement or problem. This is an interchange and discussion of ideas, especially when open and frank, as in seeking mutual understanding or harmony.

The importance of dialogue is variant. Dialogue is an inclusive process. As the climate change talks demonstrate, dialogue brings together a diverse set of voices to create a microcosm of the larger society. To bring about sustainable change, people have to develop a sense of joint ownership of the process and become stakeholders in identifying new approaches to address common challenges.

Indeed, dialogue entails learning, not just talking. The process is not just about sitting around a table, but changing the way people talk, think and communicate with one another. Unlike other forms of discussion, dialogue requires self-reflection, spirit of inquiry and personal change to be present.

Participants must be willing to address the root causes of a crisis, not just the symptoms on the surface.

For instance, the 1979 Camp David accords between Egypt and Israel may have ended the armed conflict, but arguably created no qualitative "below-the-waterline." difference in "Bringing Iraqis To The Table," The Boston Globe (April 25, 2008).

That is, there was peace (understood as the absence of violence) but no personal change (which would lead to genuine and sustainable peace). The importance of dialogue is variant.

Dialogue is an inclusive process. As the climate change talks demonstrate, dialogue brings together a diverse set of voices to create a microcosm of the larger society. To bring about sustainable change, people have to develop a sense of joint ownership of the process and become stakeholders in identifying new approaches to address common challenges.

Dialogue entails learning not just talking. Dialogue recognizes one another's humanity. Participants must be willing to show empathy toward one another, recognize differences as well as areas of common ground, and demonstrate a capacity for change. To foster this kind of human interaction, a respectful and neutral setting or "safe space" is preferred. That is why O?Malley brought Iraqis to Helsinki and not Basra. Dialogue stresses a long-term perspective. Other forms of conversation tend to focus on the symptoms rather than the root causes of problems.

Dialogue stresses a long-term perspective. Other forms of conversation tend to focus on the symptoms rather than the root causes of problems.

To find sustainable solutions requires time and patience. Dialogue indeed matters a lot for conflict prevention and peace building in any nation especially those long lasting war zones.

Dialogue is not a one-size-fits-all strategy. It is not a panacea for resolving all the world's crises, where there is deep political paralysis or a long history of violence. Rather, it represents just one tool in policymakers' toolbox a process that is flexible and adaptable to different contexts and countries, one that is especially useful when the parties to a conflict are not ready yet for formal negotiations. Dialogue requires that basic conditions be present first.

When violence, hatred, and mistrust remain stronger than the will to forge a consensus, or if there is a significant imbalance of power or a lack of political will among the participants, then the situation might not be ripe for dialogue. Moreover, participants must feel free to speak their minds without fear of retribution, or rejection.

Dialogue is meant to complement other forms of diplomatic or political processes, or lay the groundwork for future and more formal talks, not replace them. Sometimes dialogue occurs within more formal negotiations, as has been the case with the ongoing talks between Columbia and Ecuador after a March 2008 cross-border incursion damaged relations.

As Jimmy Carter told the Bi-National Dialogue Group of Ecuador and Columbia.

The process is different from other forms of conversation. In dialogue there are no winners. Whereas the purpose of negotiation is to reach a concrete settlement, the aim of dialogue is to bridge communities, share perspectives and discover new ideas. "Time and again," as Nelson Mandela once said, "conflicts are resolved through shifts that were unimaginable at the start."

Cardinal Onaiyekan said, Boko Haram in Nigeria other places had caused hatred and divisions among the people, and "reconciling" will be one of the main issues that the government will have to face as soon as the fight is over. In addition to reconciliation, he said, the authorities will have to focus on "deradicalizing" people who had turned to Islamist extremism.

The Cardinal added that people in the country were wondering how it was possible that Boko Haram still hadn't been defeated, since he said "it is only a small group in a small part of Nigeria", and that Nigerians "expected" the government to defeat them soon. Cardinal John Onaiyekan, the Archbishop of Abuja, has warned that despite recent advances by the military, the "problem [Boko Haram] was not over", and said that more security forces should be stationed in the remote north-east areas where the Islamist group is most active. However, the cardinal also said that people are confident that the "insurgency will be defeated", with thousands of displaced Nigerians already making their way back to their homes. He spoke to Claire Gilbody Dickerson.

The echoes of the conference have continued to reverberate in our Parishes and even beyond Nigeria. We enjoin all the Delegates, Institutions and Dioceses to continue to infuse the grassroots and the general public with the life-enhancing fruits of the exercise. We must continue to bear courageous witness to the love of God for humanity by sending his only Son that all might be saved. We commit ourselves to hosting more of such conferences to positively animate and energize our Church and society in order to safeguard them from anti-life ideologies and activities.

A. DIALOGUE DO MAKE A DIFFERENCE IN SOME AREAS OR SITUATIONS

The importance of Dialogue requires that basic conditions be present first for the issue at stake. Dialogue is meant to complement other forms of diplomatic or political processes, or lay the groundwork for future and more formal talks, not replace them.

Sometimes dialogue occurs within more formal negotiations, as has been the case with ongoing talks between Colombia and Ecuador after a March 2008 cross-border incursion damaged relations.

When violence, hate, and mistrust remain stronger than the will to forge a consensus, or if there is a significant imbalance of power or a lack of political will among the participants, then the situation might not be ripe for dialogue. Moreover, participants must feel free to speak their minds without fear of retribution, or rejection. Dialogue is meant to complement other forms of diplomatic or political processes, or lay the groundwork for future and more formal talks, not replace them. Dialogue can facilitate recovery from crisis. After four years of recession and rising unemployment, Argentine President Eduardo Duhalde convened a "historic national dialogue" in2002, inviting the Catholic Church to facilitate the process and UNDP to play the role of the secretariat. "I want to be one more worker in this convergence that unites the main members of political forces, business, labor and social groups to deal with the destruction that has brought us to the brink of anarchy and violence", the president told Argentines. The dialogue did not heal the socio-economic crisis overnight but it did help relieve tensions, develop a set of social reform options and prepare an emergency economic plan. Dialogue can help avert violent conflict. In response to a tense and deteriorating situation in 2003-2004 widespread poverty and a political stalemate talks were convened in Mauritania. Under the auspices of UNDP, about 400 members of Mauritania's government, opposition and civil society convened over a span of six months.

The entry point for the dialogue was to advance the Millennium Development Goals (MDGs) a set of UN benchmarks to combat global problems like poverty, illiteracy, and HIV/AIDS by 2015. The MDGs ended up providing a safe point of departure to bring the political factions and other stakeholders together. Moreover, a culture of communication and cooperation was created, allowing the opposition to tackle more sensitive issues like corruption, social discrimination, and uneven development.

Dialogue can help address environmental concerns. To outsiders, the Galapagos Islands appear to be a peaceful and idyllic locale, best known for their varied wildlife. But in recent years the volcanic archipelago has been embroiled in a different sort of eruption a feud between nature preservationists and pro-development natives. Talks were convened in the late 1990s, bringing together conservationists, fishermen and adverse set of political actors. The result was a Special Administrative Law that required all sectors of society to collectively manage a marine reserve and take part in the decision-making process. Problems remain but the dialogue process helped restore locals'confidence in their government and reconcile economic with environmental interests.

Dialogue can assist in conflict resolution. In response to a dispute between rural villagers and urban inhabitants in the San Mateo Ix-tatan region of Guatemala, a country still reeling from decades-long civil war, a dialogue was convened in 2001 by the Organization for American States.

Power had shifted to the cities, and rural representatives, many of them former guerilla members, wanted more attention paid to poverty relief and economic development. The dialogue, which was observed by the Catholic Church and the media, addressed these concerns while in the process providing a catharsis of sorts, as participants shared the pain and suffering they experienced from the civil war. The dialogue paved the way for greater communication and built trust between the two feuding sides.

Dialogue indeed matters a lot for conflict prevention and peace building in any nation especially those long lasting war zones.

The Top 10 countries where terrorist attacks kill the most people since 2013 are; Iran, Afghanistan, Pakistan, Somalia, Nigeria, Syria India, Philippens, Yemen and Thailand. Iraq suffered more deaths due to terrorist attacks than any other country in the world last year. The UNO and NATO are doing their best to bring the situation to the desired peaceful atmosphere.

B. NIGERIA A NATION OF OVER 175 MILLION INHABITANTS

Poverty and corruption are complicated by the country's great diversity. There are over 300 ethnic groups in 36 States, and the population is nearly evenly divided between Muslims and Christians.

The Muslim population is concentrated in the North, while Christians and followers of African traditional religions live predominantly in the South.

Speaking of the great division between Christians and Muslims in Nigeria, Robert Ruby and Timothy Samuel Shah explained the importance of that division as well illustrated by the fact that religion-not nationality-is the way in which most Nigerians choose to identify themselves. In a May-June [2007] survey conducted by the Pew Forum on Religion and Public Life, 76% of Christians say that religion is more important to them than their identity as Africans, Nigerians or members of an ethnic group. Among Muslims, the number naming religion as the most important factor is even higher (91%). Whether Christian or Muslim, Nigerians find great strength in their religious and cultural heritage.

In this context, the efforts of two courageous individuals, Pastor James Wuye and Imam Mohammed Ashafa, provide a compelling story and enlightening example of the potential power of interfaith dialogue as a tool for peace building. The Initiative for Peace building (IfP) is a consortium led by International Alert and funded by the European Commission.

International Alert is an independent peace building organisation that has worked for over 20 years to lay the foundations for lasting peace and security in communities affected by violent conflict.

Mediation and dialogue are the most established strategies of conflict resolution. Grounded in the principle that the conflict parties need to resolve the conflict themselves with procedural assistance from a neutral and impartial third party, mediation and dialogue appear to be a fair, humanistic, cost-effective and democratic means of conflict resolution, as opposed to arbitration or military intervention by any group.

C. THE ISSUES OF CONFLICT RESOLUTION AND LEARNING OUR LESSONS

Conflict on the other hand can be described as a situation of true or perceived disagreement through which the parties involved identify a threat to their interests, values/ethics or concerns. The variant issues to the problems of conflict resolutions and the resultant problems or consequential aspects could be seen below regarding the causes of the nation's conflict.

D. SOME OF THE KNOWN CAUSES OF CONFLICT IN MOST AFRICAN NATIONS

Religion can be explained as any specific system of beliefs about a divine being, often involving a set of rituals, a code of ethics and a philosophy of life which adherents/ followers must accept without question.

Religious conflicts in Nigeria have been traced to the under listed causes. These are:

a. Relative insecurity and Non-Challancy
b. Vengeance
c. Egoism and Poverty
d. Religious fanaticism
e. Land issues
f. Unemployment/under employment especially of youths
g. Wrong interpretation and/or understanding of the tenets of the holy books
h. Misinformation/ignoramus
i. Perceived feelings of marginalization
j. Increased politicization of religion
k. Ethno-religious reasons and other possible conflicts clothed in religious "garments"

Actually, we human beings should know naturally, that conflicts is a part of human life, and occurs in every human activity.

Very crucial is that there should be laid down rules or procedure to ensure that whenever they occur, the individual or the group involved should find a way to resolve such a conflict very quickly.

For instance, the lasting boundary dispute between Anambra State and Kogi State, in which exists heavy shootings, kidnapping, killing and missing of some important personalities in their various community in an instance worthy of mention. The authorities of both States, have met severally for a cordial understanding cultural and epistemological dialogue and the resolution of this problem but the situation remains the same, yet unsolved until the Federal Government Special Committee for resolution of ethnic or land conflicts came into the matter; and peace is seemingly coming back gradually to this area.

The reality of tolerance and better understanding of one another could be a healing root. But tolerance or toleration is a complex concept, which often expresses different degrees and forms of conscious restraint towards others. Thus, it is conceptually a form of attitude toward what is thought to be different. It is a product of series of discussions between the leadership of the two main religious bodies in Nigeria these are the Nigeria Supreme Council for Islamic Affairs (NSCIA) and the Christian Association of Nigeria (CAN). They are not government parastatals but are supported by government to ensure peaceful existence among the nation's citizenry.

The devastation and other negative consequences of religious conflicts over the years informed the formation of NIREC in 1999 by Nigeria Supreme Council for Islamic Affairs (NSCIA) and Christian Association of Nigeria (CAN) to ensure freedom of religion and welfare of all men and all citizenry. Nigeria Inter Religious Councils are helping in no small measure to finding a lasting solution to conflict resolution and peace.

It is a product of series of discussions between the leadership of the two main religious bodies in Nigeria, that is, the Nigeria Supreme Council for Islamic Affairs (NSCIA) and The Christian Association of Nigeria (CAN).

The Inter Religious Councils help in finding a lasting solution to conflict resolution and peace in conflicting situations, thus:

a. To honestly and sincerely endeavour, by themselves, to understand the true teachings of the two religions-Christianity and Islam including their peculiarities and personal mannerisms through dialogue, discussions, workshops, seminars, conferences, pamphleteering.
b. To create fora and channels for the peaceful resolution of any friction or misunderstanding that may arise from time to time.
c. To serve as an avenue for articulating cordial relationships amongst the various religious groups and between them and the government, etc.

d. To promote and inculcate moral, ethical, social and cultural values of the two faiths for the rebirth and rebuilding of a better society.
e. To provide a forum for mutual co-operation and promotion of the welfare of all citizens in the nation.
f. Toleration is widely considered a highly relevant value in moral, religious and political thoughts D. Heyd refers to the virtue of toleration, particularly from the moral point of view, as that of allowing for a judgement more inclusive than the one based on a common value system shared by all members.

Objects of toleration can be individuals, people, beliefs, action, view points and similar entities that are considered different from one or one's own. Tolerance can be treated both as a personal virtue and a social structural or political measure. Nigeria is a multi-ethnic nation with diverse cultural backgrounds. Instead of harnessing our diversities towards viable national development, we have become slaves to our ethnic origins to which our allegiance is highly focused to the detriment of nation building.

Tribal and ethnic consciousness has resulted to ethnic prejudice and mistrust, religious and political problems and socio-cultural conflicts. These vices have pervaded all spheres of life in Nigeria, be it employment, education, religion and admission into federal institutions. The early formation of the Nigeria nation by the early colonial masters contributed immensely to the ethnicity and intolerance attitude of Nigeria's ethnic groups towards each other. It is very unfortunate, that, right from the time of the birth of Nigeria, the seed of continuous squabble has been sown among the ethnic groups that make up Nigeria by the British and independence probably due to their policy. For many years now, terrorism has indeed become a persistent and nasty reality in global politics and this ought to and should always attract and capture the attention of both the State and Federal government. This has been a long standing problem in Nigeria since independence. The number of violent conflicts has declined in recent years as the willingness of governments, international organizations, and other actors to engage in dialogue has reached higher levels. If hearts and minds in South Africa and Northern Ireland can come unhardened, then the possibilities are endless. Take it from Albert Einstein, who correctly noted that "problems cannot be solved by the same level of thinking that created them."

Among the roles of religion in society that was emphasized is social cohesion, social control, and creation of meaning. Since social conflicts is a possibility in the midst of social order, the role of religion in social conflict, as an agent of social change which was also explored with instances from the United States civil rights movements and liberation theology. We also noted that religion was the basis of Roman, Greek, Western, Arabic and Asian civilizations.

With particular reference to the Nigerian context, the role of the supreme Being, gods, goddesses, spirits, ancestors, talisman magic (juju) and witchcraft is in the maintenance of the traditional social order that were highlighted. Finally, it was pointed out that with the introduction of Islam and Christianity to Nigeria, the resultant confusion in the conflict of values made the maintenance of the traditional social order less effective.

Consequently, among the burning issues and areas of contention today between Muslims and Christians include: Nigeria's membership of Organization of Islamic Conference (OIC), introduction of Sharia legal system in some Northern States, the Boko Haram menace and the planned introduction of Islamic Banking System by the Central Bank. Thus, while religion serves as the basis of social order, it can also give rise to and generate a lot of religious crisis/conflict in a pluralistic society such as Nigeria. Incompetent hands have been piloting the affairs of the nation on trial and error basis. Nigeria has been so unfortunate to have had series of unpatriotic, misfit unscrupulous, self centred and corrupt leaders. Nigerian leaders through utterances and actions encourage destructive tendencies, rivalry and disunity.

Here Chinua Achebe too maintained that he was an eye-witness to the momentous occasion when Chief Awolowo stole the leadership of Western Nigeria from Azikiwe in a broad- day light on the floor of Western House of Assembly and sent the great Azikiwe scampering back to the Niger where he became for Nigerian leaders usually, one who struggle for power at all costs and consequently does not give opportunity to the right men who would have rendered the best services to the nation.

The difficulties and differences in languages or means of communication also play a great role. The multiplicity of language and dialects spoken all over the country also militate against ethnic tolerance. Language in other nations is used as a tool for unity, but in Nigeria, it is the basis for discrimination, segregation, separation and deprivation. The elites of the nation should create or find an easier way or tendencies which masses were supposed to integrate into a united country. The departing colonial masters had created an excessively unstable and unbalanced political structure where by the Northern region was twice big as the East and West together.

Regional boundaries were arbitrarily drawn and in some cases not made to correspond with existing ethnic boundaries.

Case in point is the Yoruba who were so divided that some of them live in Nigeria while others live in Benin Republic.

Till date, this structural imbalance has proved very difficult to correct and that is responsible for incessant boundary clashes and politics of ethnic rivalry in the country. The people's attention has been shifted from issues of national consideration and nationhood to ethnic and tribal rivalry.

Religious fundamentalism particularly among some Islamic sectarian groups has contributed to violent religious uprising in some parts of the country, especially in some Northern States. Towards the end of 1980, for example, the Mohammed Maitasinene and his sectarian group unleashed havoc on Kano and its inhabitants. He and his disciples appeared to have attacked both Muslims and non-Muslims who did not share their beliefs.

Foreign observers like UNO noticed that Nigeria is one of the countries where religion has wrecked much havoc on the advancement, unity and prosperity of her citizens, and the development of the nation as a whole.

A good vision had been echoed at the nation's independence in 1960 in our first national anthem thus in this manner thus: ''Nigeria we hail thee our own dear native land, though tribes and tongues may differ in brother hood we stand... "Nigeria, all are proud to serve our sovereign mother land'. All these noble ideal demonstrate our country's national motto of unity and faith, peace and progress, which forms the road map for promoting ethnic tolerance and integration. But how far have these ideals been realized?

It is unfortunate indeed that these entire, ideals, noble have continued to hit the rocks as our present socio-economic and political terrains are characterized by ethnic rivalry, intolerance and conflicts.

Tolerance remains a fair, objective and permissive attitude towards those whose opinions, practice, race, religion, language, culture, beliefs or practices differ from or conflict with one's own. It is willingness to accept feelings, habits or beliefs that are different from one's own. Acknowledging the fact of the State of Nigeria before and after the Colonial Masters buttresses the fact that Nigeria as a nation never existed until 1914 when Lord Lugard amalgamated people dwelling in a certain part of Africa. The people dwelling in the major parts of the area that would comprise the would be created Nigeria include, the eastern, the Western and the Northern areas; people with different and distinct historical backgrounds.

They had nothing in common, no cohesion whatever. In the African Nigerian nation, the leadership conflict and power struggle is till date a problem.

This has been a long standing problem in Nigeria since independence.

Incompetent hands have been piloting the affairs of the nation on trial and error basis. Nigeria has been so unfortunate to have had series of unpatriotic misfits, unscrupulous, self-centered and corrupt leaders. Nigerian leaders through their utterances and actions encourage destructive tendencies, rivalry and disunity.

Achebe maintained that he was an eye-witness to the momentous occasion when Chief Awolowo stole the leadership of western Nigeria from Nnamdi Azikiwe in broad day light on Nigerian leaders usually struggle for power at all cost and consequently do not give opportunity to the right men who would have rendered the best services to the nation.

More so is the Religious fundamentalism particularly among some Islamic sectarian groups has contributed to violent religious uprising in some parts of the country, especially in some Northern States. Towards the end of 1980, for example, the Mohammed Maitasinene and his sectarian group unleashed havoc on Kano and its inhabitants. He and his disciples appeared to have attacked both Muslims and non-Muslims who did not share their beliefs, observed that Nigeria is one of the countries where religion has wrecked much havoc on advancement, unity and prosperity of her citizens, and the development of the nation as a whole. He noted that between 1980 and 1995 not less than fourteen convulsive religious conflicts, many lives and property were lost. The impediments were as a result of the consequences of the forced amalgamation. The consequences of Lord Lugard's amalgamation of the distinct ethnic groups into one nation without preparing the people in that regard has created a situation whereby a fundamental problem of trust and tolerance of other people's way of life has been instituted. The implication of such a forced union is clear. Nigeria has never been one. Each of the ethnic groups is still distinct and sees itself as only a part of Nigeria.

It was as a result of this that Madiebo observes, that the federation of Nigeria as it exists today, has never really been one homogenous country; for its widely different people and tribes are yet to find any basis for their unity.

For whatever reason different ethnic groups with divergent backgrounds were amalgamated into one country, Britain sowed the seed of political instability, ethnic intolerance, and the fruits of which the inmates of Nigeria are reaping today.

Moreover, in the same line of thought, Azide opined that it was obvious that the British colonial government were consciously creating two aspects of Nigerians, one conservative and tradition-bound, the other more egalitarian and modern. The British never cared to initiate unifying factors. What was uppermost in their mind was a conducive atmosphere to facilitate their economic mission. Ever since that fusion, there has been mutual distrust and intolerance among Nigerians. There has equally been no loyalty to the nation. The Igbo man sees himself as mainly Igbo and the Hausa man not a Nigerian. The Yoruba man also sees himself as a Yoruba. With this frame of mind there is loyalty and tolerance to the tribes and not the nation. Everybody therefore sees the center-Nigeria as a national cake, a gold mine where everybody according to his own national cake, a gold mine where everybody according to his own carelessness, intolerance and oversight, without reference to any regulation, struggles aggressively and intolerably for shares to be hauled back to his ethnic groups or tribe or self. As a result, there are some awkward and concerted efforts to show tolerance to African tradition, the common interest of the people and tolerance towards other people. The negative clamor for federal character, quota system, geographical spread, etc to be reflected or borne in mind in the distribution of national amenities is both insinuation of what is and its perpetuation. In other words, there has been no change of attitude to the deep narrows in the national wall. Regarding insecurity it is clear that from the foregoing, that the governance of our public interests has no semblance of responsibility, it means that public institutions meant to ensure justice end up enthroning injustice.

This injustice comes in many guises; in the massive privileges the governing class gives to itself; in its recklessness and its impunity; and also in the lethargy of the governed whose irrationality prevents them from seeing how they are being systematically short-changed by the governing class. But however it is clothed, the word of St. Augustine is very important in this regard. It means that the absence of justice and what is human community is but a bond of robber.

It means that the absence of justice gives way to violence and ultimately general insecurity. Violence takes place where the populace has ceased to hope to get a better deal through civil and legal means. It is a situation where dialogue and persuasion have ceased to have the upper hand. Nigeria is endemically an unjust society, and there is no doubt at all that it has also become a very insecure nation. Suffice it here to dwell briefly on just 3 examples.

The first is the Niger Delta problem; popularly named the issue of "resource control." Nigeria was hitherto using a formula of distribution of its income which gave 50% to the region in which the resource was derived.

But when oil was discovered in sufficient quantity, the formula was changed by General Gowon to 0% given to derivation. Sometime in the past it was between 1 and 3%, and in many instances, this paltry percentage was not even given out.

Nigerian governing class was content to pipe oil to the golden eggs, from this obvious injustice lasting for decades came the story of kidnapping and taking of oil workers as hostages.

It was the birth of kidnapping in our country. First oil workers were taken for ransom, and soon there were not enough expatriates to kidnap. But criminals in Nigeria learnt from this reaction to injustice the trade of kidnapping. Today, no one is safe in the country; and one will be living in illusion to think that our State of injustice of skewed derivation principle will make one to easily forget other acts of injustice in our polity and in our history. Virtue is acquired by repeating virtuous acts. It means that you cannot be a good man if you are not consistent in doing good. A society cannot be just if it is not consistent in upholding justice. A society that tolerates one act of injustice paves the way for another and often worse injustice. In this regard, Nigeria has easily forgotten that some of the States that are today calling for justice over derivation presided over the massive stealing of the properties of other Nigerians from today's South East who were fleeing the Nigerian civil War under the euphemism of abandoned property. The war was after all justified on the grounds of keeping Nigeria one. When the war of unity was won, thousands lost their houses for the simple reason of being from one part of the country other than from the other.

It is till today shocking that this brazen act of injustice was supported by the might of the Federal Government, perhaps as war booty to its camp followers, while other Nigerians who were not affected directly look on in utter unconcern. Today the act has been perfected and forgotten, but note that it is same the Federal Government of Nigeria which presided over the massive impoverishment of the Niger Delta region.

It is this improvement which led to the violence of Ogoni crisis-to the culture of kidnapping and thus to the increase in the level of violence in our society. This increase of violence by MEND, MOSSOP and other groups must have in some uncanny manner influenced the brazenness of today's Boko Haram in the North east of the country. We will not be thinking properly to look at such phenomenon merely from the point of view of religious or Islamic fanaticism.

Of course the country, especially Christians living in the North have suffered terribly from scourges of senseless fanaticism.

But how many people have been prosecuted for wanton destruction of life and properly in the past on grounds of Islamic fundamentalism. Is it that nobody has ever been caught? Again here impunity reigns in the psyche of our leaders who think you can solve a problem by simply sweeping it under the carpet. The impunity with which many States of the North declared Sharia rule and got away with it is the same that propels the actions of the Boko Haram sect today.

The Scottish philosopher Edmund Burke said that the society is like a contract between the living, the dead and those to be born.

Thus its history should not be trivialized; with the inability that once the event is over it is by-gone and remains so. Our past as a nation must conspire to shape our present as a consciously developing country.

The phenomenon of Boko Harram, more than any other factor is due to the continued impoverishment of our population through mismanagement. We have seen that Nigerians who lived in the 70s are better of than those who lived in the 1990s and those who lived in 1999 (when our position in the HDI was 146) and better of than those living now when our HDI rating has dropped to 156. The continued impoverishing of the society makes it very easy to recruit suicide bombers because a level of the population is left behind that is ready to die for a piece of bread or for the promise of 72 virgins in paradise in a sort of Rabbinic where kings will be their servants and queens will be their nurses. For the security of any polity and any clime, it is most dangerous if not stupid to make even a citizen especially the young to entertain little or no hope for the future.

Is it not surprising to observe that relationship between government neglect and suicidal violence? The insecurity into which the sins of bad governance has dragged us seems to have no end because our security

forces are clueless. They are not able to go underground, gather information about the groups and dislodge them before they strike. As usual what we have seen so far is joint police/military patrols in affected areas.

A new squad donned with red berets has also be formed, but where they do their anti-terrorism duty is on horrible highways, stopping cars and collecting tolls as if that has anything to do with fighting terrorism. We do not need to delve into other variant acts of violence that breed insecurity. When you look into all of them, you will notice that at the deepest root lie some acts of irresponsible governance, some failure to take people's welfare at heart, and to be honest and just.

When you talk about Jos Plateau in Nigeria other situations like that you will notice that our nation has consistently played the ostrich about the question of indignity while forcing everybody to disclose his state of origin.

We continue in this manner to divide our people deep in their consciousness and phonily engage in double speak about national unity.

Up till today, the ethnic groups that make up Nigeria still see themselves as strangers to one another and have no trust in each other.

None wants to tolerate another, each wants to dominate other. Lack of trust also brought suspicion which gave rise to the killing of one another. This was what led to the civil war of Nigeria and Biafra.

The effect is manifesting in all angles, the rise of Boko Haram issues which is now tormenting all parts of the nation; reckless bombing, kidnapping, destroying properties and the wanton killing of people.

In dreams he sees some of his relatives in the appearance of human forms.

He cannot shake off the belief that they are not still alive.

Generally, in African traditional religious, there is a belief in the hierarchy of spiritual beings. Thus the Africans believe in the existence of the Supreme Being. He is the creator of the universe and everything in it.

Some people maintain that "many translations of the Africans names for God suggest that God is the Creator Almighty in heaven Africans also believe in the existence of those lesser deities.

Besides, the traditional African believes in the existence of other spirit forces such as the ancestors; *"agwu"*, that is, one of the spirits believed to, among other things, populate the universe. But these spiritual beings are not of equal importance and power to the Supreme Being. They are rather regarded as mediators through which the human being makes supplication to the Supreme Being. Moreover, the traditional African prays and worship because he is aware that he is a creature who is in relationship to other beings whose protection he enjoys and who are the source of his life on whom he depends. The beings in the universe exist for the sake of human being. Their work, among other things, is to protect and enhance the fullness of human life. Man's main relationship with these spiritual beings is through the veneration of the ancestors and sacrifices. Thus, the deities and ancestors are the medium through which the traditional African approaches God. This explains the reason for many shrines everywhere in the traditional society for the deities and for the Supreme Being.

At the hierarchical structure of these beings, man is at the lowest level. A necessity is that, to survive, one must live a life of balance with the spiritual beings and eschew from his life and activities all forms of social evils and abominations.

The meaning of peace in African traditional societies is a necessity. Peace is very often taken as the absence of open war or conflict.

This is perhaps because war is arguably the most antithetical conditions to peace of any kind. In African world, peace is valued and cherished even in the presence of many tribal conflicts. The traditional African cherishes harmony, Oguejiofor sees harmony as living in accord with various spheres or levels of reality therefore, to obtain peace, one must live in accordance with the right principles in his relationship with the supernatural, the deities and other spirit-forces, ancestors and one's fellow human beings as well as with other elements in the universe.

These elements like plants, animals are not just subjected to man's whims and caprices. For him, there is no strict dichotomy between heaven and earth, the world of the ancestors and the world of man. The spirit world is the guarantor of earthly existence and it is imperative on human beings to maintain harmonious existence with these beings. Any infringement of this obligation on the part of the human being is believed to set off a chain reaction of disorder in earthly affairs: personal, familial, communal, national and so on. Such calamities are regarded as the foundation of the absence of peace. Thus they are not often viewed as having natural causes. War, on the other hand, is not isolated from the African reality or world-view as absence of peace. Thus, Ferguson writes that a number of African tribes see war as a national calamity sent by God in punishment or retribution for some offence committed by the community or its representatives.

In African world view, the universe occupies a special importance. One cannot live at peace or a fulfilled life without adequate material means.

Thus he has to live a long and morally upright life blessed with children, have a good or natural death and accorded a befitting burial and funeral.

In this case, African traditional religions differ from some religious such as Christianity in which the adherents can live a miserable life here on earth to enjoy eternal bliss in the hereafter.

African traditional religions have no conception of goodies in the sky after one's death. With this conception, peace is not viewed as merely the absence of internecine organized wars. Thus the war to live a fulfilled life here on earth is necessary, otherwise, life is viewed as precarious and harmony must be sought with the natural and supernatural forces, which impinge on human life. The evil spirit must be appeased and warded off and the infringement of the spiritual/temporal order must be expiated. To put it succinctly, the promotion of life and enhancement of it is the cardinal principle of African traditional morality and life. The goal of all moral conduct is therefore the fullness of life. In Africa, human life is considered fully sacred when it is marked by spiritual, material and social blessings; when the network of relations with the spiritual, human and material beings is as it should be. And this is the meaning of peace in (ATR)-African Traditional Religions.

Thus a peaceful harmonious existence as enunciated by Oguejiofor must include adequate material means to live noble and worthy life and to die a dignified death in order to live in peace with the ancestors and be qualified to await reincarnation and live out another cycle of life.

Thus in traditional African societies, peace is not an abstract, theoretical concept, but rather a down-to-earth and practical concept. Peace is conceived not in relation to conflict and war, but in relation to order, harmony and equilibrium. Onah maintains that peace in traditional Africa is a religious value in that the order, harmony and equilibrium in the universe and society is (sic) believed to be divinely established and the obligation to maintain them is religious. It is also a moral value since good conduct is required of human beings if the order, harmony and equilibrium are to be maintained. Any action that is capable of hindering another from attaining peace or the fullness of life is considered a breach of peace.

Between 1980 and 1995 there were not less than fourteen convulsive religious conflicts that have occurred in the country. In each of these religious conflicts, many lives and property were lost. The impediments were as a result of the consequences of the forced amalgamation.

The consequences of Lugard's amalgamation of the distinct ethnic groups known as Nigeria has been great and the fusion of different ethnic groups into one nation without preparing the people in that regard has created a situation whereby a fundamental problem of trust and tolerance of other people's way of life has been instituted. The implication of such a forced union is clear. Nigeria has never been one but on the way to that purpose.

Each of the ethnic groups is still distinct and sees itself as only a part of Nigeria. Nevertheless, for whatever reason, different ethnic groups with divergent backgrounds were amalgamated into one country.

Moreover, in the same line of thought, Azide opined that it was obvious that the British colonial government was consciously creating two Nigerians, one conservative and tradition-bound, the, the other more egalitarian and modern. The British never cared to initiate unifying factors. What was uppermost in their mind was a conducive atmosphere to facilitate their economic mission. Ever since that fusion, there has been mutual distrust and intolerance among Nigerians. There has equally been no loyalty to the nation.

The Igbo man sees himself still as an Igbo man not a Nigerian also a Yoruba man sees himself as a Yoruba. With this frame of mind there is loyalty and tolerance to the tribes and not the nation.

Everybody therefore sees the centre-Nigeria as a national cake, a gold mine where everybody according to his own carelessness, intolerance and oversight, without reference to any regulation, struggles aggressively and intolerably for shares to be hauled back to his ethnic groups or tribe for self. The problem of terrorism here plays its negative roles. Terrorist activities create enormous hiccups in both national and international economic, political, social networking. Not long ago, David Mark, the Senate President of Nigeria addressed the issue when he said that despite the fact that Nigeria is not at war, Nigerians are now refugees in neighbouring countries as more than 57,000 people have fled to Cameroon, Chad and Niger Republic as a result of insurgency by Boko Haram, according to the United Nations. The world body also disclosed that about half a million people have been internally displaced in the country which it described as a very alarming situation. Spokesperson of the United Nations High Commission for Refugees, UNHCR, Mr. Adrian Edwards, who spoke with reporters in Geneva said of 57,000 people who fled Nigeria, 17,000 are registered as Nigerians while the rest are nationals from neighboring countries who have been living in Nigeria for ages. He disclosed that Niger received the majority-some 40,000 concentrated in the Diffa region, a desert in the country's eastern edge.

According to him, many of those fleeing to North-Easterm Nigeria are traumatized and left with very few possessions, adding that besides the Lake Chad area, some of the new arrivals are from the Borno State capital Maiduguri. He said that since Nigeria declared a state of emergency in the three States in May 2013, more than 57,000 people have fled to Cameroon, Chad and Niger.

Some 17,000 of these numbers are registered Nigerian refugees. The rest are nationals of the surrounding countries who had been living in Nigeria for decades. Edwards noted that newly arrived refugees interviewed by the staff of the UNHCR in Niger Republic have spoken of atrocities on the shores of Lake Chad in Borno State. According to him, "one woman described corpses strewn through houses and floating on the water. She said people feared staying even to bury their dead or find missing relatives.

Others recounted fleeing a village shooting incident and said women and children were being kidnapped and taken away by unidentified assailants.

We've had some other accounts of shooting in villages there with women and children being kidnapped and taken away.

So, it is really a spread of this horrible conflict we are seeing outside of the towns and into some of the rural areas of North-East Nigeria.

It's hard for us to get full visibility of the situation inside North-East Nigeria, simply because we don't have the access. And you have to remember that in addition to people fleeing Nigeria, you have got close to half a million people internally displaced inside the country. And that's according to the government's figures. So, these are really very high numbers and reflect what seems to be a very alarming situation. The latest attaches are reported to have begun in mid-February and were continuing five days ago. In all, some 2,000 people have crossed into southeast Niger's Diffa region over the past four weeks. In addition to the attacks on Lake Chad, some of the new arrivals have come from areas near Borno's State capital, Maiduguri, that have been affected by fighting. He maintained that the UNHCR reiterates to all parties to the conflict in North-Eastern Nigeria, the vital importance of protecting civilians from harm.

He said the UNHCR was working with partners, including the International Rescue Committee, the governments of the neighbouring countries, to try and ensure that countries keep their borders open and also ensure that they help people on arrival.

Accounts of the inflictions of organized, precise and well-orchestrated pain on a person or persons, communities or a country by either one or more individual, armed gangs, with the sole aim of sending a clear message across, abound in history. This message could either be a weapon of an individual, group or State. Nowadays, whenever terrorism is mentioned, our immediate thoughts instantly create scenery of bomb blast-inferno and littered mangled bodies.

It is important for the Nigerian and African nations to note, that the major component of terrorism is simply fear, institutionalized into anxiety. Individuals, groups and even a country can be exposed into this situation, and curiosity could result. Both physical and mental terrorism create and breed a dangerous State of tension and anxiety, which leads to decreased longevity. Terrorists target civilians, facilities or systems (cyber terrorism) on which civilians rely. The objective of terrorists is neither the people they will kill nor the physical material they will destroy; instead their true target remains the emotions of those who see or read about these acts of violence and then become afraid of them. Other effects include these:

a) Hyper-vigilance due to natural or global fear, anxiety, danger, working against globalization tenets.
b) General Insecurity/Destruction leading to reduced natural development/understanding.
c) Easiest alibi/tool for Western (United States) global hegemony. (d) Veritable weapon/tactics for the under-trodden towards international recognition/ problem solution.

All these are mitigating factors working against the idea and spirit of globalization. Because of the deep secrecy in finding and undertaking terrorist operations; individuals or States seen or posing as targets, actually direct more energy and resources in updating their security apparatus.

To checkmate the national or international terrorists, economic inducements and sanctions can be used interchangeably as the case may be in achieving better results in this war against terrorism.

Terrorist-prone groups' organization could be enticed with both tangible and intangible inducement. Such a 'flame' could be put off easily while still smouldering.

However, economic sanctions, wherever proven important, and needed, should be considered as last resort, sequel to its blanket effects on targeted population (innocent citizens suffer more than the culprits), and this should not be.

Ingenious engineering and training of specialized terror management groups, highly motivated and logistically activated by individual States is recommended. Such groups will dwell on the collection, collation of information, and even have the will and mandate of sorting out both established and potential terrorists.

Such, is also sequel to the fact that almost all nations that easily employ full scale military action, are always seen and known to be the 'mighty' thereby promoting the idea that 'might is power', in international politics. Many countries, especially those of the south and less developed nations in such a scenario become agitated, and so end up being reluctant to explore further antiterrorist efforts. The history of toleration in modern society is traditionally associated closely with the rise of individual as the locus of natural rights and personal autonomy. At the same time, the ideal of toleration is also very serious related to the protection of the rights of religious groups, which in reality also covers the call of restraint in the attitude to people belonging to other religious, racial and ethno-cultural groups. Hence the rights to be tolerated apply to the two levels of human interaction; namely, the level of personal liberty of individuals and the level of the rights of a group to maintain its collective identity.

In line with the understanding of psycho-philosophical cultural conflicting human problems of the nation, Wittgenstein argues and even rejects the notion of a State of complete clarity; thus, for him, conceptual clarity engenders unclarity.

The misconception of human language and misinterpretation can bring disorder and this can endanger any situation and usher in violence. For Wittgenstein, metaphysics as the effort to describe the essence of things on critically misleading preconceptions of the essence of human language, could bring misunderstanding and confusion and risking violence. On the other way round when understanding is there, this can give room for discussion and a good forum for dialogue.

Different ideas of toleration specifically exhibit ambivalent features that lead to what is commonly regarded in philosophical terms as the paradox of toleration. The Senate President of this nation, David Mark during his tenure pleaded the Insurgents to end the war and stop unleashing terror on helpless and defenceless citizens to end the hostilities. He reminded the insurgents that violence or crime anywhere cannot produce good result. No matter the amount of anger in a man's mind, resort to violence or killing another cannot be a solution. There are many channels of communication to dialogue.

We can still come to a dialogue table and resolve our differences. The spate of attacks and killings across Nigeria is becoming intolerable and indeed unbearable. The situation is degenerating. We cannot pretend not to know that the nation is endangered. We must all speak out with one voice against this growing terrorism, "for whatever reason, let wise counsel prevail."

We are not at war with each other. Nigeria's and indeed Africans ought to be their brothers' keeper always.

This time-tested position should not be compromised. Let's respect human life. "It is not too late to reverse this ugly situation especially in Borno, Yobe, Adamawa, Katsina and Benue States".

He, however, implored security operatives across the countries to remain vigilant and determined to protect lives and property even as he urged citizens to cooperate with them. Still on the base of ethnicity and ethnic intolerance, each ethnic group established their own media which often carried the message of their region that formed them.

The mass media were sometimes partisan and they carried the message of the region that established them. Few messages which reflected the national interest were carried. Many militia groups were formed by the different ethnic groups due to ethnic intolerance that were existing among Nigeria's, examples of such militia groups includes MASSOB, Egbesu Union, Niger Delta Militia groups, Yoruba organization Afenifere and Oodua People's Congress (OPC), etc. MASSOB was formed by the Igbos agitating for liberation from one Nigeria to stay on their own and answer the Biafran nation.

The Yoruba formed Afenifere and Oodua led by Senator Abraham Adesanya, aimed at fighting for marginalization of Yoruba and total boycott of the political process. The general frustration and injustice some group or ethnicity like the Niger Delta suffer in Nigeria is due to the misrule or some complaints against the northern oligarchy that has had the reign of power since independence.

Even till today, the ethnic groups that make up Nigeria still see themselves as strangers to one another and have no trust in each other. None wants to tolerate another, each wants to dominate the other. Lack of trust also brought suspicion which gave rise to killing of another. This was what led to the civil war of Nigeria and Biafra. The effect is manifesting in all angles; the rise of Boko Haram issues which is now tormenting all parts of the nation, reckless bombings, destruction of properties and killing people massively. There is that ethical concepts, fairness in togetherness with tolerance and solidarity can that secure the understanding of other points of view necessary for cordial social co-existence among different individuals and groups. Solidarity builds a certain nearness to fellow human beings in sharing the joys and sorrows of others in practical contexts of human experiences.

Tolerance helps to bridge the distance to fellow human beings, which usually separates people from one another because of certain individual differences and special characteristics.

Real meaning of tolerance is a fair, objective and permissive attitude towards those whose opinions, practice, race, religion, language, culture, beliefs or practices differ from or are conflicting with one itself. It is the willingness to accept feelings, habits or beliefs that are different from one's own or itself. Ethno disputes and cultural problems come in here. By this we mean, ethnicity relating to cultural factors such as nationality, culture, ancestry, language and beliefs. It was often used to describe minority groups of distinct cultural tradition and origin that co-existed with larger majority groups. Today, ethnicity tends to describe any groups that are characterized by a distinct sense of difference owing to culture and decent.

The 7th schedule of the 1999 Nigerian constitution contains oaths of Allegiance taking of which is required of certain public officers as enunciated therein. This is an oath "to preserve, protect and defend the country's constitution." Contained thereunder are also oaths of different offices geared toward devoting oneself to the service and well-being of the people of Nigeria. The code of conduct for these public officers is provided for in the 5th Schedule of the constitution. We confess that in this write up, we are particularly concerned with the role played by these officers in the enforcement of these rights for the said enforcement is part and parcel of defending the constitution. There is no gainsaying the fact that the present democratic process has, in the main, failed to defend the constitution in many ways especially in the areas of fundamental rights either by omission or by commission. It goes without saying that the spate of deliberate killings of innocent citizens is most abominable.

Apart from those who had their lives extinguished through dastardly acts of armed robbery, kidnapping, ritual murder and police brutality and also through hunger, there are in recent times very many cases of political assassinations.

In Nigeria, ethnicity also involves the identification of Nigerians with the dominant or subordinate majority or minority ethnic groups, all of which co-exist with the same society. Some cases or problems of dissention could equally be found in some places, even in the capital market which arose in Lagos a few years ago, conflicts also occur, between operators and investors, and among operators. In this case, in order to sustain and enhance investors' confidence, such a conflict should be resolved promptly.

There is always need to cherish, encourage and preserve ethical values of fairness, tolerance and solidarity in a strong nation. And here one can willingly refer to the Wittgenstein's espoused form of ethical or cultural relativism that prohibits "external" criticism of our form of life as inviolability interpretations in the words of Crary, though Wittgenstein speaks of Alteration of perception\ sensibility as the goal of good philosophical practice of Edwards in 1982, and to be able to change to new way of looking of at things; and approaching sense and nonsense. This is the philosophical means which indicates that something is faulty and in this meaning irrelevant or a thing is amiss either with a language or with his relation to language for better interpretation and understanding for the expectant constant tolerance and harmonious living.

One has to consider with priority, capacities of securing a possible understanding of other points of view that enable the possible development of mutual trust; it becomes highly necessary that tolerance and solidarity must be promoted as universal ethical values in the African nation like Nigeria's institutional practices, in order to achieve a fair and just society.

But whose duty is it to promote these values? Of course, it is the duty of every member of this society- whether as a single individual or as a member of a social group-to actively contribute in promoting these salient ethical values for our common good. In fact, every group has specific duties, which can articulate in an orderly manner. One of those clear cases also at hand is that of Niger Delta.

Geographically, the Nigeria Delta area is located along the Guinea Coast, stretching several kilometres into the south-eastern and south-western parts of Nigeria. This area is technically identified as the 'Oil-belt of Nigeria' because of its rich reserve of mineral oil.

The following States make up the Oil-belt zone: Delta, Rivers, Bayelsa, Akwa Ibom, Cross River, Abia and Imo.

The major ethnic groups who inhabit those States include Urhobo, Ishekiri, Isoko, Ijaw, Ika-Ibo, Edo, Andoni, Gokana, Ikwere, Efik, Ibibio, Kalabari, Ogoni and Igbo. Put together and excluding the Igbo, they constitute about 25% of Nigeria's total population. Most recently, the oil-belt has been described literally as' a hot bed of war', because of frequent crude oil-related conflicts in this area, especially since the decade of 20th century.

Most of these conflicts surrounding crude oil mining and refining have often arisen between the local ethnic communities and the multinational oil companies on the other hand.

Sometimes, however, conflicts erupt between different communal groups mainly over the ownership of particular oil-rich lands. These conflicts originate mostly as a result of long years of economic exploitation of the affected ethnic communities and the total neglect of these communities in the provision of adequate economic and social amenities that are due to them. These economic exploitation and total neglect lead to their impoverishment, which is totally unjustifiably considering the fact that the lands of these communities provide more than 90% of Nigeria's total wealth.

The communities do not just agitate for their equitable shares of the proceeds of the wealth accruing from the crude oil; they equally protest the unchecked environmental pollution and ecological destruction of their environment by the oil companies. In the 1990s, the minority Ogoni ethnic community engaged in what can so far be considered the most vocal and practically outstanding courageous struggle against this economic exploitation, neglect and unethical destruction of the community's environment since the start of exploration and mining of crude oil in the areas. The Ogoni community struggle brought it into conflict with the then federal military government led by the late dictator Gen. Sani Abacha. The conflict reached its climax in the hanging of the leader of MOSOP- Movement of the Survival of Ogoni People- Ken Saro Wiwa and others in 1995. Because of the enormous international attention, which this conflict drew, and the widespread outcry and condemnation of these brutal killings, it will be necessary to examine the whole issue of the Ogoni conflict more closely. This is based on the fact that Ogoni ethnic community is located in the former Rivers State of Nigeria.

As earlier mentioned, it suddenly came to the limelight of the international community during the crisis that led to the killing of some of the leaders in 1995. However, the problem of the Ogoni people did not start with crisis in 1995. For a very long time, the inhabitants of oil-rich Ogoniland have been engaged in a bitter struggle of emancipation from mindless economic exploitation and unfair social struggle of neglect by the federal government.

This long struggle first gained international recognition in July 1992, through the activities of their chief spokesman Ken Saro Wiwa, who was also popularly known as an environmental and human rights agitator. The deplorable situation of this community has been widely described as a classical case of "killing the goose that lays the golden egg." Equally, one can correctly describe the relationship between the Ogonis as well as similar victims of this mindless exploitation by successive Nigerian governments and international concerns as parasitic.

In a parasitic social relationship, the social parasite tends to progress at the total expense of his or her (helpless) host, who gets nothing in return. It is therefore, a relationship in which the social parasite (in most cases an unjust and insensitive more powerful guest) is satisfied to gain all, while (less powerful) host eventually loses outright.

In the present case, while the agents of exploitation feed on the resources of their hosts, they give almost nothing in return but leave the victims underdeveloped and their environments subject to a slow and torturous death through environmental pollution. Long years of economic exploitation of the resources of Ogoni ethnic community are by both Nigerian governments and oil companies, (95% of which are foreign oil companies) that results in gradual but steady destruction of life chances; which culminates in long-term socio-economic underdevelopment that hampers the ultimate survival of this community. Though, the unethical activities of the two groups of parasites mentioned above, Ogoni ethnic community has today not only been economically exploited, its ecology has also been mercilessly destroyed through irresponsible environment pollution by uncontrolled oil spillages and mining operations. Accordingly to records of a certain government- sponsored statistical study on Ogoni Crisis' in 1995, the whole of Ogoniland produces 25, 890 barrels per day or 3.84% of the total crude oil produced in Rivers State, which, according to this reports, stands at 673, 624 barrels per day. With this account, the producers of this study actually intended to specifically highlight the significantly low volume of crude oil production in Ogoniland in relation to both local and total national production (estimated to be 1.27% of the total national production which is two million four thousand (2, 004, 000 (barrels per day").

But in doing this, they either failed to recognise it, or rather tended to reduce to relative insignificance, the obvious socio-ethnic problem that is central to this problem; namely, the absence of distributive and remunerative justice, which is actually the crux of the struggle by Ogoni ethnic community. In contrast to this government sponsored view, the former Head of State and Commander in Chief of the defunct Republic of Biafra, Rt. General Chukwuemeka Odumegwu Ojukwu rather tends to represent the mind of a great majority of well-meaning Nigerians on the Ogoni crisis as he argues that mineral-rich lands belong first and foremost to the owners of the land. If the whole nation must benefit from it, there should be a fair structure for distributing the mineral wealth among the parties involved.

In a normal fair and just condition of social relationship, an adequate share of oil wealth should be able to provide Ogoni land and its inhabitants enough for normal and decent standard of living, a standard that can be compared with that of any developed country. The Ogoni land, which produces part of Nigeria's oil-wealth, is "said to be badly impoverished, without infrastructural facilities, such as good roads, electricity, good drinking water, schools, and hospitals."The community ranks among the most economically backward and least developed in the whole of Nigeria.

Mass illiteracy due to lack of adequate educational facilities and massive unemployment makes the future of Ogoni youths very bleak. Instead of blessing, the mineral oil from Ogoni land has brought only pains, agony and untold sufferings to its people.

Furthermore, it has caused enmity between different interest and ideological groups among the leaders of the community, an enmity, which the government and the oil concerns especially the international oil. Concerns happily used to divert public attention from their unfair treatments of this ethnic community that is the victim of their exploitations. This community's bitter experience of the pain of long years of neglect by those who should care about their welfare actually reflects the similar experiences of several other hundreds of helpless minority oil producing communities, whose voices, the Ogonis have presently come to symbolise. In most recent times, those responsible for their deplorable situations seem to actually acknowledge their faults. There seems to have been a ray of hope in the mid 1990s, as the 1994/95 Constituent Assembly sought to ensure some fairness in the distribution of resources. It recommended raising the oil-income quota of oil producing areas from the disappointing 1.15% to at least 13%.

The real impact of this is yet to be felt among the people concerned.

However, mutual development, peace and the common good of every one in the community or region is needed, other than acrimony, hate and enmity. Depending on the particular nature, ethnic nationalities may chosen to pursue their demands either through peaceful and diplomatic means, or in extreme cases, through attempts at secession and violent conflicts.

In addition, in many other African countries, minority groups have been involved variously as either perpetrators or victims of discriminations, in violent communal conflicts.

Instances here are the protracted ethnic wars in Chad and Sudan, the armed struggle for political self-determination by the minorities in the eastern region of Somalia (mainly Ogaden) and the Burundi ethnic conflict between the Hutu majority and the Tutsi minority, which has claimed about 150,000 lives. So, religion as an agent of and instrument for peace has helped a lot as regards the expected calm atmosphere. Very importantly, equally, on the international level is the needed cordial talks and dialogue in any political and social situation. An example is the middle East–where more than a few conflicts that persist and should be addressed.

A speedy resumption of negotiations between Israelis and Palestinians is hoped for, so that with the courageous decisions and availability of both sides as well as support from the international community, an agreement may be reached that respects the legitimate aspirations of the two peoples, thus decisively contributing to the peace and stability of the region.

Reference to the important issue of the City of Jerusalem was not and should not be overlooked. Particular worry for the conflict that plagues Syria should be expressed, for which a political solution is hoped for that privileges the logic of reconciliation and cogent dialogue.

In Nigeria also, there have been long lasting conflicts, like the Niger-Delta issues, the boundary disputes of Bakassi-Penisula conflicts between Nigeria

and Cameroon, the newly discovered mineral resources-oil town- a boundary disputes of Anambra and Kogi States, the regular and incessant killings of innocent Christian believers by the Islamist Terrorists called Boko Haram Sect. In conclusion, the significant progress made by the Bilateral Working Commission, which is preparing an agreement regarding issues of common interest, was appreciated and its rapid conclusion in timely taken care of fashion.

But why so much fuss about Islamist terrorisms, religious fanaticism, careless life and people clinging more to secularization than virtuous life? Part of the reason might be that the hold of some religious communities on our lives has grown more tenuous.

But African nations and some countries in the world would be foolish enough to dismiss the darker possibility that a tiny subgroup Muslim fanatics will or might continue to pose a threat for many decades to come.

The Federal and State government in these countries should be ready for them, either to be daily awake to catch them and correctively

punish them to be a lesson and deterrent to other young Muslim-Islamist

fanatics preparing to join terrorism, or the Federal and State government should henceforth embark on monthly or quarterly deportation-sending on individual or a group back to their native country immediately for such heinous crimes committed. Nigeria has for long now, experienced political, cultural and digital revolution. Nevertheless, the Human Rights, these rights guaranteed by the constitution are inalienable.

This means that such rights are not awarded by any human being and cannot be surrendered under any circumstance. Violations of the rights of citizens occur from day to day as human beings interact with one another.

The police regularly commit Human Rights violations including unlawful killings, torture and other ill-treatments, include enforced disappearances.

The justice system is under-resourced and riddled with delays. Prisons in Africa especially in West Africa, (example, Nigeria), are overcrowded; the majority of inmates are on pre-trial or into the so-called while awaiting trial jail terms; detainees, have been held for many years. Few hundreds of people remain on the death row, many sentenced after unfair trials. Conflicts in the Niger Delta threaten the safety and the lives of residents. Human Rights defenders and journalists face intimidation and harassment.

Widespread of violence against women widespread and the government fails to protect the rights of children. Forced evictions take place across the country. The issue of State Security Service is however changing the way security agencies view the rights of citizens. In the cases like the present upsurge in bombings in some northern States perpetrated by Boko Haram, sectarian violence, intra and inter-communal strife where virtually everyone is a suspect, it is difficult without modern gadgets, intelligence and information to insolate the perpetrators of evil from law abiding citizens.

Those who stay beholden to only the story of colonialism, and apartheid and ethnic chauvinism cum warfare will never allow themselves to know the Africa that now also tells a story of equality democracy and capital cities that are crowded and cosmopolitan as those of any continent. Actually, nonetheless, a military coup intervenes to halt the common ruin of all. The Nigeria-Biafran war of 1967-1970 is a morbid extension of the inter-ethnic and intra-class squabbles on the ground.

Among the solution to our problems is that the citizenry should be studying the cultural and political integration of this nation. Concerning the situation of things, religion has been blamed for many conflicts in this country. But, contrary to a certain opinion, religion is not a threat to nationhood. There has been an abuse of religion and the practice of religious truism. It is not religion that threatens our peaceful coexistence. It is the misreading and misuse of sacred texts of venerable religious traditions by preachers who are either inadequately formed or not at all formed for the preaching ministry in a multi-religious entity such as Nigeria.

Ours is a country full of places of worship, of churches, mosques and shrines. But this is nothing if we do not heed the word of God, and worse still, if the same word is misinterpreted and abused through incompetent and or mischievous preaching. These sacred texts can and should be used to form religious adherents to respect and promote the dignity of every human person and the sanctity of other people's belongings.

This nation should cherish, acknowledge, commend and encourage more the initiatives of dialogue undertaken by the Nigerian Inter-Religious Council (NIREC) towards a peaceful coexistence, particularly between Muslims and Christians in Nigeria. The Council has been able to bring together not only Christian and Muslim religious leaders, but also Christian and Muslim youths. The issue of support for the Council's plans to bring together Christians and Muslims was re-visited. We see in these initiatives proactive measures against violence, and a strong foundation for peace and stability. It is our hope that these initiatives will have reverberating effects throughout the length and breadth of our country. Our world of today is engulfed in unnecessary conflicts, clashes, discord, fierce opposition and combat against each other. This is as a result of mankind undermining justice. World over, people are disenchanted, oppressed and in the process of searching for a just and equitable society, they become entangled and sucked in by the agents of oppression and tyranny.

This has led to countless uprisings, anarchy and civil unrests. For instance, there were series of newspaper reports as regards the serious demonstration and subsequent conflict in Greece in recent time.

This was as a result of oppression of the rich by the poor, the strong against the weak and lowly. In the Peoples Democratic Government of Iraq, before and after the death of Saddam Hussein, there has been terrible and brutal conflict. In Nigeria, for the past fifteen years, there has been ferocious and murderous battle as a result of the crude oil in the Niger Delta. Some of the youths in the area have been agitating on the reason for the total neglect of the people by the government.

Now, these restive youths are now branded as militants. They are militants because of their demand for justice and fair play in the distribution of wealth from the area.

The people from this region are permanently in pain, anguish, and torment as a result of the supposedly natural wealth that God has bestowed on them. From time to time, there have also been oil spillages such that the land and rivers are in permanent pollution. Today, the militancy has degenerated into hostage-taking, blowing up of oil wells, kidnapping, and total war against the government's joint task force protecting these oil installations.

According to the Guardian News Paper of 21st January, 2006, these are atrocious wars. Wars that are supposed to be nipped in the bud, but quite unfortunate, it has been allowed to monumentally degenerate into kidnapping and hostage-taking and serial killings. Yet, another silent but ferocious war raging all over the world according to the Punch Newspaper of January 15th, 2008 is the battle of armed robbers.

In Nigeria – from North to South, East to West of the country, nowhere is safe; as the papers went further to assert, this ugly phenomenon has now become a hydra-headed monster, defying any worthwhile solution. Today, we see and hear screaming headlines as "Banks Under Siege", "Robbers on the Rampage", Robbers kill 4 Policemen and make away with bullion van", "Village sacked as a result of armed robbers", village head kidnapped and two sons killed." As the Guardian Newspaper of 13th November, 2008 stated in an article Robbers Kill 4 and rape two Women by Kennedy Emetulu, these robbers tend to get away with all their atrocities. In the face of all these, according to the Daily Champion Newspaper, government seems helpless and purposeless. And just last week, as reported by This Day Newspaper of 9th December 2008, robbers once again attacked a bank, killed three and made away with both foreign and local currencies.

Up till this day, police still cannot get a clue to the whereabouts of these daredevil robbers. Three years ago, as reported by the print and electronic media, the Attorney-General of the Federal Republic of Nigeria was killed in his own house by armed robbers. Again, the perpetrators of this dastardly act have not been accosted and brought to book till date.

Who can rescue us in the face of these daunting challenges? When are we going to have a society without killers, assassins and daredevil butchers and murderers?

As if these criminalities were not enough, religious militancy is yet another brutal and violent battle raging. Just last week, the Christians and Muslims were as it as the Guardian of 5th December, screamed in its headline -Slaughter in Jos-350 people killed.

The Nation Newspaper also reported that more than 380 souls were lost as the battle between Christian and Muslim group were fought in Jos township.

As asserted by the Guardian of April 13th, in Iraq, there has been a raging battle between the Sunni Arabs leaders and the Shiites.

The whole scenario is further escalated when one of the leaders of the Sunni group, Saddam Hussein was taunted and ridiculed before being executed by his captors who essentially were made up of the Shiites.

In Darfur, Sudan, the government is set for a showdown with the rebels and other militants wanting a bite of the national cake.

In South Africa, as stated by the Punch of 15th November, 2008, the criminals have taken over major streets, and occasionally mauled down a popular world acclaimed music superstar, Lucky Dube. To say the least, it was a huge loss not only to South Africans but to the entire entertainment world. Indeed, between last year and this year 2009, so many lives were lost to senseless killers and militants all over the world. The former Pakistan prime minister was brutally assassinated by a mindless suicide bomber on the 27th of December 2007.

According to the Nation Newspaper of 29th December, it was a national disaster not only to the Pakistani nation but to all lovers of justice and equality. Today as always, there has been an on going war or battle between the Hamas and that part of Israelite nation.

Al Qaeda is against American installations; and the Talibans is against anything America and all those opposing them in any way; but in all we need a peaceful world where all will be happy forever without terror of any type. But can the world continue like this? Should mankind continue to wreck havoc on themselves in the name of careless living? On what can be done concerning the duty of the religious groups or Intelligent Peace Committee groups has a major role to play in the promotion of religious tolerance, fair play and in the protection of the rights of people against all forms of discrimination and inequality.

The guiding spirit in this respect should always be the opinion for the weak and least advantaged. The fact that many violent conflicts that have occurred in different parts of the country and that different forms of discrimination and social injustice have their roots in religious intolerance, equally explain why religious bodies must assume greater responsibilities for the realization of mutual trust in Nigeria. The Agenda of Inter Religious Dialogue is the intensive bid to promote 'love and brotherhood' among the different religions in the country.

Religion and society peace pact is evermore necessary.

The Islamic and Christian religions definitely bear the bulk of this responsibility as the two largest religions in Nigeria.

The two religions are also involved-in different ways and degrees- in many violent conflicts that have ravaged this very nation.

2.2

Human Rights Problems in the Present Nigeria Nation

It is solely the prerogative of man to treat a fellow human being in a justified and Godly way. Human Rights and Human Dignity go hand in hand and have one goal. If these are not to be impaired, they need to be protected both by the State and the citizenry. At times, this does not come so easily as one thinks. Sometimes, the rights are denied or tampered with by State and citizenry. We are to see here how and why Human Rights have been held in Nigeria and its prospects in the future within the context of the emerging world of the twenty-first century.

In this view, Elizabeth Reichert rightly said that as we entered the global age, an age characterized by ethnic cleansing, suicide bombings, air strikes, the war on terrorism, kidnapping, suppression of civil liberties, and the decline of the welfare State to comply to the dictates of the free market economy, there is a need for new understandings and new approaches. This will be made more possible when people understand the concept or meaningfulness of rightness.

Many a time (in one's life), one is told that one is 'right' in making a particular decision or in following a particular course of action. Though, at other times, one may be said to be 'wrong', in either case, a judgment is made and since it is ethical judgment, it is often classified under ' value judgement. So, when we say that a person is 'right', what actually do we mean? What canon of measurement do we employ in such an affirmation?

Is 'rightness' an objective equality in a thing or a subjective one in an agent? Is it a permanent quality, or just a transient quality? In other words, is it possible for a thing to be right today, and wrong tomorrow? Or, could it be right in this particular context, say, culture, and wrong in another context?

If so why? These philosophical questions help us to realize the 'strangeness' embedded in their 'familiarity.'

Many problems that seem endemic to one State or one country can only be understood internationally, as common problems with common solutions.

Social welfare, in the sense of the well-being of a people, and human rights are inextricably linked. People cannot enjoy a sense of security and well-being if their rights are systematically violated by the very State representatives from whom they would seek protection. Nor can they enjoy the benefits of human rights such as exist in a democracy if their social welfare needs such as food, shelter, and clothing are not met.

Human Rights entail that which are due to a human being by just claims based on moral values and principles. In a normal parlance, right is something which a man has no right to deprive his fellow human being acess to without out sledge of hammer as different to justice. There are certain deeds in the society which should never be invaded, those things which are supreme and sacred. Some of the Human Rights are connatural with the human person. That means, they flow from nature of man; and so are fundamental to man; as human person. All the Human Rights should be enthroned in each country's constitution and be protected by man. The Human Rights rules in Nigeria are flouted at random. The Church in many of her documents upholds the United Nation's Declaration of 1948.

Pope John XXIII States "Each individual is truly a person; endowed by nature with intelligence and freewill.

On this ground, he has rights and duties which together flow direct consequence of his nature.

These rights and duties are universal and inviolable and all together inalienable. The fathers of the Second Vatican Council stated:

> there is a growing awareness of the sublime dignity of the human person who stands above all things and whose right and duties are universal and inviolable. He ought therefore, to have ready access to all that is necessary for living genuinely human life. For instance, food, clothing, housing, the right to choose his state of life and set up a family the right to education, to work, to his good name, to respect, to have proper knowledge, the right to act according to the dictates of conscience and safeguard his privacy and rightful freedom even in matters of religion.[124]

---

124 Vatican Council II, Declaration on Human Liberty, Dignitatis Humanae, in: A. Flannery., (Gen. Ed.) Conciliar and Post Conciliar Documents, p. 799.

There is also culture of authoritarianism and effects on Human Rights. As understood in social psychological contexts, it is almost antithetical to the accommodative expression of the human individuality and individual differences, and by extension, to Human Rights as opined by Eysenck, Arnold and Meli (1975), describing authoritarianism as a collective term for various anti-democratic and potentially fascist social attitudes. They went on to described such attitudes as characterized by (a) a rigid, indeed, inflexible adherence to conventional norms; (b) a desire to submit uncritically to authority; (c) aggressiveness expressed in the inclination to despise and condemn and penalize those adjudged to offend against traditional values; (d) rejection of more individual or personal inventive or creative attitudes;(e), superstitious and suspicious behavior; (f)a preference for positions of power and show of " toughness"; (g) encouragement of sycophancy among followers and admirers.

It does require too deep a reflection on the above description of typical authoritarian attitudes provided by Eysenck, Arnold and Meli to be able to identify those characteristics in despots, both ancient and modern.

In Nigeria, we not only have devotees of various military dictators, particularly those who benefited politically and materially from the reign of those dictators but also have an insidious anda persuasive military/authoritarian mentality in the general population. The abuse of Human Rights was seen to be a secret of "success" by the dictators and their agents, and since it became "normal" , the Nigerian population in turn has adopted an attitude of acquiescence to Human Rights abuses in Nigeria. For many, the attitude of acquiescence has turned into a more socially dangerous disposition, namely, a sense of feeling of helplessness in the face of atrocities. Thus, even in the present "democratic"dispensation, villages are wiped out without remorse. Indeed, remorselessness, and insensitivity to the plight of others are some of the hallmarks of authoritarianism and dictatorship.

Political murders are committed as a matter of course, and little or no attempts are made to re-assure the populace of justice through credible investigation and successful prosecution. Elections are rigged (theft of the people's right) in a manner so scandalous as to destroy the ethos and render the young confused and without a predictable political future. Unfortunately, there is no credible and confident political opposition; rather "opposition" candidates who lost elections are falling over each other to join or rejoin the "winning" team. Accordingly, Nigeria is now one step away from a de-facto one-party State and consequent totalitarianism which is a natural breeding ground for Human Rights abuses. The present atmosphere is either sufficiently comfortable for such former dare- devils or too subtle for them to discern any actual instances of abuse of Human Rights and the threats to those rights. What has taken over in Nigeria is a culture of authoritarianism. As a result, there is a regression to self-centeredness, elitisms, anti-intellectualism, resentment and resistance to new ideas and plurality of viewpoints. Under those circumstances, in the twenty first century, a national development has become the victim.

In any sort of authoritarianism, it would be a herculean task to attempt to produce a complete enumeration of Human Rights abuses.

Millions who suffer psychological abuses resulting in dehumanization and depersonalization, loss of self- esteem and loss of the motive to rise beyond officially imposed limitations, can never have their plights fully appreciated.

Pensioners in Nigeria constitute one category of such victims. After spending their most robust years serving the nation, they feel rejected and cast into nothingness in their twilight years. Those whose responsibility it is to give this category of Nigerians their rights think only of the country's money, naira and kobo and how these can be manipulated to their advantage.

The devastating psychological effect of their actions is lost to them. The internationally best known victims of Human Rights abuse include women, children and tribal/racial, political and religious minorities, and sometimes certain minorities.

Over the centuries and across cultures, women have been victims of domestic, social, cultural, political, religious and sexual slavery. Over those years, they have been brow-beaten into accepting inferior and second class status. Most people, including women themselves, have come to attempt this conventionalized Human Rights violation as normal and cultural, whereas both mythologically and scientifically, the power and capacity of women in most spheres of life are undeniable. Driven into desperation in recent decades, women have resorted to feminist movements and crusades for gender equality.

But such efforts are drops in the ocean compared to what is prevalent, particularly in African, Asian and Middle Eastern cultures. In Nigeria, we have unspeakable treatment of widows in some parts, and downright rejection of their humanity in others.

To avoid being too voluminous, we will mention just one case, the application of the Sharia law to Amina Lawal in Zamfara State of Nigeria where she was stoned to death because she had a baby out of wedlock.

If having a baby was a crime, are judges (men) who sentenced her to death by stoning oblivious of the natural law that Amina must have had sexual relation with a man to produce a baby? Where is he then? Has he no part in Amina's "criminal" act? Amina is sub-human, a dispensable object.

It is that subsisting idea of the dispensability of women that has led to the national disgrace of women trafficking. Children have not fared much better than women in terms of Human Rights.

They are victims of abortion, child labor, malnutrition, sexual abuse, educational deprivation, ritual sacrifice, (to mention but a few) also could be envisaged. Eya gives a Nigerian perspective to child abuse and neglect. However, the contemporary world community appears to be progressively more vociferous about the rights of children. Spearheaded by the United Nations agencies like UNICEF, the defence of children's right is now the concern of thousands of national and international Non-Governmental Organizations. In Nigeria, politicization or education of children and the youth and perpetration of systems such as the "almajir", are regarded by many scholars as constitutional violation of the rights of children. As long as Nigerians, irrespective of tribe and tongue, cannot freely, practice religion and politics according to the constitution in any part of the country of their choice, the entire nation stands in violation of human rights. Most socio-religio-political conflicts in Nigeria emanate from either lack of awareness of these rights or deliberate violation of those rights for political and economic ends.

The Church adopted and improved upon the U.N. list of these rights as summarized below. There exists the Fundamental/Liberal Rights that all men are equal in nobility, dignity and nature and so have the same fundamental rights and duties that should both be inviolable and universal.

That everyone has a right to existence, to bodily integrity and well beingfood, clothing and shelter.

a. To a good reputation, respect, privacy and honest representation.
b. To act in accordance with right norms of his conscience.
c. To freedom of expression.
d. To freedom of religion
e. To have these rights safeguarded by law.

The Civil, Political, Economic, Social and Cultural Rights: All should have rights to:

a. Free assembly and association
b. Move about freely.
c. Choose freely one's State in life.
d. Beget children in lawfully constituted marriage
e. Sound holistic Education
f. Integral development
g. Care and Concern especially for old people, orphans, the sick, the rejected.
h. Work and good working conditions, and development of talent and free initiative.
i. Take active part in public life, to contribute to common good, to vote and to be voted for.
j. Private sufficient property and the keeping of ones identity as people affirmed and share in benefits of culture.

1. SELF GOVERNMENT OF NATION.

Actually, the Human Rights in Nigeria coupled with the nation's situational problem is so to say deplorable.

The rights of the people are not upheld but since independence, there has been a constant degeneration from the bad to the worse, the worse to the ugly, the ugly to the awful.

The State as well as the citizenry and even the different religious groups in Nigeria are to be blamed for the mess of this country. On the part of the state or government, the rights earlier stated in parts of the constitution and are supposed to be protected by law but they are stifled in other parts sterile and unworkable.

The Nigerian leaders since independence have deliberately refused to uphold these rights; at times thwarting the constitution or interpreting them to favor their selfish interests to the detriment of the masses. As a result our national dailies and weeklies are fraught with reports on frequent affronts on Human Rights. It is obvious that there exists a clear class distinction between the rich and the poor, the powerful and the powerless in the Nigerian society. However, at the threshold of this year on 31. Oct 2013 from the Sun Newspaper, the United Nation on Human Rights Review gave Nigeria a pass mark saying that the nation has an exemplary record; Nigeria should always endeavor to give a good account of her rights record, when she faced other countries at the 17th session of the Universal Periodic Review, (UPR) of the United Nations Human Rights Council in Geneva, Switzerland at the end of this month.

The UPR is a new and unique mechanism of the United Nations, which started in April 2008 and consists of the review of the human rights practices of all States in the world, once every four and half years.

Nigeria was first reviewed in 2009. Nigeria delegation, led by the Attorney General of the Federation and Minister of Justice, their commitments to the Human Rights Council through its active participation in the work and activities of the council, support for the national Human Rights Commission, commitment to Human Rights instruments and support for strategies at regional and international levels to promote and protect Human Rights.

He added that Nigeria has also fulfilled its commitment by amending the National Human Rights Commission Act in 2010, granting the commission operational and financial independence, and enhanced its investigative and enforcement powers. Actually, Nigeria acceded to several international Human Rights instruments.

The constitution was amended to grant financial autonomy to the Independent National Electoral Commission, which contributed significantly in making the 2011 general elections of Nigeria free, fair and credible. Also, section 254 of the constitution was amended to provide for the establishment of a National Industrial Court. The delegation added that the government has maintained the rights based approach to economic management that is properly poor and gender sensitive, which is reflected in the economic transformation blueprint tagged or captioned it Nigeria Vision 2020.

While government is committed to improving access to affordable housing through legal and policy frameworks, which have increased the number of prototype housing units. The Federal Justice Sector Reform Coordinating Committee, FJSRRCC, was mandated to coordinate the development, management and implementation of policies aimed at improving the delivery of justice services with an Administration of Criminal Justice Bill before the National Assembly.

The bill is intended to institutionalize the board objective of the proposed National Prosecution Policy. He said that terrorism and violent insurgency have posed existential threats. These threats, which are externally-introduced, have manifested in the activities of militant insurgents and organized crime groups committing atrocities, crimes against humanity and violation of Human Rights. The delegation stated that significant efforts had been made to implement the accepted recommendations and the efforts made in this regard constituted a substantial part of our national report.

Response to advance questions, the delegation emphasized that torture, as a means of extracting information from suspects, had no place in law enforcement. The police should focus on modern and scientific means of interrogation and processes. Police officers found to have committed extrajudicial executions are usually dismissed from service and prosecuted in accordance with the law. The delegation noted that the demolition of illegal structures in various parts of the country was embarked upon in public interest.

The affected structures were those erected without permission from relevant authorities and was therefore not in conformity with the master plan of those areas. He added that experts had warned that the continuous existence of those illegal structures posed a danger, not only to the lives of inhabitants of such areas, but also to the ecosystem.

The authorities have carried out verification exercises to ensure that those who have genuine claims were either compensated or relocated to other areas and provided with alternative shelter. The rich and powerful become sacred cows that go away with every evil they hatch, while the poor and the powerless become scape goats readily sacrificed innocently to serve the interest of the former.

The majority of Nigerians are living in abject poverty, though our country is not so poor; our people are intelligent, it depends more on the Federal government's sincerity, honesty and being God fearing and law abiding.

The fundamental Human Rights, the right to life, which is arguably the most fundamental and most important of all others has been flagrantly trampled upon in Nigeria since independence.

The waging and prosecution of a thirty months civil war between 1967-1969 is unwarranted and uncalled for. Thousands of Nigerians and the then Biafrans lost their lives in that ill-advised war, where in certain situations unnecessary silence were kept, and on this we can uphold the good words of Dhavan in her book concerning the issue of Impossible Speech and the Politics of Silence analyzed within contextual canonical philosophical texts. And on the other way round here, was an endeavor to politicize silence, like, to explore how some forms of speech have made impossible within various philosophical discourses and violent consequences concerned. It is indeed clear that juxtaposing silence with power irritates our everyday correction of certain anomalies.

One easily also calls to mind the gruesome hanging of Ken Saro Wiwa and other Ogoni Human Rights crusaders, the murder of Dele Giwa, Kudirat Abiola, wife of M.K. Abiola, and contemporary, M.K. O. Abiola himself, Bola Ige, Prof. Chimere Ikoku to mention but a few recent examples. There is also recurrent ethnic clashes in which lives are lost in their numbers.

The Aguleri and Umuleri, Omo and Ijaw, Ife and Modakeke, and the Aguleri and Okpebe Anambra State and Kogi State struggles and incessant fights for the ownership over minerals resources and oil found between the boundaries of both States.

These misunderstandings and clashes continue to rage unabated. Then there are religious unrests especially between Christians and Moslems in the North, though some of them have political and ethnic undertones.

During such mayhems, or catastrophes, lives and properties are lost. These are but a few outstanding cases. Out in these cities and villages, thousands die in the hands of armed robbers and hired assassins. Sometimes people point even accusing fingers on the government who do little or at worst bent on postponing action endlessly.

The greater population of Nigerians also lives in sub-human pitiable situations; in fact dehumanizing conditions without adequate food, shelter and clothing lack of employment opportunities and non payment.

People literally die of hunger and the inability to get adequate medical attention. There is also a breakdown of infrastructural amenities. Apart from pockets of such amenities in a few cities, there is generally no good roads and health care delivery, erratic power supply, no pipe born water etc.

Nor the children provided with education not to talk of qualitative education. What about the indirect entrenching of examination malpractices in the curriculum and the incessant strikes by teachers?

The civil and political rights of Nigerians are even worse for it. Still fresh in mind is the 2003 election as a living testimony of how far the leaders go neglecting the rights of the people.

All the rights of the people have been rubbished; be it freedom of movement, freedom of speech or freedom of religion. Children's right to education is not respected and women are still regarded as second class citizens at best to be seen but not heard.

May we then, neither neglect nor forget to mention the concept of Amnesty and its place in Human Rights discourse.

This regards the application that lends support to the argument that an unlimited prosecution of international crimes may result to a threat to peace of security and in such instances; the domestic amnesties may be recognized.

Article 16 vests power in the Security Council to request that proceedings before International Courts be deferred for a period of twelve months, with the option of a renewal, where it is believed that such prosecution would threaten peace and security.

Then there is environmental pollution in oil producing areas without provision of amenities. The Nigeria populace is a no people beaten black and blue, suppressed and enslaved. The citizenry does not help matters. Because of lack of proper education, people are so ignorant of their rights that they do not even know when it is denied or what to do if they are aware. The leaders, service the structure that destroys education so that the situation continues. And because people lack self worth, they easily lend themselves to instruments of denying others their rights like: armed robbery, assassinations, thuggery etc.

The Church has been making efforts to conscientise people of their rights and help them to claim them. Her efforts however remain largely on the level of admonitions. No serious action has yet been taken.

Thus, Hilary Okeke could say, "The Church in Nigeria shares in the low level of awareness and respect for personal rights which characterizes the Nigerian society in general." The emergence of a battalion of Human Rights organizations and Human Rights activities lend credence to the alarming rate of denial of Human Rights in Nigeria.

The effects of the situation is that once Nigeria with this world order-globalization and is able to serve the interests of the so-called first worlds, its leaders feel rest assured of protection and so, they can afford to play with the citizenry and their rights. On the solution or the stoppage of any ugly situation in the country, the international communities especially the United Nation henceforth furiously made this assertion that members of the Islamist Sect, Boko Haram and the Military could face Human Rights charges.

The UN High Commissioner for Human Rights said this on November 6th 2013 in Geneva in reaction to the killing of about 30 people whose wedding convoy was allegedly attacked by members of Islamic Boko Haram in Borno State at the weekend. Cecile Pouilly, a spokeswoman for the UN High Commissioner for human Rights said, the atrocious attack was inexcusable and that both sides of the conflict are suspected of committing Human Rights violations. The warning that members of Islamic Boko Haram could face Human Rights charges was reinstated.

Nigerian authorities are also suspected of abuses in their response to the attack. The Church and Human Rights protagonists should also invest their resources in this regard in creating awareness about Human Rights.

They must also be ready to lead people to struggle for rights. This struggle should take the form of even civil disobedience and a readiness to make sacrifices. On the issue of corruption and transparency and upholding justice, human rights principles and fair-play, the Nigerian authority for freedom of information for Socio- economic Rights and Accountability Project, (SERAP), opined that a declaration be made; that the detailed information about the spending of recovered stolen public funds since the return of civil rule in 1999, and to publish widely such information, including on a dedicated website, amounts to a breach of fundamental principles of transparency and accountability and violates Article 9, 21 and 22 of the African Charter on Human and People's Rights (Ratification and Enforcement). This matter confirms the persistent failure of successive governments starting from the Obasanjo government, to respect Nigerian's rights to a corruption-free society and to uphold constitutional and international commitments on transparency and accountability.

This matter is also an important step towards reversing a culture of secrecy and corruption that has meant that high ranking government officials continue to look after themselves at the expense of the well-being of majority of Nigerians, and development of the country.

This is a crucial precedent that vindicates the right to transparent and accountable government and affirms the human rights of the Nigerian people to live a life free from want and fear. In Sections 2(3) (d) (V) and (4) of the Federal Office of Inquiry (FOI) Act, a public official is under a binding legal duty to ensure that documents containing information relating to the receipt or expenditure of recovered stolen funds are widely disseminated and made readily available to members of the public through various means.

2.3

Christians, Muslims and Human Rights in Africa – Nigeria Today and Islamic-Muslims Boko Haram Terror – Network Saga

Today and Islamic-Muslims Boko Haram Terror-Networks Saga Nigeria is a great, The nation is originally blessed, grew fast to be populous but also a complex country. Due to this fact, those who live in it know that it is difficult to describe certain conditions in our country. Many are often amazed and at times quite impatient with some foreign visitors who make themselves experts on Nigerian affairs after a brief stay in or a quick ride through the country. It reminds one of the fables of the blind men and the elephant.

One could now ask what the situation of Human Rights in Nigeria is in general. How do Christians and Muslims react to that situation, as individual citizens, and as religious bodies within the community?

What are the main areas of serious concern for these religious bodies in the midst of the many social problems characteristic of a fast growing and constantly changing society like ours?

How do we explain the diversity of approaches and concerns, and the instances of bitter rivalries between the two? Before going further on this pertinent issue let us have a succinct glance at the situation and state of the Nigerian nation before and after the colonial masters and the yearning for independence. So, Nigeria as a nation never existed until 1914 when Lord Lugard amalgamated people dwelling in a certain part of Africa.

The people dwelling in the major component part of the area that would comprise the would be created Nigeria include, the Eastern, the Western and the Northern areas were people with different and distinct historical backgrounds. They had nothing in common, no cohesion whatsoever.

They even practiced different religions and had different political and economic systems. The Igbo constituted the eastern parts while the Yoruba constituted the western and the Hausa constituted the Northern areas. On this matter, Azide here said that the Yoruba and Igbo practiced what is known in scholarly circles as African traditional religion, the Hausa had been under the influence of the Islamic religion for over two century. Again, while the Hausa and the Yoruba had an elaborate and organized political setting, which for the Hausa was centrally located in the emirates and Oba for the Yoruba; the Igbo, on the other hand, ran a different system which had nothing to do with centralization.

When the British colonizers came, they discovered these differences in culture and politics and therefore, developed different administrative system to administer the areas.

The southern parts were synthesized and ruled directly while the northern parts came under a process of administration which Lugard formulated and introduced as "Indirect rule" that is "rule through the native chiefs, who are regarded as an integral part of the machinery of government. The above were the different systems of administration used in administering the different component parts of the area which the British colonized.

The arrangements were adequately based on the distinct nature of the different areas. All the same, in 1914, Lord Lugard amalgamated these different and distinct areas into what his wife called Nigeria. With the passage of time, these differences notwithstanding, the British colonial masters went ahead to merge these different ethnic groups into colonies, and the colonies ultimately into a unified unit administered by a common government. That was the origin of Nigeria, and therefore in forming it, the interest and option of Nigerians were neither consulted nor taken into consideration. There was no referendum; the people were never given the opportunity to show whether or not they wanted to be unified.

The amalgamation was rather heterogeneous and not homogenous.

The British amalgamated these distinct ethnic groups just for their own selfish interest in the economy of the people and not for the unity of the people. What are the future prospects for greater mutual understanding and closer collaboration for the promotion of the rights and dignity of man, for genuine human progress for showing forth the glory of God? There exists the elusive decision or sceptical argument as regards the size and distribution of Christians and Muslims in Nigeria which has reflected very much the constantly changing realities of our country.

One thing is certain, both religions are growing fast.

At present, they have between them swallowed up almost all who until recently have maintained the religion of their tribal traditions- called in some circles 'pagans'. Already in the 1962 census, over 80% of Nigerians claimed to be either Christians or Muslims and the percentage is higher now. It is also certain that strongest concentration of Muslim is to be found in the North while the South-East is almost entirely Christian. Other areas are mixed; especially in the Yoruba areas to the South-West. Beyond these general assertions we are left with conjectures and estimates.

However, one of the greatest problems of planners in Nigeria is the availability of accurate statistics. The population is now estimated at about 175 million, which some think is a conservative figure; while others think it is inflated. In the absence of accurate statistics, both Christians and Muslims currently engaged in a game (or war) of numbers.

Christians seem and claim to be more than Muslims in number while some Muslims claim that they are more than the Christian in the population; such unsure and untenable figure. People really do not know exactly but have estimated until a thoroughly righteous census could be conducted.

Perhaps the confusion is partly due to the difference in approach to membership figures between Christian and Muslim. While Muslims tend to count everyone as a Muslim until he says he is not, Christian figures are generally taken from official Church registers. Thus, more people claim to be Christians than the Churches have on their registers and Islam claim among its members many who have never considered themselves Muslims. My estimation is that there could well be about 43% of Nigerians who would claim to be Muslims, and then 49.5% Christians, and about 7% who are either pagans or Atheists or still undecided.

The relevant figures in Barrett's Encyclopaedia of the Christian World are as follows: Muslim 45% and Christians 49%. Christians though more in numbers should strive to maintain always the expected cohesive unit. It is around questions such as these that we shall build our description of and reflection on the Nigerian situation.

There is a real fear that our superficially healthy Human Rights atmosphere is already seriously infected and that if adequate cure is not administered now, it will soon break onto the surface. Serious symptoms of these are evident. Here are some examples:

a) Ignorance: In spite of the investment that had been made in education in Nigeria, many people are still illiterate or poorly educated. At times, the educated elite has taken advantage of the situation to improve its own condition at the expense of the poor masses.
   Typical example is in politics, where a smart fellow steals the votes of his village with sweet talk and empty promises while he enriches himself. The people are supposed to be happy that their own son is dining with the great men of the nation, even if they starve at home.
   Thanks to God, that the nation changing fast with better education. More people are demanding that politicians and public office holders be in fact what they claim to be as servants of the people.
   There is a general consensus that their record of performance, with some notable exceptions, leaves much to be desired.
   They will find it increasingly difficult to get away with gross misuse of power.
b) Poverty: Nigeria has acquired in the outside world a reputation for being a rich country, especially because of her oil revenue and other mineral resources. And yet there is a lot of poverty around. It is intolerable to have little and watch others flaunt their wealth in one's face.
   A few people seem to have got more than their share of the nation's wealth, and seem to enjoy showing it off in extravagant spending: buying big cars, sprawling mansions, expensive clothings etc. The sense of frustration is high, especially among the educated and socially alert low-income city dwellers. The situation could easily become explosive.
c) Hardening Social Strata: A new phenomenon is slowly developing in the gradual emergence of rigid social strata. For a long time, ability and talent were decisive factors in social advancement. Many of the men now on top came from very poor family backgrounds before. The gap between the rich and the poor is increasing. Cities now have their rich suburbs. The children of the poor have a rough ride through public schools. Even the salary structure reflects and perpetuates this disparity. At times, people talk here of "local apartheid" from the way some "big men" treat their "house boys or maid", the description is hardly an exaggeration. The society in general, seems equally true of Christians and Muslims

> as religious groups concern for Human Rights does not feature high in their pre-occupation, except in some indirect ways, to which we shall presently refer. In this, they are very much part of the Nigerian environment, with its known proverbial capacity to absorb crisis of all sorts with calmness. Nigeria as a political entity is a product of colonialism. Nevertheless, global political developments, the Second World War as well as Atlantic Charter stimulated the quest for self-determination and national independence.

The struggle against colonialism was therefore a struggle for Human Rights of people.

Nigeria gained political independence from Britain over 53 years ago and has operated five constitutions each which had provisions for Human Rights firmly enshrined. The question then arises, to what extent have the political actors respected or promoted Human Rights in their exercise of political power? It is crystally clear that since independence in 1960, Nigeria, had a chequered history, civil strife leading to civil war, abuse of power leading to exchange of baton of power from one regime to another in quest of political rulership. These culminated in the emergence of 14 years of civilian era and 29 years of military inter-regnum.

Of course, sermons galore flow from Churches and Mosques against the evils of our society-and huge audience are always available. But it is doubtful if either the Church or the Mosque can be said to be reacting adequately and concretely to the issues and problems mentioned above. What action, there is in favour of Human Rights as such tends to cut cross boundaries of religious affiliation? How do we educate adherents of both religions in the country to enhance enduring peace and mutual understanding at all levels of human existence so as to achieve our goal of transforming sheer human interaction to solid human subsistence?

How do we promote smooth human compatibility, made easy by traditional tolerance between adherents of different religion?

It is absurd for religion to be a source of disunity where hitherto existing traditional-cultural environments had made mutual co-existence an interesting factor for cordial human relationship irrespective of religious affiliations. In the Southeast, especially among the Igbo nation, there is obvious Christian presence, which is not really antagonistic to the presence of religious other affiliations. Islamic presence, by way of Mosques is already felt in central Igbo city centres like Enugu, Onitsha, Umuahia, Owerri, Aba, Afikpo, etc.

The multicultural interactions can also serve as basis for occasional religious misunderstanding and any conflict should be seen as an urgent necessity and be enhanced always. The Catholic Bishops Conference of Nigeria (CBCN) is also another organ for the transformation of human existence into human co-existence in Nigeria and the world as a whole.

It is on record that the CBCN has issued not less than thirty official Communiques and Pastoral Statements to support the struggle to realize positive Christian-Muslim relations in Nigeria.

In general, it is remarkable that the statements are aimed at a solid support for unity and peace in the country. The CBCN has also emphasised the right of each religion to co-exist with others.

I do believe that the efforts of CBCN are a great challenge to all and sundry to avoid religious antagonism, especially through insistence on the promotion of religious fanaticism, bigotry and intolerance. It is important to proffer means of ensuring a correct understanding and harmonious co-existence of peoples and religions to reduce drastically, tensions and conflicts in the society. We all have experienced such occurrences in one form or the other.

This is an important task of the various religions in their bid to promote mission and dialogue. The incessant outbreaks of conflict in the country can be described as sheer ignorance or mere timidity. The problem arising from unhealthy relations between Muslims and Christians in Nigeria demand cogent responses from ecclesiastical leadership in both religions and this is the importance of interreligious dialogue. The significance of this encounter is rooted in the truism that interreligious dialogue opens doors to a better understanding of the faith and religious tradition of the other, as well as widening ones horizons, which helps one to learn about people in a way that is possible only and through this personal encounter. It may also lead to new and expected discoveries about oneself, in a way that enables one to see oneself in new way. That is why the political structure is also expected to be essential in the promotion of harmony, peace, and co-existence. Religion in Nigeria must never apply any political expediencies or bureaucratic influences to inflame hatred and fanatical orientations. For Norman Solomon, 'too often when religious leaders hold sway over government, whether by usurping power or by influencing the rulers, diversity is thwarted-not only the diversity of faiths, but diversity within each faith. An instance was in the great wars of religion in the 16th century Europe during which Christian Princes wrought havoc on the Christian people in misguided and ultimately abortive attempts to stamp out diversity and establish one universal Church. Another extreme to be avoided also is that of humanists, who in trying to assert the richness of diversity turned their backs on tradition, for there is no religion without a very rich tradition.

Christians and Muslims often find themselves in community development projects, social welfare clubs and voluntary organisations which try to assist the poor and the underprivileged members of the society. But these are rather in the line of social assistance or self-help projects. Concerning the religious bodies, Christians and Muslims are making contributions which promote Human Rights at various levels.

The Christian Church has an enviable record of education, health services and general social upliftment of those who have come under her influence.

Although some recent official policies of the government have tended to control, reduce or even neutralise the social impact of the Church on the Nigerian community, she continues to seek ways of maintaining her presence. Muslims came late to the scene in the field of running modern social institutions like schools and hospitals; but they have made giant strides in recent years. One also notices that every year, Muslim Communities are establishing new schools, with funds generated both from within and outside Nigeria.

As regards help for the poor, it is noted that some Muslim Community in Nigeria does take the Islamic precept of Almsgiving rather seriously. Beggars litter the front of Mosque and many rich Muslims provide daily meals for large numbers of destitute. While this may not be an ideal solution for the problem of economic disparity, it does achieve the immediate purpose of filling some empty stomachs.

On this terrain, these two groups have been working, one quite independently of the other. Collaboration has not been given a fair trial due to mutual suspicious and rivalries. At times, they even work against one another. So, by far, the greatest pre-occupation of Christians and Muslims in Nigeria as religious groups seems concerned with the struggle for survival and supremacy. One feels a sense of critical urgency about the present historical moment. Both sides feel convinced that these are the years when decisive battles are to be fought–and won or lost forever. It is as if we are the last lap of a long-distance race when each competitor puts in all his energies.

To understand our present frame of mind, we need to go into a bit of history.

On the question of at least reducing or dousing the religious tension between Christians and Muslims in Nigeria, both the Christian and Islamic theologians should work daily round the clock on their adherents and members anywhere for a strength of faith and imbibing prayerfully and practically the spirit of live and let live. For this present age, the cold relationship between Christians and Muslims in Nigeria has indeed taken a different and dangerous shape.

This has indeed aroused in concerned Nigerians, the need to search for a better solution aimed at enhancing harmonious understanding between the two major religions, especially between Christians and Muslims. This remains a necessity. The strength and vulnerability of the missionary status of Christianity and Islam during the centuries have perhaps evoked the contemporary need to make them aware of their involvement in the promotion of justice, peace, and love in the world.[125]

It may also not be out of place for them to see this role as an obligatory aspect of their function as missionary faith.

A brief reflection of history did show that the pre-Nigerian days or Nigeria per se, owes its political entity originally to Britain which, in 1914 decided to put under one Governor the various parcels of land and territories that had come under her control during the previous decades.

Before then, the territory was inhabited and controlled by different nations and peoples, each with its own history, culture and religion.

Both Islam and Christianity had found their way into the territory by the time the Britain took control.

---

[125] Who are Nigeria's Boko Haram Islamist group? 2016 -*Boko Haram* promotes a version of *Islam* which makes it "haram"... freed in October *2016* following talks involving the militants, the *Nigerian*... www.cnn.com/2014/06/09/world/boko-haram-fast-facts; www.bbc.co.uk/news/world-africa-13809501.

It was noticed that the first to arrive in this country was Islam in the Northern area but failed to spread successfully as they expected. Its first contact with what is now called Nigeria dated as far back as 9th Century when Berber Muslim merchants led trade expeditions to the Kamen-Borno region around the lake Chad.

Then followed a gradual and peaceful infiltration of a theologically fluid type of Islam, and that accommodated itself to much of the local religious customs. This same type of Islam found its way into Yorubaland to the South-West of Nigeria, where real converts were rather few. There it hardly scratched the surface of the people's culture and religious tradition. The turning point came in the North at the beginning of the 19th century when Usman dan Fodio set in motion a movement to purify Islam in Hausaland. He ended up with an empire, the Sokoto Caliphate over which he became not only a religious teacher but also a temporal ruler. The explosive mixture of religious fervour and imperialist fury devoured most of Nothern Nigeria. It was halted in the North East by the Bornu rival (and Islamic) empire, and by the Yoruba Kingdom in the South.

Indeed, Christianity started in the ancient Kingdoms of Benin and Warri around the 16th century, and did not finally come to stay until the mid-16th century when freed slaves came or were brought back to the West Coast of Africa. Courageous missionary enterprises were–undertaken, some even as far as inland as Kano, but the tittle success registered was mainly along the coast.

British Rule: say around 1900, Britain imposed her Pax-Britanica , stopped all tribal wars, halted the political expansion of the Sokoto empire, and with it, the concomitant spread of Islam south-wards, and east-wards. Some Muslims in Nigeria maintain that all Nigeria would have been as Muslim as the North if the British had not stepped in to intervene at that time. But on the other hand, it can also be said that by recognising and upholding the authority of the Muslim Emirs, Britain prevented liberation movements that might have arisen against Fulani domination of many parts of the North. The argument works both ways.

In the mean time, Christian missions flourished under British protection and were actively encouraged wherever it served British imperial interest, which caused Lord Lugard, the British Governor, to forbid direct Christian evangelization to people in places considered Muslim. For the sake of peace, Britain did all she could to keep Christianity and Islam separate in the North, for whom religion had always been, rather a private affair.

The clearer fact is that, religious bodies should endeavour to assist in the establishment of a true democracy, one which ensures security for persons and property, especially through honest mediation and promotion of mutual co-existence. Christians and Muslims should create associations for dialogue and the promotion of peace and justice in the bid to transform human existence into human co-existence.

The Federal Government has occasionally played some vital roles in the promotion of peace and justice in the country. But it should take definite and decisive steps that would ensure sanity and mutual interactions between various groups and affiliations.

Honest collaboration is inevitable in the transformation of human existence into human co-existence. Terrorism bred and nurtured in states, blossom into international terrorism. Consequently, individual governments should have and maintain a robust cum viable security apparatus, in order to aid and stimulate global relationship and development. All in all, international terrorism causes innocent civilians colossal losses in life and property and change to the friendly relations between states and people. It threatens the society and the territorial integrity of the state, and is a major hidden peril affecting international peace and security.

Given that terrorism is an international problem, it needs international solution vigorously and collaboratively.

In view of this, all states should engage in a constructive pro-active public diplomacy, which will even further task all western countries to engage in a total re-evaluation of their foreign policies. Partly due to its perceived international arrogance, hypocrisy and greed, the U.S. has demonstrated a propensity to its own role in encouraging terrorism and greed.

The U.S. has demonstrated a propensity to its own role in encouraging terrorism both as a reaction to its foreign policies, and even, at times, as a direct tool in the implementation of its policies. Related to this double standard is the on-going U.S. support of the government of Colombia, Turkey and various Middle Eastern allies guilty of terrorism.

On a larger scale, by her large annual weapon's supply to both Third world and Middle Eastern countries, the U.S. provides potential terrorists easy access to weapons.

Actions and behaviours of states on the international stage should be more important than what they tend to preach and portray. The world should collectively have the 'liver' to condemn the condemnable, correct and caution all acts of state and international terrorism, regardless of whom the culprit is. The United Nations' Organization should put in place equitable mechanisms; the United nations' charter guiding international law (Principles and practice) must be reviewed and put in use by all states. Added to this, all members of the United Nations must adapt and implement available anti-terrorist domestic legislation.

In a situation whereby all States are obliged to, and truly respect all international law principles, including that of state sovereignty, territorial integrity and non-interference in the internal affairs of all countries, international terrorism will start loosing steam.

The current trend of 'non-negotiation' with terrorist groups appears not only as a misnomer but equally inimical to the demands of Article 33 of the United Nations charter, whereby parties to any dispute shall first of all seek a solution by peaceful means, including negotiation. Be that as it may, in the nowadays setting, the United States and most Western powers, always practice 'non-negotiation' with terrorists (as their principle). Constructive engagement, through classified strategies has always proved to be of advantage in defusing terrorist attacks classified strategies has always proved to be of advantage in defusing terrorist attacks and potentials. It is on record presently that the U.S. government is engaged in promising negotiation with the Talibans in Afghanistan. A resort for good reasoning is to live Godly for ever lasting peaceful atmosphere. All nations should endeavour to have in place, well-enhanced internal security network.

With such ideas obtained, the police forces of all countries should accede and undertake extensive and effective co-operation through the Interpol, towards containing international terrorism by crime investigation, searching for and arresting targeted international terrorists.

Economic inducements and sanctions can be used interchangeably as the case may be in achieving better results in this war against terrorism. Terrorist-prone groups and organizations could be enticed with both tangible and intangible inducements. Such a 'flame' could be put off easily while still smouldering.

However, economic sanctions, whenever proven important, and needed, should be considered as a last resort because, sequel to its blanket effects on a targeted population, innocent citizens suffer more than the culprits.

It is evident that if both Christians and Muslims all over the world follow the strong principles of love and justice laid down for its members then their various societies would certainly be a place of mutual co-existence. In Nigeria, it is imperative for the government to change its mentality in relation to governance and that is change of lavish and corrupt lifestyle, development of the country through improved infrastructure and the peoples' welfare; withdrawal from hitherto complicity in crime and evil, whether in the Niger Delta because of oil wealth or in the North because of misguided religious politics of dominations; lack of concern for justice and rule of law; etc. It should not be forgotten that the high hopes expressed by Nigerians more than a decade ago with the inception of democracy after so many years of military rule have not been fulfilled and seem not to be in view due to rigged elections and manipulation of electoral results. I want to suppose that we have experienced so much misfortune in the history of our country to urge all of us to strive to turn our existence into a co-existence that can be passed as a legacy to generations unborn.

If variety is not recognised and promoted in Nigeria, our dream might remain a nightmare in the pursuit of this goal.

The first Republic1960-1966: This is the period between Independence and the military coups of 1966. The new atmosphere affected the relative strength of both religions.

However, on the one hand, the post- independence concepts of freedom, equality and democracy tended to undermine the authority of traditional rulers. Even though the independence constitution tried to make provisions for them by constituting them into something like an Upper house, called the "House of Chiefs" where many of them felt quite insecure. In the Muslim North, where they were also religious leaders of their communities, there was a tendency to seek added leverage from the religious basis of their authority. Thus the Emirs became fanatical defenders and promoters of Islam and intransigents of Christian influence which they saw, rightly, as a threat to their position.

Equally, the concept of freedom of religion was taken seriously by Nigerian Christians. Previous British arrangements with Muslim rulers, setting up rigid spheres of influence and closing certain Muslim areas to Christian evangelization were considered obsolete.

In the meantime, the Christian bodies continued to enjoy full freedom at home and generous support from outside. On the whole, it was a period very favourable for Christian expansion.

The Civil War and the Oil Boom of 1966-and 1979: The outbreak of the Nigerian Civil war was intense and coincided with the discovery of sizeable deposits of oil in Nigeria. The later was probably partly a cause of the former; and there are many who believe that there would have been no"Biafra" if there were no oil in the region. This affected Christians and Muslims in different ways since national unity was the "casus belli", the Federal Government was anxious to play down all differences among Nigerians, including religious ones.

While the Biafran propaganda machine was effectively getting people abroad to see the conflict in terms of the ' Muslim North "trying to swallow up the Christian South" with the aid of Russian arms and MIG jet- fighters, the Federal government kept insisting that this was not so. The clearest argument was the fact that the head of the Federal Government, General Gowon, was himself a Christian.

Massive troop movements within the country; North-South interactions and unity were to some extent forged.

The heroic efforts of Christian humanitarian groups to relieve suffering in Biafra were often misinterpreted on the Federal side as indicating active support of 'rebels."

Missionaries who decided to stay with their flock during the conflict were branded as "mercenaries" and ejected from the country as "personae non gratae" after the war.

The net-result of this was that enemies of the Church (and were not necessarily Muslims) were able to paint her in bad light-even though Christians were giving more than adequate proof of their courage, loyalty and patriotism on the battlefields, Islam reaped advantages from this situation; at least indirectly.

The Second Republic: 1979 Onwards: We started what we call our second Republic with peaceful return to civilian rule in 1979.

Already doing the debates of the Constitution Drafting Committee (CDC) and later of the Constituent Assembly which drafted and worked out anew Constitution for the country, issues affecting Christians and Muslims received very close attention and heated discussion. There was no topic more hotly debated than the Shari'a, the Islamic Law, and its place in the Nigerian Legal System. Since then, there has been much evidence of a growing awareness and increased alertness on both sides, each being anxious that the other does not enjoy any undue advantages attention and heated. On the whole, the Christians are feeling in recent years that the political climate within the country tends to favour Islam at the expense of Christianity. But complaints come from both sides. Before gong into the nature of these complaints, it would be useful to give a broad outline of the situation of Christians and Muslims in Nigeria.

In the light of the above discussions, I would like to suggest to the Nigerian political and religious leadership of the need to be extra-ordinarily careful in the guidance of the society entrusted to them. To amplify this suggestion, I would like also to mention some instances of major leadership failures of the past in the handling of religious conflicts like, 1. the Bauchi Pogrom of 1990-1991: This is one of the major lapses of successive governments in Nigeria, whether military or democratic since the independence of the country in 1960. The price has been very dear and chilling. One of such occasions of carelessness was the Bauchi Massacre of 1990. There was nothing that should have prevented the school authorities in Bauchi State from acting swiftly with the cooperation of the local police to prevent the episode.

2. The Zango-Kataf Crisis of 1992: Worthy of note is that "a Zango is essentially a trade camp, a transit along the way to the major business centres in the North. Zango later became the real settlement.

Thus, in spite of the usage of the possessive noun to qualify the Kataf, the Zango does not belong to the Kataf." In order to understand the location of this crisis, I would like to explain the meaning of the Zango in the context of the Hausa of the Northern Nigeria and Islamic tradition.

In fact, every city of any size in West Africa has large centralised Hausa community, usually reffered to as Zango or Zongo, a term which originally refered to the stopping point of trade caravans.

3. On May 16, 1992, the eventful day of the riot and religious crisis escalation, a group of Muslim youths had attackted and vandalized a yam field belonging to Christian farmers of Kataf people. Naturally, the reaction

was fierce and strong against the long-tolerated Hausa-Flulani economic and political domination in the area.

At the end of the trouble, about 1, 000 Hausa- Fulani, mainly, Muslims were brutally killed and thus, paid for their deeds with their own lives. Investigations showed that the Zango-Kataf had the backing of a high-ranking retired Nigerian Army General, Major General Zamani Lekwot, a Kataf indigene.

As a result of revelations leading to the conflict, the Justice B. Oputa Panel convicted him of organising and arming the farmers against the Muslims and have continued the avowed retaliatory killings of their Muslim brethren by which the Zango-Kataf. It was clear that the government of the day did not do much to stop the spread of the violence. Neither the violence nor the army had been effectively mobilized to check the outbreak of hostilities, thus disrupting cordial human co-existence. 3. Kaduna Sharia Crisis 2000:

The massacre of people in Kaduna in February 2000 after the unpopular introduction of the Sharia Law in some Nothern States of the Federation was another indication that mutual co-existence between Christians and Muslims in Nigeria was still a mirage.

No Nigerian is unaware of the massive flight from the northern part of the country; a situation that almost provoked another civil war because of the ethnic reprisals across Igboland to the Atlantic in Lagos.

It is not to be forgotten that the Catholic Bishops of Nigeria, after their meeting in January of the same year, called for a summit of Christian and Muslim leaders to seek ways to deal with the religious cause of violence, particularly the introduction of the strict Islamic law in most northern States of Nigeria, which is secular by constitution.

The honest appeal by the Catholic hierarchy was not realized, at least before more harvoc than expected was unleashed on the civil society.

4.Zaki-Biam 2001: Another violent development was between the Jukun and the Fulanis on the one hand, and the Tivs on other.

The crude manner with which the Federal Authority handled the incident by sending a truckload of soldiers to quell the unrest in October 2001, and the arrest of the militants possibly attracted the rage of the people who ambushed and killed about 22 soldiers (another manner of lawlessness and open confrontation with the State) that were concerned.

President Olusego Obasanjo was highly blamed for the almost inhuman approach which the Nigerian soldiers applied to handle the incident of tracking down the Tiv-Militia. Miss World Competition Riot, November 2002: It was one of the most shameful acts of religious destruction that Nigeria has experienced. Most Muslims opposed the beauty competition categorising it as immoral.

However, some analyst have also criticised the international community for organising such an event in the holy month of Ramadan, against the will of most Muslims who live in the North. At least 100 people were killed while so many Christian Churches were burnt down.

The incident raised the question of the role of the international community regarding increase in religious hostilities in Nigeria, and their professed readiness to promote peace, reconciliation, and economic growth.

In dealing with the complex situation in Nigeria, therefore, a lot of caution has to be taken, not only locally but also internationally.

6. Boko Haram Islamic Sect (July 2009): One may often or constantly ask oneself why some Nigerians allow the sentiments of religious bigotry to override the reason of their human existence and its essence.

No other incident could have provoked my yearning for an answer than the violence of July 2009 perpetrated by the Islamist sect called Boko Haram. Whereas so many countries have developed systematic ways of taming such uprisings, Nigeria seems to witness, every new blood-letting as a novelty.

All knew that it was the Boko Haram- a fanatic terror group that ran amok and crazy, attacking police stations and destroying everything on their way and imagination, demanding an immediate end to Western institutions, and seeking for the imposition of a religious code (the Sharia), for more than 350 different cultural and religious groups in Nigeria.

The violence exhibited by the Boko Haram in the name of religion replicated the dexterity of the bloodly clashes between the Niger Delta-Militants and the Nigeria soldiers at the creeks and coasts.

The two groups really showed the world how weak and callous the government is in caring for the citizenry. It is total manifestation of the degradation Nigeria has witnessed in the past decades-politically, economically, and even religiously.

The Islamic Sect-Boko Haram, is synonymous with terrorism and insurgency in Nigeria. The phenomenon Boko Haram connotes an opposition militating against the progress and against developmental and peaceful environment in the country.

The eventualities and probabilities (*mutmaßlich*), of Islamic Muslims Terror-Networks are popular in local and international media and also in the print, online and electronic media. A search on the internet will also show pictures of their leaders, their statements, audios and videos that are easily accessible but could invoke fear and trepidation in the mind of the public. While the activities of the group is clearly restricted to about three states in Northern Nigeria: Adamawa, Borno and Yobe, there are erroneous impression as if the activities of the group are felt in the remaining 33 states and Federal Capital Territory, Abuja. In the realisation that the terrorists may be gaining undue publicity, the National Security Adviser (NSA), Col. Sambo Dasuki (rtd) recently inaugurated a forum of Spokespersons in Security and Response Agencies (FOSSRA) was charged to be proactive and responsive in public information management. He was reported to have said that the next stage of war on terror should include advocacy and media engagement through accurate, timely and responsible information to dissuade our people from criminal activities as well as to silence the propaganda tools of terrorists.

How come the insurgents have succeeded in their propaganda campaigns? The answer is not farfetched: Fear, violent crimes and casualty figures are major ingredients that quench the journalistic instincts for breaking news and lead stories.

In achieving such media exposure, within the space of a fortnight, countless lives have been lost to senseless attacks in Konduga, Kauri, and other villages in Borno State and some parts of Adamawa States. Indeed, Borno State with their 14 Local Government Areas and variant communities is where lots of hefty terror-networks is reside and it is where the Boko Haram wars and steady unrest stocked. Other areas in the North-East where most troubles and killings are witnessed are Taraba, Adamawa, Bauchi, Yobe, Masha, Gombe, but Jos Plateau, Kaduna and Kano can not be simply excluded.

The vulnerable citizens continue to remain helpless. Even military personnel are not safe; as some of them were alleged to have been mauled while on national assignments to protect Nigerians and their country. Concerned over the monumental atrocities committed by insurgents, Governor Kashim Shettima of Borno State in an emotional outburst inadvertently claimed that the sect is more sophisticated and motivated than the Nigerian military. The fact that the troops on ground are trying to reduce civilian casualties in their battle against the terrorists is the major barricade to their effort.[126] This is due to the fact that insurgents always seek refuge in villages and across borders alongside innocent civilians. Thus military personnel are severely constrained in identifying suspects from innocent citizens in civilian settlements. Selective engagements in such situations are strenuous and difficult to avoid heavy civilian casualty. Few months ago, the military received bashing for the massive operation in Baga fishing community while flushing out the suspected terrorists in Borno state.

This and other accusations of extra-judicial killings against the military have heavily restricted the fight against the terrorists.

Without justifying the violence of Boko Haram, one observes immediately the dangers arising from the state of illiteracy, poverty and impoverishment suffered by the people. Having no good jobs and no positive religious orientations, the one group fights for their material welfare which they see in Oil while the second group mischievously misled the ravaged and ignorant masses with some of the ill-gotten wealth from Oil.

Boko Haram cannot be mentioned without considering the frustration that led both the leader Mohammed Yusuf and the led (the masses)-a frustration I strongly associate with the sheer anarchy called democracy in Nigeria.

The sect took laws into their hand because there was none to checkmate them. Or, if there was one, then either ignored or deliberately allowed to be redundant and ineffective. The so-called Boko Haram is a complete evidence of lack of law and order like any other terrorist acts. The disorder displayed by the sect was a clarion for the constituted authority to regroup and salvage the nation from further Boko Harams. In an International Conference of Multi-disciplinary forum; a controversial question arose whether

---

[126] *Nigeria: Boko Haram , Borno State – Genocide Watch.* genocidewatch.net/category/updates/byregion/africa/.../nigeria/ *Nigeria* — One of the girls kidnapped by *Boko Haram* more than two . . . - Here's a look at *Boko Haram*, a militant *Islamic* group working out of *Nigeria*, . . . *Nigerian* Girl Abducted by *Boko Haram* from Chibok Is Found . . . 18 May, *2016* LAGOS, www.cnn.com/2014/06/09/world/boko-haram

some of the known heavy Islamic-Muslim nations are exporting or are exporters of terrorism or mayhem to others? Many experts on this issue deliberated on this issue basing their arguments on why most of victims caught perpetrating or these criminal acts are often from a particular religion or known country suspicious and notorious as such satanic acts; instead of seeking for peace progress and welfare of their own God given nation and all God's creation.

A human right and pro-life authority spoke vehemently; saying that, should the heads of States of all Islamic States and Muslim nations steadily many times annually, could caution as a deterrent to any other country, summon always the very country concerned for urgent serious dialogue, corrections; and admonitions and then sanctions those painting Islamic Religion 'black' even before the UNO or NATO or Human Rights Internationals comes in, then the world will enjoy lasting freedom and peaceful co-existence. Those countries causing such criminal acts, scattering their citizens, terrible panic often in a weekly, monthly and yearly and many people dying should think-thought their wrong ways to human life.

Any nation whether Islamic or Christian nation that is always at war and terrorist acts is a perpetual sick nation; that lacks and hates peace and this does directly and indirectly affect their development, population growth, economy and making their own country a seemingly constant refugees and asylum seeker elsewhere and anywhere that may accept them; but as well be a tantamount of a notorious typical bloodthirsty and war-terror mongers and individual or other country should cast doubts on their way of life for others.

In this meaning of steady cautions and summons of the Federal Government's Leaders (parliaments) of those terrorist countries for a serious query from the international community with a follow-up corrections those religious radicalisms, aggressiveness and terrorisms from any individual or groups can be greatly avoided and conscientiously abruptly be stopped for lasting peace of all people in the global generation.

A change of heart to live peacefully and happily as God's own children is a possibility because it does not cause anything to live a good life and to always let your fellow human beings live in peace too. A good security and intelligence net-work could have prevented what happened in Bauchi, Borno, Gombe, Kaduna, Kano, Katsina, and Yobe where they had their operational bases. They declared a "Jihad" of mass destruction, distorting as it were the true meaning of "Jihad" in Islam which means "struggle or striving in Islam for moral, spiritual, or political goal." The Boko Haram incident should remind us of the outbreaks of religious violence in the 1980s, mostly rooted in the call for the imposition of Sharia as the constituted and constitutional legal code for Nigeria.

Even the outbreaks of 2004 in Yobe and Borno States where some youths regarded them as "Talibans" can be said to be forerunner or preparatory to the Boko Haram drama of 2009.

One common feature runs across these disturbances in the North, even after the adoption of Sharia Law by several northern States.

That is, Nigeria's secular institutions do not deliver justice. Sharia Law has been hoped to be a better alternative. But the irony of it is very glaring.

How and in what way? Boko Haram, which can be seen as an evolution of the Nigerian "Taliban" (as it is called in Hausa) judged the Sharia a great failure. We recall that the Boko Haram initiated their violence in four Sharian States in the North where its criminal law is operative.

Concerning the Islamic Muslim Terror Networks, a prominent Muslim cleric, Sheikh Ahmad Gumi, said that Boko Haram is 100 per cent a Muslim problem, accusing some people in the North of "cooperating with and working to protect them. Gumi, explicating issues on Islamic Movements nationally, globally or Internationally particularly in the Africa-Nigerian Region saying that in the current April 2016 edition of the Interview, "Boko Haram as it is now cannot prosper in Ibadan-Nigeria, because the locals will expose them. We have to understand, he said, "that these people are from amongst us and that the society was not doing enough to bring these elements out. I can tell you that Boko Haram is 100 per cent a Muslim problem he reiterated, and more so not over sight the incessant horibble menace of the Fulani cattle herders around the country. Gumi, who also described the agitation for Biafra as "analogue," challenged Muslim leaders to do more to combat Boko Haram.[127] The problems of unrest, terror-networks of Boko Haram, ISIS, etc, touch various nations like in African and other continents of the world; Orlando, New York in USA, Nizza and Paris in

[127] Viewing Fast Facts on *Boko Haram* to get information on the militant *Islamic* group based in *Nigeria*, whose purpose is to institute Sharia, or *Islamic* law. … *Boko Haram Fast Facts. CNN Library. Updated 1:28 PM ET*, Mon October 31, *2016* …

France, Munich, Ansbach, Wuerzburg in Germany, London in UK, Madrid in Spain, Brussels in Belgium, Toronto in Canada. Others are Mumbai in India, Djerba, Bali, Mombasa, Toulouse, and in Africa, Nigeria, Mali, Kenya, Cameroon, Ghana, etc. These ugly news should not and ought not to be a laughing matter, it is a threat to humanity. This can be termed the "perpetual or lasting' 'sins of the Islamic Muslim world against humanity concerning the bombings, and terrorising of the innocent citizens of the world.

Everyman or woman is free to enjoy that freedom of existence, safety happy livelihood regarding human dignity and human rights in any enviroment one finds oneself.

This is what all Muslim clerics-the Imams; all the Islamic theologians and Psychologists ought every Friday Mosque-prayers (*Wudhu and Salat al Zuhr*) service an at the Muslims daily-hours of prayer be preaching more for saving and protecting one's and another's life in every place; all should be adopting this most important urgent maxim of *Live and Let Live,* and that is letting and allowing others-and your neighbours Live in peace; and as well every priest in every Christian Church to strongly preach more on the need for daily happy-peacefully living for all the people of God. To really acknowledge that God is the sole giver and owner of life, any human being ought to daily protect their life and other people's life. Commenting on the controversial bill to regulate preaching in Kaduna State, Gumi said the bill had gone too far and was an infringement on the constitution. "If you are trying to fight terrorism and extremism," he said, "you don't clamp down on the freedom of speech, freedom of thought and freedom of propagation of thoughts. Another root of corruption and impunity in the nation is clear; that though a good number lawless individuals hates the rule of law and do whatever they like even under the cover of politics or their religion; and such people oftentimes go scoot-free unpunished but these undue liberties are enshrined in the constitution to be observed and to be obeyed."

The International Security Watch, Federal Forces and other detectives should also quietly often control and monitor what is going on in various Mosques on Fridays and Churches on Sundays concerning the type of preachings, doctrine or indoctrination the Imams in Mosques and Priests in Christian Churches deliver to from their pulpits.

It is not a secret that ordinary Muslims who hoped that the Sharia would be remedy to the ills of the secular society when it was introduced a decade ago are completely disillusioned by their leaders, most of whom they consider worse than non-Muslim leaders.

It would not even be an exaggeration to uphold the view that some of those States belong to the worst governed in Nigeria.

Corruption and immorality are not lacking among its elites. So, frustration became rife among the underprivileged. In the words of Oyinka Medubi, everyone must understand that we owe them a moral duty; and perhaps, this may help to develop in each individual a Nigerian identity and the good understanding of one another and a better livelihood.

Nigeria, however, is getting to know themselves better and to work together more than ever before.

The process of increased interaction is likely to continue into the future. The result of this on Christian-Muslim relations will be to force both sides to take one another more seriously. There is really no rational alternative to mutual respect, tolerance, understanding and collaboration. Our contacts are teaching us to appreciate the good points of each side.

There is no such formal structure for collaboration between Christians and Muslims. But informal opportunities crop up at every turn, especially for joint action for matters of local concern. There should be proffered remedies for violation. By this we mean that where Human Rights violation has occurred, the most effective step to take, is to contemplate the recourse matter. And according to section 46 of the constitution, any person who alleges that any of the provisions of Chapter IV of the constitution has been, is being or likely to be contravened in any State in relation to him may apply to high court in that State for redress. For the purpose of the enforcement of the rights of citizens, the Chief Justice of Nigeria made the Fundamental Rights (enforcement procedure), rules which made access to court easier and simplified the rules on enforcement of fundamental rights.

The general principle of law which the courts have adopted over the years, is that statutes which seek to deprive the citizen of their right to freedom is to be construed as strength against weak and can seen as bad intention of the legislation. Effect would only be given to the spirit and intent of the legislation. A person whose right is breached has the option to pursue any one of the ways open to him to enforce his rights including *(mandamus prahibitio certiorari)*- a prohibited command of an injunction and action for damages. The court is obligated to hear the person who comes to it with allegation that his fundamental rights have been infringed by government or its organ or agencies or any person and possibly remedy the wrong done him. An action for the enforcement of fundamental rights is maintainable against an individual as it is against a government or any of its agencies.

On the theoretical level, there is and there should be an effort to create a model of Christian-Muslim relationship that will not be conditioned by the rough history of our respective pasts.

Practically speaking, education and public enlightenment is necessary. There is need for the inclusion of Human Rights education in the curricular of both primary and secondary schools and police colleges throughout the country.

Apart from this, the enforcement of the remedies under the rules comes in sight. The Fundamental Rights, (Enforcement Procedure) Rules of 2009 provide a peculiar procedure for enforcing breaches of fundamental rights.

Under the law, the remedies are varied and include bail to a detained person or his production in open court, and injunction, certiorari to quash proceedings etc. There are many Nigerians, convinced Muslims and Christians who are anxious to make sure that we show the world that Christians and Muslims need not necessarily be at each others throat.

The next topic brings us into the comparism of Aquinas thoughts and the Modern understanding of Justice and Human Rights.

Chapter Three: Thomas Aquinas Life and Works

3.1

Life and Times of Thomas Aquinas

The brief survey of Thomas Aquinas writings on his numerous scholastic works and personality, and successful life coupled with his various excellent performances is a necessity as this will lead us explicitly in between the lines of certain explanations in the course of this research work. He was born in 1225 at Roccasecca, near Naples in Italy. He was the 7th child and the youngest son of Landolfo, the head of one of the most illustrious families of southern Italy and nephew to Fedredric Barbarossa.

Aquinas epitomizes scholasticism and academicians, and educationists singled him out as philosopher and theologian per excellence.

It can be generally asserted that Aquinas philosophy is a rethinking

of Aristotelianism which does not however deny the originality of his thoughts. For his education; he attended the University of Naples, where he followed the course in liberal arts. Despite the intense opposition from his family to discourage him from joining the Dominican Congregation, Aquinas eventually got his way, and ended up becoming one of the most important religious thinkers of the middle ages. One broad characteristic of his work in philosophy is a tendency to seek the " middle way"on questions that have been given a wide range of answers. Today this philosophical method is labelled "moderate realism"[128]

It is in this context that we shall survey his ethical teachings, especially his views on Justice, Human Rights and Common Good and we should not forget that his religious commitments led him to look beyond philosophy for the reasonable final answers. He did some of his studies in Paris, before moving to Cologne in 1248 and three years later he lectured on Matthew's gospel and began to write the "Summary Against the Gentiles", *Summa Contra Gentiles,* example the *Book III, 114-138; In X Libros Ethicarum;*

---

[128] Aquinas. T., Summa Theologiae, I- II Quest. 93 a1.Aquinas. T., Summa Theologiae, I-II Quest. 93 a1.

Questiones Disputate de Malo, Aquinas dealt more with theoritical analysis of ethical activities in a long series of works among which are the Scriptum in IV Libros Sententiarum and other treatises.

In his major works, Aquinas provided important arguments in favor of the Christian faith for the benefit of missionaries working amongst Moslems and Jews. In 1266, he began one his most important writings, usually known by its Latin title, *Summa Theologiae.* Thomas developed a detailed study of key aspects of Christian theology (such as the role of reason and faith), as well as detailed analysis of key doctrinal questions (such as the divinity of Christ). This particular work is divided into three parts, with each of the first two parts being subdivided. Part one deals chiefly with God the creator; Part II with the restoration of humanity to God; and Part III with the manner in which the person and work of Christ bring about the salvation to humanity.

Between 1256 and 1259 the two hundred and fifty-three scholastic disputations which constitute his treatise *De Veritate* and the *De Pontentiae* and at this time, at the request of the famous missionary, Raymond of Pernafort, in 1259, after three years of theological teaching, as master at Paris, Thomas, returned to Italy. Thomas also commented clearly on the Scriptures, lectured on Cannon Law, and at the request of the Pope he compiled the *Catena Aurea* of the glosses on the Gospels, and wrote a work aiming at the reconciliation of the Greek Church with Rome. On the institution of the feast of *Corpus Christi,* he was chosen to provide its liturgical office, for which he wrote the hymnes, *Pange Lingua Gloriose, Corporis Mysterium, Sacris Solemnis juncta sint guadia* and the *Verbum Supernum Prodiens.* With Papal encouragement Thomas then began his exposition of the works of Aristotle which really influenced him.

At the Papal curia he met his conferere, William of Moerbeke, who at the suggestion of Thomas began a new translation of Aristotle direct from Greek. With the help of good texts, free of the corruptions that characterized the versions taken from the Arabic, Thomas between 1256 and 1269 also wrote his comment on the physics, Metaphysics, on the soul, Ethics, Politics and the Posterior Analytics. He had occasion to answer both Augustinians and Averoists while expanding his theological doctrine through Scriptural commentaries, the many disputation he held at his time, and in particular, the *Summa Theologica* which he had began in Italy in 1267.

Against the Averoist, Thomas equally wrote two treaties, *De aeternitate mundi et De unitate intellectus,* to prove that Averoist work did not sound good philosophically. The purity of Thomas doctrine gained him the name "Angel of the School' 'he was called to Italy by his superiors in 1272 and charged with reorganisng all the theological courses of his order.

There at Naples in the university he as well lectured on the Psalms and works of St. Paul, he commented on Aristotle's "on the Heavens and on Generation and Corruption"and then worked on the third part of Summa.

He emphasized more on man's behaviour and interaction towards his fellow man as contrary and arbitrary injustice which stems from deprivation of justice, rights and fair-play in our society. Aquinas really moved into a quest for a panacea which is a desiring solution to the problem of Human Rights and the co-existence between man and man, justice and fairness, and the common good.

Aquinas as well wrote his special treatises at the request of his friends, regarding what he had done as he had done, throughout his life. He then wrote about his career for his students the *De Ente et Essentia,* for the king of Cyprus he composed the *De Regimine Principium*, in the Platonic tradition he had connected on the treatise of Beothius and the *Liber de Causis,* which he showed was not a work of Aristotle, the part of his treatise on man especially the one of " Treatise on Prudence, Law and Justice", and his work on *"De Regimine Principium"De Principiis Natura* between 1265 and 1273, the pars-Prima Secunda-Secundae are among his popular and famous works. As his life drew to its close, he composed numerous minor works on theology, including the *compendum theologiae.* This is the nucleus and the whole quintessence of his formidable synthesis on the insights of his classical philosophy and Christian theology.

Thomas Aquinas writing career came suddenly to an end on December 6, 1273. He, however, enjoyed great popularity as a teacher and left behind a great monument for humanity. He then declared that he could write no longer. Urged by his companions to complete the *Summa,* he replied by saying "I can do no more, such things have been revealed to me that all I have written seems as straw, and I now await the end of my life."[129]

---

[129] Great Books of the Western World; cited by J.M. Adler., (ed.), Aquinas: I, nr.17, Encyclopaedia Britanica, Inc, Chicago, London 1996, p. v.

It is possible that he may have had some sort of breakdown, perhaps brought about by overwork. Despite that, he still commented on the Song of Solomon at the request of the Monks. In all of these works of his, his teachings are basically the same.

He takes the approach of moral theology which deals on what is moral, good or evil in terms of its accord with the divine law, revealed through the sacred scriptures and interpreted in the Christian tradition.

But Aquinas did not consider moral theology to be a part of philosophy for he based his teachings on what the theory of natural law or eternal law defines as "the divine wisdom directing all actions and movements."[130]

His formulations of the idea of justice is based much on the writings of Aristotle found in Book Five of Nichomachean Ethics.

In this traditon which stated that '*all things have a specific nature which does not change*'' Aquinas called justice a moral virtue defined as: " the constant and perpetual will to render to everyone what is due to him."[131] Aquinas believed that the natural law, which is "the rational creature's participation of the eternal law", made it possible for all men to have sufficient knowledge of what is morally right or wrong in order to regulate their own actions.[132] Uncompromisingly, Aquinas makes divine reason the touchstone of his reflections and "right reason"(*recta ratio*) the justification of ethical thoughts. Where the supreme standard is the eternal law, in volitional activities, the proximate standard is human reason (*regaula proxima est ratio humana*).

Suffice it to say that Aquinas formulated the natural law theory from his view that man participates"of a certain share in the divine reason', but this share could thus be limited to such law itself and therefore not partake of justice. Aquinas itemized it all in his analysis about man that human reason distinguishes man from other higher brutes which lack rationality. It is a part of being reasonable, which Aquinas admonished all to maintain and to respect the goods of others, even if an all powerful legitimate has not ordered so. It is worth mentioning too, that in Aquinas ethical writings or principles, whenever man's action proceeds to its end to be in accord with the order of reason and eternal law; the act that is right and justifiable.

---

130 Aquinas. T., Summa Theologiae, Pars IIa – Iiae, Quest. 58. Art.3.

131 Aquinas. T., Summa Theologiae, I-II, Quest. 9,1 a 2.

132 Cf. Aquinas. T., Summa Theologiae, I-II, 21, 1c.

However, when it is twisted away from this rightness, its is an unjust act, a sin.[133] We should also keep in mind that within the tail end of his life on earth, that he offered us another major key works on theology with its special importance thoughts called the "*Quinque Viae.*"

The Five Ways (arguments for the proof of the existence of God), the principle of analogy, which provides a theological foundation for knowing God through the creation remains explicit.

He died on March 7, 1274. Having surveyed the Thomas Aquinas writings productive acumen and industriousness, let us now see the contemporary notion of Justice and Human Rights in the next topic.

[133] Cf. Aquinas. T., Summa Contra Gentiles III, 121-122.

3.2

Human Rights and Justice and Common Good in Aquinas Thoughts as Concerns Nigeria

Following the aphorism of Thomas Aquinas, the object of justice is right of others.[134] Justice is then very much comparable to the human right.

This is because of the sole purpose of acknowledging and consideration of the integrity of human person and dignity. Human Rights is seen here as the definitely moral or legal claim of a person to have or get something or to behave in a particular way or manner.

Human Rights also introduce the concept of economic and social Human Rights. Everyone, by virtue of being human, is entitled to social security and the economic, social, and cultural rights necessary to obtain dignity and pursue individual development. Common good plays a major role in Aquinas thought.

What common good is all about, its philosophical antecedents and solidarity as a firm commitment to common good.

Furthermore, a leap is taken to understand in concrete terms, the concept of common good. No human power may obstruct the realization of man as a human person and the foundational goal of social order is the human person.

Common Good and one's welfare has a meaningful purpose here.

The notion of 'Common Good' here seems to flow from the concept of sharing. In other words, the inescapable pressures of human limitations, needs and scarcity appear to generate a necessity of the common good. If resources are limited, relative to individuals who need them, this may call for 'ethical adjustments". Human behavior is like a river that tries always to maintain its normal levels. "Ordinary animals, the Igbo hold, scratch

[134] Aquinas. T., Summa Theologiae IIa IIae, Quest 57, Art.I ff

their backs at trees when their backs irritate them but, men on the other way round, turn their backs to their fellow men." Implicit in the notion of common good are two levels of consideration. The first level concerns the necessity of using the limited resources sparingly.

Scarcity imposes a certain degree of necessity in human living. Here, greater emphasis is laid on "apportioning" and allocating", "assigning." Rearden is right when he highlights that "scarcity of resources combines with needs to produce the obligation of using resources economically and especially of developing them.

The greatest allocation of the common good to the underprivileged is based on communal aspiration to secure as much as minimum requirements for survival as possible for the lower class.

It is in line with Rawls' philosophy that 'each person possesses an inviolability founded on justice (or fairness) that even the welfare of the society as a whole cannot over ride. The second consideration shows that in the pursuit of the limited resources, everybody seems to mind their own business. Even if one does mind others 'business' it is ultimately those of one's family, town, clan, tribes, or those of one's close associates. The common good, unarguably exists for those who are often outside these class of consideration–family, town, tribe.

If the common good is like the common welfare in so far as both are 'common', it is different from it in almost every other respect. "Welfarism" according to Azikiwe is "a social system where the State assumes the primary responsibility for the individual and social welfare of its citizens.

Here, the emphasis is more on the State, or the community.

In modern communities, welfarism is more on the State, or the community.

In modern communities, welfarism is needed to cater for those aspects of life which are beyond the capacity of each individual, especially the less privileged. Thus, "it is a complex of policies, attitudes, and beliefs which animate the State to provide for the inhabitants whose means are inadequate.

Common welfare, has ethical relevance in so far as it helps the society to evolve policies, and plans that foster the continued survival and flourishing of the individuals, especially the less advantaged. In Igbo traditional community as in other African communities, thatch houses are built for individuals by collective efforts. Pathways and bridges are constructed communally. Marriage transactions are a corporate rather than individual undertaking. Thus, "common welfare", unlike "common good" involves social mobility, consideration, and dynamism directed in favor of the individuals, especially the less privileged.

It concerns those areas of life, which left alone, the individual's discrete entities could meet up with. Here, we mention education, security, health, electricity, pension. Common good, on the other hand is more of static structures or properties devoted for common usages and less dynamic. Common welfare presupposes a certain measure of human touch, human acceptance, care and concern.

Hence, common good presupposes respect for the human person. Totalitarianism leads to chaos while common good and elimination of inequality brings about social order.

In a society where the members have the spirit of common good, common values are shared adequately; and are enjoyed by all, and there is order in that society because they pursue the same goal.

The protection of the human person and of human dignity at all stages of human life require insertion and participation in; not insulation and separation from the community. Hence Barber noted that the community prospers when its members turn within and tend only to their private cares.

Common good is a term that can refer to several different concepts. In the popular meaning, common good describes a specific "good" that is shared and is beneficial for all or members of a given community.[135] This is equally how common good is broadly defined in philosophy, ethics and political science.In the Nigerian context, there is too much individualism and egocentrism; hence there is no peace, no adequate justice, no transparency and as such, social order is lacking. Furthermore, Nigeria as a country lacks the spirit of common good, everybody thinks for his own good and prosperity with little or no interest about the "good" of our neighbor, hence, no solidarity among the members of the society.

The fact that human right provisions are not lacking in various Nigerian constitutions has also been clearly demonstrated by our delineation of these provisions in the 1999 constitution. But to show the yawning gap between

---

[135] B. Barber., Strong Democracy: Participatory Politics for new Age. Berkel: University Press, California 1984, p. 78.

the paper tiger and what obtains in practice, we made our observation of the forms of violation and disrespect with which these basic rights are being greeted in the present democracy. What now remains for us is to proffer some suggestions that may be a panacea to the unfortunate anomie. First and foremost, there is the need to enthrone the rule of law. This means that the present situation in Nigeria where disobedience to court orders and injunctions especially by the ruling elites is the order of the day, has to be thrown overboard. In our society, no one should construct ones lifestyle as if one is not subject to the ordinary laws of the land.

This is especially important in a polity where many violations of fundamental rights are perpetrated by some members of the ruling class. Thus, the practices of the rule of Law will succeed if and only if, inter-alia, the leadership is responsible.

As far back as 1983, Achebe observed in a booklet entitled "The Trouble with Nigeria"[136] that the most basic problems raised by his observation have not been properly addressed. No wonder we today still experience executive lawlessness, legislative anarchy and reckless judiciary within the halls of government.

Sometimes, there are fisticuffs either between the executive and the legislature or between the executives and the judiciary.

This is a clear indication that there is either a reign of bad will or that many are quite ignorant of the tenets or the principles of separation of powers, checks and balances and generally of the essential features of democracy.

There is no doubt that unless these issues are put straight, genuine

respect for basic rights of citizens will still be in abeyance. Akin to the need for responsible leadership is the necessity for the generation of people-oriented policies by the leaders. This is because some policies are good and their problem becomes that of implementation.

The effect is that poverty paradoxically becomes pregnant in a country blessed with abundant human and natural resources. And unless this poverty is eradicated not necessarily by giving fish to the hungry but also by making him to learn how to fish through creation of employment opportunities, then it is inevitable that the Hobbesian state of nature where

[136] C. Achebe., The Trouble With Nigeria, Enugu: Fourth Dimension Publishers, 1983, p. 67.

life is not only "brutish, short and nasty" but also "where man is a wolf to his fellow man" *(homo homini lupus)* shall have been re-established. There would certainly be inaugurated a greater tendency for infringements on Human Rights. If only people would know that the life span of man is very short, most problems would not have arisen. God is the creator of man, and man is created *'imago Dei'* as God's image. It is because we all are created equal in the image of God that everybody must have a respect for the right of other people. Your right ends where my own begins and vice versa.

Human Rights with its concerns is of great regard; is an essential factor of societal development. This is particularly true as every form of positive development must have human being as its target. Quintessence of humanness lies in the quality and dignity which any human being enjoy in Nigeria today. Having great regard and respect for human rights is an important index of national and individual development.

It seems that a measure of a country's claim to be democratic is based on how the Human Rights of its citizens are honestly respected, protected and exercised and executed.

The result will certainly constitute a formula for sustainable human development in Nigeria today. The discourse is premised on the idea that every process of development must target the disunity of the human person as its *terminus ad quem.* Human being as a "social animal" need one another and their own self development depends upon their being social beings. The realization that one's development is dependent upon the cooperation of others leads man to reflect on the importance of the public interest. People draw upon and gain from their fellow men, while at the same time leaving themselves free to pursue their own choices and potentials. In this way, everyone benefits. Hence, common good can be understood in terms of social order. Social order implies a set of rules and institutions within which each individual is left free to pursue his/her own choices and develop as a human being.

The notion of common good first emerged in the writing of the Greek philosopher, Plato in the fifth century. Over the centuries, philosophical debates have continued as to the nature of the "good" and what constitutes the "common good." For Plato, justice was a supreme virtue that was embodied in the common good and his ideal system of government envisaged rule by philosopher-kings who used their wisdom to act justly for the good of all. Justice understood traditionally as a virtue and related to good, has ever since been the foundation of a good political and social order and as such to be in every one's interest. For Thomas Aquinas, the notion of justice as being the mutuality or reciprocity shared among the members of society was further refined, when he argued that "the virtue of a good citizen is general justice, whereby each person is directed to the common good. Furthermore, Aquinas understood the connection between virtue and the common good as directed by justice "so that all acts of virtue can pertain to justice in so far as it directs each person to the common good".[137] R.J.Araujo also noted that Marcus Tillius Cicero shared some of Aristotle's thought when he suggested that a commonwealth or social order emerges from the social spirit of people who make the commonwealth their "property", which is established on the principles of respect for justice and partnership for the common good.[138]

Good human reasoning brought Aquinas's understanding of common good into the contemporary era.

In plain terms, the basic position that the human person and the community are not in conflict with one another means be that their vital interests are complementary rather than contradictory. The common good is common because it is received in persons, each one of whom is mirror of the whole. The end of the society is the good of the community, of the social body.

But if the good of the social body is not understood to be a common good of human persons, just as the social body itself is a whole of human persons, this conception also would lead to other errors of a totalitarian type.

The common good of the city is neither the mere collection of private goods, nor the proper good for a whole that like the species with respect to its individuals or the hive with respect to its bees, relates the parts to itself alone and sacrifice them to itself. It is the good human life of the multitude, of a multitude of persons; it is their communion in good living.

---

137 T. Aquinas., (*Summa theologiae,* q.58, a.2.).

138 R. J. Araujo., "Justice as Right Relationship: a Philosophical and Theological Reflection on Affirmative Action", in *Pepperdine*; (http.//www.unffl.org/vol ii *Law* Review, 448-450, 474-476, London 2000.

Aristotle, argued for example that the good of the community should set the direction for the lives of individuals, for it is a higher or more "divine" good than the particular goods of private persons; seeking a balance between the rights succeeding generations of philosophers have wrestled with ever since. The above discourse discloses that so many men (philosophers) of different epochs and times have ventured into discerning what the common good is and it is not yet settled as shown in the contemporary interest and attention to the subject. These rights should be realised by national efforts and international cooperation, with consideration of the organisation and resource of each State.

Human Rights are thus the standards laid down by society for the treatment of her members, and these standards derive from, and reflect in the political organisation of society, the economic and social system, the cultural values, as well as the moral stipulations and historical circumstances, which may differ. It means that the perception between societies of what constitutes Human Rights may equally not be uniform except when general objective standards are established; upon which the Human Rights of otherwise different societies can be compared.

The quest for such common objective standards had found expression in the various treaties and conventions between states; some bilateral, others multilateral, which attempt to generate a consensus in meaning, and to determine the various dimensions operative mechanisms and procedures for the evaluation of the degree of achievement of this worthy objective.

Human rights are possible only in the context of the duties that the citizen performs as his contribution to society and the obligations that he renders to the State and civil society in return for the protections given to him and the conditions created around him for his optimal self-fulfilment;

hence, the practice of linking Human Rights to duties and obligations. Along the same line, it is because of the apparently complex nature of these rights that people became indifferent to distinguish between its various dimensions, including the political and civil, the socio-cultural, economic and others. The political rights relate to the role of the individual in political society, his capacity to participate in the electoral, legislative and governing processes of the country and his general involvement in the inputs, processes and feedbacks within the political system.

It is a measure of the level of development of the political systems that citizens are free and able to participate directly or indirectly at the various levels of policy-making and implementation. So to participate effectively, citizens must enjoy the rights of freedom of association, of speech, and assembly, in the conditions of the rule of law. Socio-cultural rights include artistic expression, the use of indigenous languages and their inclusion in the approved curricula of schools. The preservation of local cultural artefacts, history and folklore, as well as the encouragement of related sports, are all some of the main components of cultural rights. A programme of free and compulsory education for all citizens at least up to the pre-university level is an essential prerequisite for the full realization of cultural rights within a society. And for an individual, as such, security of life and property, not only guarantees the freedom of peoples and a peaceful environment for society, but ensures that the accumulated benefits of culture are passed between generations unhindered and undiluted.

Regarding the relationship to other rights, one observes that there are several other rights which had come to be viewed as either prerequisitory, parallel or supplementary to Human Rights but which in due course became considered by many as embodied in the latter, and these include civil and civic rights, civil liberties, natural rights and the right to life and property. Civil rights are the rights automatically enjoyed by a person as member of civil society. Unlike the rights conferred by the State, so long as the individual or group meets the society's expectation, their civil rights cannot be tampered with either by the State or by the society, instead, both are obliged to protect and advance them.[139]

Civil rights on the other hand, relate to the capacity and entitlement to participate in the conduct of affairs of the community to which one belongs, in other words, civic right is one of the practical applications of the principles of civil and other Human Rights to service of the civil society, community and people. It means, in effect, that except in the conditions of the optimal development of civil rights and appreciation of the essence of civil society- a community of people that predated, and exist without, the State- it would seem impossible to rise in service of the community, which is one partial manifestation of that civil society. What then can be said on natural rights?

---

[139] O. Igwe., Politics and Globe Dictionary, Enugu, Nigeria, 2002, p. 64.

Natural rights, once again according to the *Politics and Globe Dictionary,*where Igwe makes mention of the rights as being supposedly beyond any regulation or interference by the State, a components of Human Rights, and a development from the concept of natural law. What are the natural laws themselves? These laws had been defined as laws that exist in nature or made by God, which are therefore, unalterable, quite unlike positive laws made by man and, so, subject to changes and diverse interpretations. It is these natural laws that create natural rights. In a single sentence, this piece addresses several key issues in Human Rights doctrine, although little research exists to explain these particular rights.[140]

A government must try to provide residents with social security and the means to realize important economic, social, and cultural rights, this would include the rights to work, housing, health care, holidays, and allowable observance of cultural traditions. To realize these rights, government should cooperate with each other through international organisations. Wealthier countries would be expected to assist less wealthy countries through transfers of assistance. That means that social workers have significant involvement in these issues, with the NASW (National Association of Social Workers), supporting a national health care policy that ensures the right to universal medical coverage.[141]

Hence, all aspects and variations of the rights of man have undivided common roots in a general commitment to his welfare and insisting upon the joint responsibility of the individual State and society in promoting it.

Therefore, fundamental Human Rights can be rightly considered as generally the same as Human Rights, and related to civil rights, natural rights, people's rights and civil liberties and individuals and groups within a free society.[142]

Based upon this principle, and not withstanding the necessary theoretical distinctions that have to be made between them in scholarship, their

---

[140] J. Wronka, Human Rights ans Socail Policy in the 21st Century- A History of the Idea of Human Rigths and Comparison of the United Nations Universal Declaration of Human Rights with United States Federal and State Constitution. Rev. ed. Lanham, Md., University Press of America, 1998, p. 13.

[141] National Association of Social Workers, (NASW Code of Ethics. Washington, D.C. NASW Press, 1996. cf . also, Social Work Speaks- National Association of Social Worksers policy Statemetns , 2000-2003. 5th ed. Washington, D.C. NASW Press.

[142] O. Igwe., Politics and Globe Dictionary, Enugu, Nigeria, 2002, p. 165.

simulations application in practical policy remains the most central responsibility of political leadership. Regardless of their diverse nature and character, the road to the rights of man had never been straight and smooth; on the contrary, it had been a long tortuous path filled with struggle and bloodshed, bitterness, despair and triumph.

If there was no notion of Human Rights, may be man could have been in the Hobbesian State of nature, and in which life was "solitary, poor, nasty, brutish and short" a place where "force and fraud and its cardinal virtues", and the only rule that men acknowledge is the good old rule, to live righteously.

Primitive society as characterized above was a very harsh environment where justice was immediate, swift and severe, a place where a subject might have been stoned to death years before his innocence would be established. The slave- owning societies of slavery, serfdom and feudalism may be imagined to be higher orders of development by some people.

At least, where slaves existed, free men ought to have existed too, and being free means the possession of some rights at the very least.

Moreover, a serf could purchase his freedom and, by so doing equally free his offspring from further bondage. A similar situation existed under the feudal system where the nobility, monarchy and warlords enjoyed a considerable amount of freedom over and above what was accessible to the generality of peoples. Mankind had also gone through the horrible experience of the industrial revolution and colonialism. During the industrial revolution, able-bodied men, together with women, the aged and the sick in addition to children, some of whom were as young as seven years, would work for upwards of eighteen hours in hazardous environments with little or no concern for their hygiene, health and happiness.

People were dying like fowls in exchange for pittances that could not fulfil even the most fundamental of needs.

There had also been several wars of such terrible magnitude that in some cases the survivors started envying the dead weapons of mass destruction were employed while unlawful and prohibited tactics and instruments became the norm, with no side conceding responsibility or suggesting remorse. The death, torture, execution and abandonment of children, the sick and the aged; the deliberate use of starvation as an instrument of war, show trials of innocent people in a phoney judicial process, forced exile and deprivation of citizenships, entities, genocides and indiscriminate bombing of civilian areas, and the twisting of history to cover the crimes of the victorious and exaggerate the mistakes of the defeated, had all been some of the notable 'fruits'of war in the last few centuries. There is no condition as iniquitous to the notion of the exercise of Human Rights as war and other hostilities, because in such conditions, the penalty for the most minor of misdemeanours might be the ultimate sanction of execution, with no intermediate consideration. It was considered by Feldman, that "the preparation for aggressive wars goes hand in hand with breaches of Human Rights and freedoms of broad segments of the population, and the starting of such wars results in the abolishment of Human Rights and fundamental freedoms.

It is hardly surprising, then that having gone through many of the calamities summarized above the resultant conditions of men would start to touch the conscience of scholars and statesmen concerning the ideal human society to recommend and the correct human condition to pursue. People in all societies and cultures began searching their minds and asking themselves fundamental question of life what good and righteous life is all about.

If there is need for collective life at all in the State or the society, why can't there also be a common minimum standard for treating all their members, and why should such a minimum standard not accord with the principles of justice, equality and fair-play?

Why should we continue with certain inhuman practices that society could do without; what is the essence of collective life, of democracy, of civilization? Civilized nations started to take individual actions to promote and assure the observance of minimum standard in treatment of citizens, and to generalize their positive experience in this regard to cover all nations.

One of the earliest national attempts to promote the Human Rights of citizens was the *Magna Carta* which the assertive English nobility compelled the powerless King John to sign on June 15, 1215.

That document "subsequently became the basis of English and British constitutional development, the freedoms liberties and rights enjoyed by their peoples, and the duties and obligations they render in return.[143]

The nobility was the only conscious revolutionary force at the time, and they knew that it was almost impossible to achieve any rights for themselves without equally ensuring the freedoms and rights of the generality. Hence,

---

[143] Cf. O. Igwe., Politics and Globe Dictionary, Enugu, Nigeria, 2002, p. 246.

we also have granted to all the freemen of our kingdom, for us and for our heirs forever, all the under-written liberties, to be had and held by them and their heirs, of us and our heirs forever.

This was followed in 1689 by the Bill of Rights (actually, a Declaration of Rights), among whose provisions were

a) That pretended power of suspending laws, or the execution of laws, by legal authority, without consent of parliament, is illegal.
b) That the pretended power of dispensing with laws, or the execution of laws, illegally.
c) That the freedom of speech, and debates or proceedings in a parliament, ought not to be impeached or questioned in any court or place out of parliament.

Although the rights and freedoms appear mostly in favour of parliament, they most importantly laid the solid foundations for their eventual application to all citizens. It will be recalled that in the 18th century, the American colonists had clamoured for no 'taxation without representation', in effect to the participation of the people in decisions concerning their welfare.

In the 1789 in particular, the French revolution which had been based on the cardinal principles of *liberte* (freedom), *egalite* (equality), and *fraternite* (brotherhood), subsequently created the 'Declaration of the Rights of Man and of the Citizen', establishing principles which were not only applicable to the French, but beneficent to all mankind.

An international term introduced by the United States Declaration of Independence in 1776 and the Declaration of the Rights of Man and Citizen in 1789 of the French Revolution was observed.[144]

It was adopted by the United States constitution and extended by the 16th constitutional amendment in 1913, and is the subject of international declarations. The first of these was the Declaration of Human Rights and Declaration of Human Rights and Duties worked out in 1929 by New York Institute of International Law and submitted to Inter-Ameraican Legal committees.

In article 1, it clearly proclaimed that it is a duty of every state to recognize equal rights of an individual to life freedom and property and to fully

144 E. J. Osmanczyk., Encyclpaedia of United nations and International Agreements. Philadelphia- London, 1985, p. 352.

grant and protect these rights on this entire territory regardless of nationality, sex, race, language or religion.

In article 2, it stated that this declaration together with the resolution of Inter-American conference in Chapultepec, March 8, 1945, on the need to establish international protection on Human Rights, laid the foundations for a draft of the Univeral declaration of Human Rights submitted to the United Nations (UN), Human Rights Commission. On Decemeber 10, 1948, this Commission prepared the Human Rights Universal Declaration.

This Declaration was a United Nation General Resolution and forms the basis for the fundamental Human Rights adopted by member States including Nigeria.

It is the duty of every State to recognize equal rights of the individual to free execution, whether in public or private of any faith, religion or worship, the practise of which is not in violation of public order and good manner.

More so, the 1776 American Declaration of Independence had proclaimed thus that we hold these truths to be self-evident, that all men are created equal, that they are endowed by their Creator with certain inalienable rights that are among these are life, liberty and pursuit of happiness.

That to secure these rights, governments are instituted among men; deriving their just powers from the consent of the governed. Africans especially Nigerians, have not been found wanting in emulating the theories of other nations, even if there is no serious official commitment to their practical implementation.

And so too are matters concerning Human Rights discourse.

Thus, the 1979 Nigerian Constitution contained two chapters on what was called 'Fundamental Objectives and Directive Principles of State Policy' And the Fundamental Rights where it enumerated eleven of such rights and freedoms including the right to life, fair hearing, acquisition of property, etc, and the freedom from discrimination, etc which, of course, had all been observed mostly in breach. Some other African and Third World countries had similar constitutional provisions on Human Rights which are hardly paid attention to by their governments.[145]

[145] Federal Republic of Nigeria (1999), The Constitution Of The Federal Republic of Nigeria 1999, Lagos, Federal Government Press.

Although, as the foregoing discourses have demonstrated, questions of Human Rights have engaged the concerns of nations, notable figures and publicists for a very long time.

The 48 nation Universal Declaration in December 10, 1948, was the most modern and comprehensive articulation of the subject in history by a concert of sovereign States. It is was regarded as 'a common standard of achievement for all people and all nations, to the end that every individual and every organ of society, keeping this Declaration constantly in mind, shall strive by teaching and education to promote respect for these rights and freedoms and by progressive measures, national and international, to secure their universal and affective recognition and observance.[146]

As such, a common standard of achievement the Declaration has continued to occupy an exalted position in the minds of men.

Since 1948, most discussions on Human Rights in many parts of the world have taken their terms of reference from the Declaration, even though there continued to be attempts by various regional organisations such as the OAU (Afican Union, European Union), EU and the NGOs to elaborate upon concepts of Human Rights as uniquely applicable to their members or corresponding to their *Weltanschauung.*

Even the original Declaration had itself been elaborated on in 1966 by two UN- sponsored treaties-

a) the International Convenant on Civil and Political Rights, and
b) 9 the International Covenant on Economic, Social and Cultural rights- thus further legitimizing the original division by the Declaration of the rights into those that are "civil and political"and those concerned with economic, social and cultural rights.'

Many other resolutions in the General Assembly and Security Council, as well as other bodies and multitude of writing, have also continued to broaden man's thinking on Human Rights.

The civil and political rights"prohibit slavery, inhuman treatment, arbitrary arrest and arbitrary interference with privacy, together with discrimination on grounds of race, colour, sex, language, religion, political or other opinion, national or social origin, property, birth or other status. They also proclaim the right to a fair trial, freedom of movement and residence, the right to political asylum, the right to have and change nationality, the right

[146] M. Akehurst., A Modern Introduction to International Law, London, 1971, p. 100.

to marry, the right to own property, freedom of peaceful assembly and association, free elections and equal opportunities for access to public positions.

On the other hand, the economic, social and cultural rights demand "the right to social security, to full employment and fair conditions of work, to an adequate standard of living, to education and to participation in the cultural life of the community.[147]

However, no one bothered that civilized existence can brush the 1948 Declaration aside but, unfortunately, many governments often observe it in the breach, and most of the rest only do so when convenient.

In many developed countries, race is often the basis upon which the tenets of the Declaration and Human Rights of weaker minorities are undermined, while in a number of the developing societies, the so-called ' needs of development'are used as a pretext for non-compliance.

This problem of deliberate violations is behind the unrelenting spate of complaints from diverse groups and individuals in Nigeria, Africa and elsewhere.

This is to buttress the fact that all individuals and families have the right to housing that meets their basic needs for shelter at affordable level and provides for a rewarding community life. In practicing their various professions, social workers should also respect the cultural rights of others.

These Human Rights which elaborates on the generalized economic and social rights. Actually and certainly, this Human Right appears grandiose in that unemployment is a fact of life the world over.

In the normal parlance, can governments really guarantee employment and a wage sufficient to provide an existence worthy of human dignity?

Lesser developed countries would have especially difficult time meeting the requirements for the populace.

Nevertheless, the goal of ensuring that every one who wants to work has a job with sufficient income to provide for his or her family ought to and should have a merit. In other words, the right to work with a living wage makes sense as a Human Right even if the fulfilments of this right are not always possible. This Human Right also raises the issue of equal pay for equal work. This touches special care and assistance for motherhood and childhood also relate to cultural and social rights. A father might question the specific protection of motherhood and not fatherhood. However, this

[147] M. Akehurst., A Modern Introduction to International Law, London, 1971, p. 99.

Human Right seems justified in that the mother carries the child for nine months before the actual birth of the child.

Regardless of how much a father might like to duplicate that experience, this attempt at a duplication remains an impossibility.

For that reason, special protection to the mother is a legitimate right. Equally, viewed within the perspective of leadership and administration, it can be seen as claim leaders and the led have on each other to fulfil a particular obligation and responsibility for each other.

In all Aquinas' intellectual ideas regarding the issues of Human Rights and justice, it could be ascertained that he cleverly derived most of his philosophical thoughts and findings on the nature of man, and he followed the political theory of Aristotle whose thoughts he worked closely with.

In Aquinas Thoughts, man is by nature a social animal who needs justice and fair-play among other necessities which life demands when we know that justice is a virtue distributing to every one his due.

On the same terrain, Aquinas specially pointed out that justice is a moral virtue which induces man to recognize the good of his own neighbor.[148]

The common good of all virtues whether in relation to ourselves or in relation to others is always referable to common good, therefore all acts of virtue directs one to the common good.

Aquinas main view is that justice is actually and primarily the virtue in relation to the other virtues. Since law directs to the common good; justice directs this generally to legal justice. It is the legal justice which directs man to the common good which immediately mediates between the goods of the individuals.

Justice has lots of positions in meaning, that all should recognise the truth for the purpose of good conduct as far as natural law is concerned.

Justice in the knowledge of Aquinas, relates to the moral aspect of man.

To be just means then paying what one owes to the other, it is therefore, giving one his due. This, now ushers in the exercise of the righteousness and peace for the common good of all or for the general public.

The expression '*bonum commune*' or 'common good' covers all the concrete goods within the reach of man in any historical situation. It includes all the needs and goods attainable by mortal man. It is the establishment of

[148] T. Aquinas., Summa Theologiae, IIa- IIae Qest. 58 Art. 1.

both the infra-and supra-strucutres of the society which help the individual to develop his potentialities which channels the establishmnet of things that will make man's life worth living.

Aquinas again rightly explained "Quaedam rationis ordinatio ad bonum commune, ab eo qui curam communitatis habet promulgata."[149]

The above quotation means that-(it is the right of reason for the common good, promulgated by him who has the care of the community). The generality of the common good is the virtue of the State which ought to be practical. This common good is maintained for the peace and order so that happiness is assured for all people in the community. For a better practice as regards common good or human relations, Wilhelm Vossenkuhl meaningfully and explicitly in his philosophical thoughts addressed the issue well, by asserting:

> the moral standard of men indeed concerns the ethical matters and this goes in different ways about goodness and being good; and precisely is not only about the moral good but also in all that reflects the various aspects of goodness that is meant for good life of a man.[150]

Man is an individual substance of creation and a phenomenon. In Aquinas distinctive knowledge, man is also a physical substance with an intellectual knowledge. What man is in his unique conception and worth was what Aquinas insisted upon for the unity of human nature.

Common good and justice have to play lots of key roles in human nature and its existentialisms. The common good is that of fundamental value governing social life. John XXIII defines the common good as: all those social conditions which favour the full development of human personality.[151]

In this sense the real life today with due regard to human rights as John Paul II said could unite with Gospel message for its perfection in the ambience located near the complex field of the science of moral theology and social ethics. It is in both theory and practice, a distinct discipline for the better livelihood of man.[152]

---

149 Aquinas. T., Summa Theologiae, Ia- IIae Quest. 90, Art 4.

150 Vossenkuhl. W., Die Möglichkeit des Guten Ethik in 21. Jahrhundert München 2006, p. 253.

151 John XXIII, Mater et Magistra, AAS 53, Rome, 1961, p. 417.

152 Cf. John Paul II, Laborens Exercens, 1981 nr.3 and AAS 80, Roma 1988, p. 541.

As man's civil society ought to be built and to be directed towards the realisation of natural and supernatural ends Aquinas on his explication on the doctrine of justice and common good also said as mentioned above, that the object of justice is the right of others.[153] Aquinas basic proposition, technically called 'the judgement of Synderesis'; -an intellectual quality enabling any man to intuit the first principles of practical reasoning which states that: " good should be done and sought after; evil is to be avoided."[154]

For any society to achieve certain objectives, it must have common good and share common beliefs, attitudes and mode of actions.

Ipso facto, human beings are not angels, there must be certain rules and regulations which we call norms or laws that could serve and guide the actions and activities of the members of the society.

Also in the very portion of the *Summa Theologica,* Aquinas explains the doctrine of the common good by making distinction between justice as applied to the particular and to the general.

This goes to mean, that the first pertains to one's relations and to the particular individuals.

The second aspect equally applies or pertains to one's relations to others and in general to members of a community.

In Aquinas, the particular good of the individual members is related to the good of the entire community such that whatever is good of the part being referred to, can be directed to the good of the whole. In so far as the good of all virtues whether in relation to oneself or in relation to others; can be referable to common good, justice directs man to the common good. Justice actually in this sense of reasoning means a general virtue in relation to the other virtues.

If the law directs to the generality and welfares of all, therefore, this general justice is legal justice.

The legal justice directs man to the common good immediately and also to the good of the individual meditatively.

The notion of common good was central to the theology of Thomas Aquinas that was to dominate Catholic thought even centuries after his death. Aquinas studied and wrote at a time when scholars had re-discovered

153 Cf. Aquinas. T., Summa Theologiae, IIa IIae, Quest. 57, 57, Art. 1ff.

154 Aquinas. T., Summa Theologiae, I- II, 94, 2.

the work of Aristotle and were attempting to reconcile it with divine revelation.

Aquinas argued that God's own self is the highest good, we can attain and that a right relation to God requires a commitment to the common good of our neighbours and of all creation.

Thus he avers that "private good is subordinated to the end of the common good: for the being of a part is for the sake of the being of the whole. Hence the good of the race is more godlike.

St. Augustine, one of the foremost influential philosophers, and theologias of early Christianity was greatly influenced[155] by the teaching and philosophy of Plato.

In great work "the City of God", Augustine contracts the city of man characterized by division, disharmony and selfishness as a result of original sin with "the City of God", the building of which is the goal of human history on which the motivation of its citizens flow from their love of God and for each other.The notion of the common good is a recurring theme in the great encyclicate of the Church from *Rerum Noverum* of Leo XIII where for example it is stated that "Civil society exists for the common good and all citizens without exception, can and ought to contribute to that common good".[156] The *Centesimus Annus* of John Paul II equally declared that the social nature of man is not completely fulfilled in the state, but is realized in various intermediary groups, beginning with the family and including economic, social, political and cultural groups which stem from human nature itself and have their own autonomy, always with a view to Common Good. The*Gaudium et Spes* defines the common good as the sum of those conditions of social life which allow members relatively thorough and ready access to their own fulfilment, thus the common good involves the ordering of social institutions toward human flourishing or fulfilment.[157]

The problem encountered by an attempt to promote the common good as motivation of human activity and social order is the concept of individualism.

---

[155] St. Augustine The City of God. Henry Bettenson, trans, Augustine New York: Penguin Books Editions, 1986 p. 94.

[156] John Paul II On the Handredth Anniversary of Rerum Novarum (Centesimus Annus). Libreria Editrice Vaticana 1991. p. 74.

[157] John Paul II On the Handredth Anniversary of Rerum Novarum (Centesimus Annus). Libreria Editrice Vaticana1991, p. 75.

Modern western culture places a high value to "do their own things". This idea has the tendency to view society as comprising of separate independent individuals who are free to pursue their own individual goals and interest without interference from others. In this individualistic culture it is difficult, perhaps, impossible to convince people that they should sacrifice some of their freedom, some of their personal goals and some of their interests, for the sake of the good "common good.

However, it is argued that the good of the community should set the direction for the lives of individuals; it is the only appropriate model for a pluralistic society in which "common good" is more important than any notion of "common good" and the neglect of community and social obligation, indeed it overlooks the fact that the very ability of people to identify what is good or noble depends on their being part of a community sharing in their arguments, conversations or dialogue.

The notion of common good first emerged in the writing of the Greek philosopher Plato in the fifth century. Over the centuries since, philosophical; debates have continued as to the nature of the "good" and what constitutes the "common good". For Plato, justice was a supreme virtue that was embodied in the common good and his ideal system of government envisaged rule by philosopher-kings who used their wisdom to act justly to the good of all. Justice understood traditionally as virtue and related to good, has ever since been the foundation of a good political and social order and as such to be in every one's interest.

The common good is common because it is received in persons, each one of whom is a mirror of the whole. The end of the society is the good of the community, of the social body. But if the good of the social body is not understood to be a common good of human persons, just as the social body itself is a whole of human persons, this conception also would lead to other errors of a totalitarian type.

The common good of the city is neither the mere collection of private goods, nor the proper good for a whole that, like the species with respect to its individuals or the hive with respect to its bees, relates the parts to itself alone and sacrifices them to itself. It is the good human life of the multitude, of a multitude of persons; it is their communion in good living.

Aristotle, argued for example that, the good of the community should set the direction for the lives of individuals, for it is a higher or more "divine" good than the particular goods of private persons. The above discourse discloses that so many men (philosophers) of different epochs and times have ventured into discerning what the common good is and it is not yet settled as shown in contemporary interest and attention to the subject. This is for the enlightenments regarding legal justice as already elucidated in earlier chapters of this work in our treatment of the classifications of justice and Human Rights and their meaningful differentiations.

Aquinas following the thoughts of Aristotle makes a distinction between commutative justice which directs the relation of one individual with another in mutual interactions, as a part which concerns the distributive justice and directs the relation of the community to the individual person as regards equity and common good.[158] For Aquinas therefore, the good of the particular or the individual is not divorced from the general good.

Aristotle, whose concepts Aquinas majorly imbibed and, imitated in his writings has his theory of morality or ethical theory on justice centring around his belief that man in his nature had a distinctive "end"to achieve or has a function to fulfil on earth. He then began his Nichomachean Ethics by asserting that: "every art and every investigation, and similarly every action and pursuits of man are considered to aim at some good. Hence, the Good has been rightly defined as that act which all things aim at"[159]

Regarding this type of philosophical cum moral postulation, we are led to ask the question, "what is the good at which human behaviour aims at?"

Plato answered this question in his "Doctrine of ideas,"where he said and maintained that this supreme principle of good was separated from the world of experience and from individual man and was to be arrived at by the mind's ascent from the visible world to the intelligible world.

Aristotle, on the other way round from his ethical theory maintains that the principle of good and right was embedded within each man; seeing justice as a state of mind of what it means to be just. Moreover this principle could be discovered by studying the essential nature of man which could be attained through one's actual behaviour in daily life.[160] He distinguishes himself in the realm of ethics by bringing it down to practical life. But

---

[158] Cf. T. Aquinas., Summa Theologiea, IIa Iiae, Quest. 61. Art. 1ff.

[159] Aristotle, Nichomachean Ethics, Penguin Classics, 1976, (Ed., J.A.K. Thomson); Bk.1, I, 1094ai.

[160] Aristotle , Nichomachean Ethics, Bk. 1. 1094a1-22.

Aristotle is of the opinion that there cannot be a universal good as such; although Plato held this to be the culmination of his Theory of Forms.[161] On this very point, the Aristotle's theory of justice in the line of Aquinas Thoughts, differs from that of Plato which has to be seen and understood, differently, as Aristotle in his Metaphysics, sharply criticized Plato's "Doctrine of Ideas."[162]

In clear texts, Aristotle makes it known in several places in his writings that all men cling to justice of some kind, and states clearly in the ethics that "there is more than one kind of justice;"[163] An example, those involving "the rightly framed law"which is a complete virtue, but not absolutely, but in relation to our neighbours.

In rhetoric, he gives it some content by saying that justice is; the virtue which assigns to each man his due in conformity with the law, while injustice is a vice whereby "man claims what belongs to others in opposition to law.[164] He believes that man is a political and social animal, who "alone has the sense of just and unjust,"and he sought to reconcile justice with the conflicts he observes about him. Aristotle makes justice a human concern.

Aristotle, however, concedes that a common element runs through all these, which he characterizes as a proper proportion or relationship between individuals.[165]

In 'Ethics', Aristotle initially from his own thoughts or knowledge divides 'the just into the lawful, equal or fair-play. These are, respectively, his universal or general (legislative), and the particular (judge- made decisions in individual cases). Aquinas equally is of the opinion that the legislative type of justice requires obedience to the law, and therefore comprehends a civic virtue.

So, justice is the will of man's power to choose the good with which the sense desires are concerned and that human dignity and rights ought to and should be held in high esteem in our modern society. In juxtaposition, a good practice of Justice and the well handling of the societal norms and lawful regulations could always launch people into happiness and bring them together for certain meaningful progressions for their well being.

---

161 Cf. Aristotle, Bk. 1, vi.
162 Aristotle, Bk, Vbii, 110b.
163 Aristotle, Rhetoric, 1366b.
164 Aristotle, Nichomechean Ethics, Bk. V, ii, (1130a18-b8).
165 Aristotle, Nichomechean Ethics, Bk. V, ii, (1130a18-b8).

Anything therefore that furthers the interest of any class to the detriment or disadvantages of the other would be totally unjust. In the ideal state, there are three classes of citizens like medical doctors, farmers, carpenters, etc., who with their own desires and type of temperance provide the State with material- products and its substance, but those occupying the lowest larger position are the class of the workers.

The citizens are naturally fitted into various classes of the state, and these classifications were based on their ability to learn and to reason well.

The rulers were to be brought into the world in accordance with premeditated standard of living.

Justice and common good, in the ideal State, therefore, is that act by which each individual conscientiously does that work for which he is best fitted by nature to do.

It is the bond which holds the State together and makes it to be in a harmonious union with many of individual persons, each of whom has found his life-work in accordance with his naturally fitness and his training. For any individual to arrogate himself a position which he is not fitted for by nature, is seen as to being unjust act on his part.

For the strengthening of the rule of law and for ushering in justice, Plato derived this idea of justice from his explanation regarding the tripartite division of the soul from human being (the desiring, the spiritual and the rational elements of the soul).

There is a mutual functional order when these three elements are functioning for the good of the individual and there is disorder when one part stops being active. There will be law and order when the three classes perform their different functions well for the good of the State; there is disorder and lawlessness, if any class interferes with the functioning of another or mishandles it.

However, Aquinas of medieval era regarding the administration of justice and common good argued on the issue of the best possible world for man and said that the universe cannot be any other better way different from what creatures are capable of their nature. He stresses that certain limitations must pervade the universe because to create certain kinds of being could set limits on others. The world is in the best way only in the issue which contains the best adjustment and arrangement possible of the kinds of things that have been created.[166]

The virtue of justice is conceived to be a civic virtue in the State as conceived by Plato and Aristotle. In support of this Aristotle commented: In the State, the good aimed at, is justice, and that means what is for the benefit of the whole community.[167]

Stressing the necessity of justice the development of man, he further said that man is the best of all the animals but when he has reached his full development, could also be the worst of all creatures especially when divorced from law and justice.[168]

If wisdom is upheld as being the virtue of the rulers, justice can and will only be attained when and where the philosopher-king rules the society.

Justice, therefore, is an important factor and organising principle in any ideal State. The truism is that the ideal State is not easy to attain, Plato advocated for an approximation of the ideal and so he postulated the rule of statesman as the second best where the Philosopher-king is not to be obtained or not reachable. For instance a statesman with a scientific understanding of the art of the government; is what is needed for the well functioning or practising of the law. This is nothing but a form of government that approximates the ideal State.

This generally means one who has the interest of his people at heart and one who has made some meaningful contributions to the government of his country.

One who has and gives a clear vision of the political reasonable pursuit of his people could achieve more for the citizens of the country concerned. This is when it comes to the issue of common good and the ruling populace, whereby the ruler helps in the explication and execution of law so that people would know how to be law abiding citizens.

Nevertheless, laws remain always the standard for justice.

Let us now cast our minds reflecting more on certain grounds of justice taken from Simonides that justice means speaking the truth and paying one's debt.[169] As far as *bonum commune* is concerned, every art should first

---

[166] Cf. S.E, Stumpf., On Thomas Aquinas Thought, Is this the Best Possible World?, State and Livelihood, cited in his Book: Philosophy, History and Problems, p. 180.

[167] Aristotle, The Justice, trans. by T. A., Sinclair, New York press, USA 1962, p. 207.

[168] Cf. Aristotle, The Justice, p. 61.

[169] Cf. Plato, The Republic, trans by B. Jowett, New York press, USA 1974, p. 9.

and foremost have the welfares and the interests of its subject at heart *via-a-vis* the rule of law too and should be treated with justice and fairness in certain problems or in situational specificity.

In the State where the rule of law obtains, the notion of law is always tied to the notion of justice and morality and this is because morality is concerned with setting standards of conducts as it is intrinsically connected with laws. We are not isolated individuals who choose to come together in society only because it is necessary to do so to protect individual rights and freedoms. Rather, individuals find their own meaning and identity and dignity as part of the larger community.

Hence, the Catholic Bishop's Conference of England and Wales highlighted that, common good implies that every individual has a duty to promote the welfare of the community as well as the right to benefit from that welfare.[170]

Furthermore, Weber emphasized that as a social being every individual has the moral responsibility to work for the good of the community.

The individual's own good is closely related to this common good. It is only when the right conditions of social life are established that individuals and social groups can flourish.

Likewise, the human person is not merely the subject of social, cultural, and historical conditions, for it is proper to man, who has a spiritual soul, to tend towards a goal that transcends the changing conditions of his existence.

John Paul II in his encyclical letter *(Sollicitudo Rei Socialis)* on Social Concern stipulates that solidarity is not a feeling of vague compassion or shallow distress at the misfortunes of so many people, both near and far. Solidarity is rather a firm and persevering determination to commit oneself to the common good: that is to say, to the good of all and of each individual, because we are all really responsible for all.[171]

The Pastoral Constitution on the Church in the Modern World further buttressed the above statement of John Paul II and added that the same solidarity that rests on individuals exists also for nations, hence, advanced nations have a heavy obligation to help the developing peoples.

---

170 The Catholic Bishop's Conference of England and Wales, 2009, nr. 22.

171 John Paul II (1996). "On Social Concern" (Sollicitude Rei Socialis), in The Encyclisals of John Paul II. Our Sunday visitor, Inc Huntington press, Indiana.

John Paul II in his encyclical letter (*Centesimus Annus*) further recommended that in order to overcome today's individualistic mentality, what is required is a concrete commitment to solidarity and charity, beginning in the family with the mutual support of husband and wife and the care which the different generations give to one another.

In this sense, the family too, can be called a community of work and solidarity.[172] John XIII in his encyclical letter (*Pacem in Terris*) Peace on Earth exonorates that the dignity of the human person involves the right to take an active part in public affairs and to contribute one's part to the common good of the citizens.[173]

Common good has sometimes been seen as a utilitarian idea, thus representing "the greater possible number of individuals."

Another definition of a common good as the quintessential goal of the state requires an admission of the individual basic right in the society, which is namely, the right of every one to freely shape his life by responsible action, in pursuit of virtue and in accordance with the moral law. Common good, then, is the sum total of the conditions of social life which enable people more easily and straight-forwardly to contribute their own quota in the society. Common good as stipulated by R. J. Araujo is the "good for all: the advantage or benefit of everyone." Thus, common good is that which is for the benefit of everyone. If so, is God implicitly our supernatural common good since it is in Him we live and move and have our being?

Yes, He is our *Summum Bonum*, or highest good, the salvation of our soul consists in beatific vision.

Furthermore, the Catholic Bishop's Conference of England and Wales emphasized that Common good is the prime responsibility of public authorities.

Common good stands in opposition to the good of the ruling class. It implies that every individual has a duty to promote the welfare of the community as well as the right to benefit from that welfare. Common good is to be understood as the sum total social conditions which

---

[172] John Paul II., On the Handredth Anniversary of Rerum Novarum (centesimus Annus). Libreria Editrice Vaticana 1991.

[173] John XXIII., Encyclicals, "Peace on Earth"*(Pacem in Terris)*, in the Great Encyclical Paulist Press, Paramus New York 1963.

allow people, either as groups or as individuals, to reach their fulfillment more fully and more easily.

Gaudian et Spes asserts that common good concerns the life of all.[174] It calls for prudence and solidarity from each, even more from those who exercise the office of authority. Every day, human interdependence grows more tightly drawn and spreads by degree over the whole world. As a result, common good, that is, the sum of those conditions of social life which allows social groups and their individual members relatively thorough and ready access to their own fulfillment, today takes on an increasingly universal complexion and consequently involves rights and duties with respect to the whole human race. *Guardium et Spes* continues to emphasize that every social group must take account of the needs and legitimate aspirations of other groups, and even of the general welfare of the entire family. The common good should be interpreted in such away that the individual should not lose the sight of goodness in the collective whole.

The common good must be for the good of concrete persons.

The purpose of law and the intention of the lawgiver should mean good and it is to be for the securing of the 'common good' regulated according to divine justice, and thus it follows that the effect of the law is to make men good in living peacefully and happily.

This is also to say in the philosophical arguments and thoughts of Samuel Stumpf, that the phase pertaining to common good has no other meaning for Aquinas except insofar as it results in the good of individuals.

However, on the same terrain, Aquinas says that the 'goodness of any part is considered in comparison with the whole, since then every goodness should concern other parts of the State, it is impossible that a man could be good unless he proportionates well to the common good.

Law itself, says Aquinas, is an ordinance of reason for the common good, and laws are made by one who has the care of the community being promulgated. In this way, although the sovereign has authority and power, the laws, must not reflect this power in a vacuous sense but have to be demonstrated by reason which are aimed at the common good.

State is formed to satisfy human temporal needs of the society and this helps man in the attainment of the common good which in turn is only a means to the final end of man purposefully.

---

[174] Vatican II, Gaudian et Spes nr. 26.

Nevertheless, for Aquinas thoughts, societies are formed not only for the sake of the good life but for the common welfare and for the common good of the entire citizen because man living in isolation would not achieve all his aims and desires in life. Pesche, regarding the operation of the state here commented in that larger human groups many important and necessary tasks cannot be achieved without the help of the State[175]

There should also be a moral responsibility of the human person in the part of the common good based on the fact of moral nature of man which is bound to secure the morality of its citizens. The rulers as regards the common good of all are not only obliged to make people good, they are also concerned with the provision of the necessary conditions which will enable people to become good. In administration of justice for the common good, the state has to establish laws in order to enforce justice and equity, and to make the citizens know their rights and duties.

Be that as it may, the State authority could be seen as very important segments such as the legislation and administration of justice, promotion of the socio-economic welfare and the care for cultural concerns, So the state authorities are also concerned with the provisions of the common defence, maintenance of justice for the common good of all the citizenry.

On this regard, man being a conscientious being, a mind, remains the essential attribute and a necessity to each other. Nicholas Berdyeav has the similar view thus: "Consciousness is the unity of self and its distinction from the not-self consciousness, is not identical with conscientized knowledge, but it always involves a relation to the logical principle which transcends the self-contained mental world"[176] The above statement of Berdyeav ushers in the existential notion of man's consciousness and interaction with his fellow human being justified and in the righteous manner. The main characteristics of consciousness are that of universality or generality and without it nothing will be accounted for the achievement of human goal.

In other words, life experiences of man in the society teaches man as the object of consciousness challenging man to be conscious of himself and the environs where one finds himself and thereby, taking cognisance of others.

---

[175] C.H., Pesche., Christian Ethics, Vol. II, Dublin 1978, p 29.

[176] N.Berdyeav., The Destiny of Man, London 1977, p. 69.

That is to say that as far as justice and common good is concerned, one has to have the awareness of the self and others around him.

On the issue of the consciousness for the common good, Sören Kierkegaard for the well being of man said:

> The most concrete content of consciousness one can have, is consciousness of onself, the self consciousness which is so concrete that no author- not even the most copious in his command of words, not even the most consummate delineator of character, has ever been able to describe such a thing, although such a thing is what every man is.[177]

Man could be able to unify his objects of experience because he is conscious of himself. For the common good, he is organised in himself, he can also organise the things that he knows and work well with his experiences ideas and intellect for the sake of justice, law and order.

The nucleus of it all, is that existence is the essence of man; this is consciousness of self awareness.

On this terrain, it should be the concern of the civil authorities to ensure that the rights of the citizens are acknowledged, respected, coordinated with rights, defended and promoted; so that in this way each one may more easily carry out his/her duties. Therefore, common good embraces the sum total of those conditions of social living, whereby men/women are enabled to fully and more readily achieve their own perfections, and in the spirit of common good sincerely concur among themselves.

Furthermore, since individuals will tend to identify and feel understood by those who share the same values as themselves, hence, value consensus provides the foundation for cooperation, since common value produce common goals.Justice, human right and common good for Thomas Aquinas remains one of the prime necessities for man on earth.

In so far as there is purpose in human existence, man encounters himself in every sphere of life to be just and to act righteously but also as a wise and thinking being, he has to decipher coherently, his own reality and to be aware of who he is and where he is.

This sounds like a paradoxical and a complex phenomenon but it is not a self-deception whenever man makes constant efforts for the happiness of all and for the better livelihood which a conscientious being in the society

---

[177] S. Kiergegaard., Concluding Unscientific Postscript, Príncepton University Press, America,1961, p. 127ff.

yearns for. Man as a factual entity and a finite being that has a concrete existence in a given space-temporal situation.

To exist or live well in all the diversities of his being is what man should and ought to value and cherish justice and common good. These are what Aquinas thoughts on Human Rights justice and common good meant for our modern society.

The next topic brings us into the Rights and Human Acts and Africas' Own Human Rights Declaration.

3.3

Aquinas Thoughts and Modern Understanding of Justice and Human Rights

Having seen from the former chapters the Aquinas Thoughts in human rights and justice and common good, let us now compare his ideologies and propositions with that of the modern society's understanding. Justice and human rights as equivocally and really, is the recognition of the worth, dignity of human person. These are the clarifications already made above in Aquinas views; though in modern understanding it designate many other things different from the ontological meanings when compared with the today's societal attitudinal character.

We could then say that justice and injustice are the normative concepts of morality which play a great part in socio-political consciousness.

It seems in a practical terms somewhat the combination of several phenomena considered from the point of view of how good and evil are ' distributed'from and among people.

Be this as it may, this shows that the modern understanding or the misinterpretation of what justice and human rights means lead to their being misused. Sequentially, from Aquinas Thoughts, Justice and Human Rights cum common good as the names imply, are principally making sure that equity is practiced; that is, the needed and expected egalitarianism of which the inverse is the injustice.

Justice undoubtedly does pertain to man's righteousness not only to do the just thing but also to be just as well.

Aristotle who is a good companion of Aquinas in his thoughts suggests that, justice implies the notion of treat equals equally and unequal unequally, but clarified that to be in proportion but in consideration to their relevant differences.[178]

He really harped more on his view that distributive justice employs geometrical proportions.

This is in accordance with what Marxist Philosophers theory believed as to giving to each according to his needs and from each according to his ability. It should be in our modern understandings, which stands clear as that natural equality of men which cements their fellowship from the fact that human person is basically the same, sharing the same, and natural sense of justice everywhere.

The British philosopher, David Hume equally emphasized that justice is the bond of society and no association of human individuals could subsist without it.[179] Furthermore, following the injunctions of Aquinas Thoughts, that justice is a moral virtue that induces man to recognise the good of his own neighbour; it all means that the adage "live and let others live" is expected of us all for a harmonious living.

Every citizen therefore, is entitled to live in freedom without fear or persecution or violence anywhere in the world.

Yet international crime and terrorism, injustice and brutality are among the things that most concern every nation today regarding human rights, human freedom and justice. These challenges, call for protection on the citizens and for swift joint action at international level and the active observation and the implementary of policy of the United Nations on the abuse of Human Rights.

The salient question is what can ultimately improve the protection of human rights for the better continuation of a reasonable nation's building? This has always been a challenging or disturbing question among human right scholars in the today's world.

Comparably with Aquinas political philosophy-(*De Regno; In Libros Politiocorum*; and *Summa Theogiae I-II),* Aquinas agreed with Aristotle that man is a social and political being with free will and free choice.

He thus stressed the idea of the limited monarchy or that kind of state which Aristotle has called the "*Politeia*", to be applied well in the state. The

---

178 Cf. Aristotle Nichomachean Ethics, Book 5, II, 113b, Penguim Classics, London 1976.

179 Hume.D., An Enquiry Concerning the Principles of Morals., L. A. Selby- Bigge (ed). Oxford 1902, p.p. 206.

purpose of the state is to provide temporal peace and welfare to its citizens; whereby the state could independently dispense justice even though there was a divine idea. He admitted the basic kinds of justice known as *"justitia distributiva", "justitia commutativa"*and *"justitia legalis."*[180]

When we compare this too to our modern state; (society) where ethnic problems, fraud, sectionalism, robbery and other ill-treatment practices persist and through which people have the rare hope of progress in life, this should call for some adjustments and amendments.

The challenging question from people is how for example the Nigerian government or some other countries in Africa or Europe in the state levels, should re-administer and maintain justice for example in some state levels where justice is least practiced; Human Right neglected or where justice is delayed and denied without qualms?

Regarding rights and liberties there is the need to guard against the tendency to lapse into the binary opposites of tradition and modernity. Multiple and diverse influences which shaped the rights discourse in many African societies, and these cannot simply be reduced to choices between tradition and modernity.

The issues of the notions of "modernity", "civilization", and the later, "development" did at various times influence notions of rights and liberties.

The extent to which individuals and groups could claim certain rights; the colonial state, particularly in the early colonial periods depended largely also on the level of " civilization"and "modernity" they were considered to have attained. Another consideration is the role of exclusion in the discourses about rights.

It is important to understand what people in today's modern world claimed as rights. They understand justice in line with conspiracy, and obstruction of justice with the mind of Thomas Hobbes in his political postulation that life in the state of nature is brutish, nasty and short, and man is a wolf to his fellow human being.

This key statement has become an indispensable truism in most countries of the world today. This is because government policies and programmes are in constant state of flux, one step forward plunges such a society into a state of anarchy, and un emedial lawlessness.

---

180 Aquinas. T., Summa Theologiae I- II. On the Issue of state and Socio-political Equity for the Citizenry in the Nation.

When lawlessness takes the centre-stage, insecurity of lives and property become the new order. In a society where the rule of law is not adhered to and justice is subverted to the detriment of the common man by political group in power, only a vibrant, fearless and virile judiciary should remain strongly the last hope of the common man. It is equally just and important to understand what they did not.

The modern world today in most countries of the world did not and have not concretely understood justice a not to be taken as a 'do or die affairs in the Nicco Macheveli's philosophical principles which stated that the end justify the means. It is necessary to recognize that some rights claims did not apply to everyone and excluded particular individuals and groups.

Some would argue that this very fact means that they were not really "human rights" since they did not equally apply to everyone in the same way at every time. Yet, they are important to us because they are customary rights, whose claims are founded on law and social acceptance that have shaped contemporary understandings of Human Rights.

Equally significant is the need to identify claims that are made and understood as discretionary privileges rather than as rights.

Certain entitlements enjoyed by members of particular social groups or classes were clearly understood to be privileges that were given and contingent on certain conditions.

There is an instance, in some African society, foreigners who settled in the community were entitled to piece of land, granted gratis to enable them to farm for their livelihood. Such an entitlement was clearly understood by all parties involved as a reasonable privilege.

With changes in the circumstances of things, this privilege could be lost. In this contextual analysis, and in other cases, however, in individual entitlements to land were understood and claimed as a matter of right rather than privilege. "Legitimate" sons born within wedlock were usually entitled to land as an inalienable right. Again, rather than a right, it pertains to a privilege rather than a right since it pertains only to "legitimate sons" This may be true when we examined this through the lens of present-day definitions of human rights.

But our concern here is not so much with how these customary notions or rights measure against today's standards but with how the people who developed this language of rights construed it themselves.

My concern is with the discourse of rights in a specific context, centered on the meaning and its application to the people and how the historical actors themselves perceived particular entitlements and the language with which they made claims to such entitlements in our societal levels. Aquinas categorically admonished that man is to follow the ordinance of reason and seriously brush aside various types of injustices and malicious acts for the good of the citizens. Though, man is a being seen as an enigma of complexity in his natural ego, Aquinas categorically and vehemently made it very clear that man has no right to dominate his neighbour whether on the ground of ethnicity, personality, power, creed, race, colour, age or status in the society.

In reaction to these arguments for cultural relativism in the definition of human rights, some writers-mainly legal and social science scholars argued that, although the humanistic values which underlie the concept of human rights, it may be universally shared.

A distinction must be made between the moral standards of human dignity, which all cultures shared to some extent, and the contemporary human rights that are enforceable legal or quasi-legal entitlements held by individuals in relation to States.

The concept of Human Rights in Aquinas Thoughts when compared to as seen and explained, is essentially a modern one founded on specific historical developments in West-enlightenments libertarianism, the Magna

Charta, the French and American Revloutions and, ultimately, the Universal Declaration of Human Rights of 1948.[181]

The good of the particular or individual good is not divorced from the general good.

Just like law, justice in its salient meaning is always for the good and general welfares of every citizen, it is never meant at all for any prohibitive or punitive function, it is never meant for any private or retroactive effects but for peace and order and happiness otherwise it denies its aim and purpose. The language of rights and justice in today's understanding has attained such importance that it underlies almost every facet of public and private discourse, from claims within the family unit to national and global political debates.

---

[181] Cf. Patterson, Freedom, Slavery, and the Modern Construction of Rights, New York press, USA 1999, p. 135.

In deed, the past five decades have spawned a global' 'rights revolution"a revolution of norms and values that has redefined our understanding of ethics and justice.[182]

Academic interest in the "rights" discourse has centred for the most part on contemporary understanding of "human rights" in a way that tends to obscure how the language of rights has historically been deployed to further more complex and contradictory agendas. Within African studies, scholars have employed various aspects of "human rights," "civil rights," and "constitutional rights" mainly within the context of post -UNDR developments. These things are in line with Aquinas Thoughts. Further more, the tradition of "rights" discourse in the continents goes much further back. In parts of Africa, the rights discourses underlined several aspects of local history-the workings of traditional social and political systems, European missionary incursion and activities, the antislavery movement, colonial conquest and control, the colonial legal system, contestations over land, press activism, and most significantly, the nationalist movement.

Human freedom, liberty and right is a means to the conditions of our own existence. Though right is an inviolable power and to many people, the right of man's liberty is fundamental. St. Paul in the scripture poignantly asserted this when he said that when Christ freed us, he meant us to remain free and righteous, stand firm, therefore, we are not to submit again to the yoke of slavery. (cf.Jn 8, 31-32). In consequence, he dwelt on justice and righteousness and the freedom from moral indigence, spiritual bankruptcy and issues on sin.

Also that man should bring into the world, liberty, peace and freedom for the construction, justice and unrighteousness to enhance total love, unity and understanding and mutualistic life among his fellow man. But man should not abuse his freedom.

Biblically put, we are slaves of no one except God and never should we use our freedom as an excuse for wickedness. Respect for every one, love of community, fear of God and honour to the emperor is to be maintained.

---

[182] Cf. Ignatief. M., "The Rights Revolution," Toronto 2000, and also his Human Rights as Politics and Idolatory, New Jersey 2001, p. 97.

There should be no room for lawlessness, nor licentiousness. As Iwe put it: “no perpetuation of iniquities in the name of liberty.”[183] So, liberty is meant for man, and law is made for man, as well as order for peace.

In comparism, what Aquinas is saying about all these, is that the social concern for the contemporary age, war, abortion, injury, bribery and corruption, inflation, racism, apartheid, terrorism, atheism, arms, race etc., should be brought to the purview, in the perspective of what being righteous, just and free really means. It is in freedom that we make our own decisions, thereby assuming the responsibility for the outcome of the decisions that should bring us to the direction of righteousness.This goes to mean that, in as far as we accept our existence, we accept ourselves for what we, as free human beings are on the right path to self fulfilment.

Authentic human existence should not see others’ freedom and liberty as obstacle but as a horizon. The law of the state guarantees and protects human dignity and the freedom of right. Everybody is born free and equal before God and therefore has a right to freedom of expression, association, religious worship, and all have a duty to respect the rights, laws in the state which are made to guarantee these rights. These aspects of the rights discourse, which predate more recent concerns with “universal human rights,” have received little attention.

Yet, many would agree that a thorough historical treatment of these pre-UNDR themes is crucial to our understanding of contemporary human rights.

A philosopher Ronald Dworkin famously argued that rights are “trumps” against the tyranny of the majority.[184] To exercise one’s rights has come to be taken as something inherently good, an index of social and political progress.

Human dignity and human rights are therefore not coterminous as dignity can be protected in a society that is not based rights.[185]

In our modern understanding people make the distinction between the concepts of distributive justice and human rights.

---

183 Iwe. N. S. S., Christianity, Culture and Moral., Port Harcourt- Nigeria 1979, p. 66.

184 Cf. R. Dworkin., Taking Rights Seriously, Harward 1978, p. 87.

185 Cf. R. Howard., “Group versus Individual Dignity in the African Debate on Human Rights,”in Human Rigths in Africa: Cross-Cultural Perspectives, An- A. A.Naimand Deng., F. M., (ed.), Washington 1990, and Howard. R., Human Rights in Common Wealth Africa New Jersey 1986. p. 19.

That is the more reason why W.Vosssenkuhl maintained that the human dignity and human rights is an important customary fact to be maintained in every society.[186] It is also in Thomas Aquinas Thoughts that distributive justice involves giving a person that which he or she is entitled to have (his or her rights). Unless these rights are those to which the individual is entitled to have simply as a human being, the rights in question will not be "human rights." On this issue Jack Donnelly said: " In much pre-colonial Africa for instance, rights were assigned on .The basis of communal membership, family status, or achievement. These were, therefore, strictly speaking,"privileges" granted by ruling elites, not human rights.[187]

Man is socially oriented. Man being a social being means that he is a being that can live in communion with other beings in good relationship. Thus prudentially forbids man's inhumanity to man. The unity of human kind and human race should be highly respected. Aquinas is of the opinion that the society or state is divinely ordained for the smooth running of man's life here on earth and to make it possible for one to achieve one's goals.

The healthy growth in human relations is all the more important.

The necessity for good human relation arises out of good practice of justice and one's right requirements of our society. The requirements of society in terms of human rationality have never changed in its objectivity.

Human nature being so diverse, the quality of love, understanding, obedience, respect, loyality etc, varies from person to person.

The psychology of human psyche, the ill-feeling of fear or being abandoned and being swallowed up in the immense chasm of one's need so as not to lose one's freedom, identity and being.

The problem is the difficulty of accepting others in their natural self and what one's right should mean.

The question is to know how, during the different stages of one's lives, and in our journey to wholeness and fullness of life, we can weaken the walls which separate us from each other, and thereby create a forum for the respect of human freedom, dignity and rights.

---

186 Cf. W.Vossenkuhl., Die Möglichkeit des Guten im 21. Jahrhundert., p. 94.

187 Donnelly. J., "Human Rights and Human Dignity: An Analytic Critique of Non-Western Conceptions of Human Rigths,"American Political Science Review 76, New York 1982, p. 303.

In the human society that expects much progress and better development, each member has to reasonably and genuinely contribute its quota for the common good of all.

This is what we could call duty for duty sake in all righteousness.

All mankind has his or her role to play in life, and a particular duty to perform; but should each neglect ones duty, then one is not being righteous to oneself and also not fulfilling the expectations of a raison d'être.

The concerns about human relationship or human interactions if not well handled in our modern understanding could keep the society in such a jeopardy and untold confusion. Psychologists had for long line expressed these problems both in the interpersonal relations and in the group relations, but the most important factor is good personality.

Man is a social being in nature, and unless he relates himself righteously to others he can neither live nor develop his potential. Man' s social nature makes it evident that the progress of the human person and the advance of the society itself hinge on each other.

The subject and the goal of all social institutions is and must be that, the human person which for its part and by its very nature stands completely in need of social life. The social life is not something added on to man.[188]

Hence, through one's dealings with others, through reciprocal duties, and fraternal dialogue, one develops one gifts and one's is able to rise to his destiny. Students of human relations also agree that one of the greatest needs of daily life is for men to be thinking good of oneself and other person, and to develop a sense of community.[189] But a sense of community could be all, but could be impossible unless every member agree to live well in a community, agree to follow its laws, and agrees to perform in the community, and such tasks are required to develop oneself and others similarly. Human person continues to grow and to learn till death.

This is to say that human beings are constantly learning till the end of his life. This evolves a change to pass through different stages, discover one identity and open oneself to others.

This growth which begins at the moment of conception, when the first cell is formed, goes on until the moment of death, through times of joy

[188] Cf. Maraus. J., On Justice and Relations , pp. 61 61-62.

[189] Loc. Cit.

and grief, through gestures of love and moment of actions, communion and suffering.

The Vat. II Council documents referring to the Church in the Modern World and of our present day society meaningfully explained:

"Among those social ties which man needs for his development are such things like the family and political community that relates with greater immediacy to his innermost nature. Others originate rather from one's free decision."[190]

The State government and the Church's religious leaders here have also their obligatory roles to play for a new better society for all and sundry.

They are to see that justice is maintained and human dignity upheld and protected. The government being an institution set by every society should direct its affairs as representative of God in all their undertakings.

As regards to a nation, the government should not only direct the affairs of the nation; it should also harmonize individual desires, assign duties and obligations to members, and to see that these are fulfilled for the protection of the right of the members.

Additionally, it should provide or direct the provision of goods and services and to see to their adequate availability and equitable distributions.

The government of the day should be there to organise things in such a way that people will compliment the work of each other for the better life of all the citizenry. The society through its agencies and policies also should harmonize and direct individual idiosyncrasies and desires to avoid clashes of interest that can result in chaos. This could be workable if the society through the government of the state assigns certain duties and obligations to each member of the society not only with one's ability, but also on merit or on exceptional consideration. The idea of human rights, properly so called has roots in the adoption of the UNDR by the United Nations in 1948.

To meet up practically well with Aquinas' Thoughts entails that the Church or the society should actively be involving themselves in the exigencies of man's daily life, with their livelihood and education, and their general earthly welfare and progress.[191]

With right reasons, the Holy Father, John XXIII also adds that the Christianity is the meeting point of heaven and earth.

---

190 Vat. II, Pastoral Constitution on the Church in the Modern World Guadium et Spes, Dec, 7, 1966, nr. 25.

191 T. Aquinas., The Baisic Writings, New York Press, USA 1967, p. 476.

It lays claim to the whole man, body and soul, intellect and will, inducing him to raise his mind above the changing conditions of this earthly existence and reach upwards for the eternal life of heaven.

Right reason here is the norm of morality. It is the true knowledge by which the objective values of human actions are judged.

It directs people to achieve their proper end and absence of right reason which shows a sort of deviation from achieving the end.

Aquinas stated thus: "the true proximate rule to norm by which we judge the objective morality of human act is right reason."[192]

On this issue, the right reason for a righteous living is taking to mean here a rule or norm of human act. It is the will that leads man to achieve his proper end. Then man's norm of morality is said to be right reason for which a person is considered to be irrational.

Consequently, we have a supreme rule and a proximate rule. The supreme rule is the eternal law while proximate rule is the human reason.

Eternal law can be considered as the wisdom of God which is absolute.

Human beings or other rational creatures in reference to Aquinas Thoughts share in the external reason by which they have their own natural inclination to their due acts and ends, this touches justice or Human Rights in all its ramifications. This is in conjunction with the practical human situations, just as the speculative reason derives scientific practical human conclusion from the naturally known in the demonstrable principles.

Aquinas' view is focused on the orientation that should help man to structure and govern his civil society.

Aquinas rightly, understand man's situation and his variant actions and remarks that because man is rational, his inclination, is as well towards the search for the truth, and to be acting righteously on the basic moral truth is simply to do good and avoid evil.

As a rational being, then, man is under a basic natural obligation to protect his life and health, in which case suicide and untold carelessness are wrong. The rule and measure of acts is the reason because it belongs to direct a man's whole activity towards his end. The natural law is dictated by reason.

But Aquinas argues that since God created all things, human nature and the natural law are best understood as the product of God's wisdom

---

192 Cf. John XXIII, Mater et Magistra , Material, Social; and Profit Sharing Roma 1961.

or reason.[193] Freedom of right and human act could be strengthening to the practice of justice in order to uphold Human Rights to a higher level of expectations.

Paul VI rightly recognised this problem and said: "in strong bonds of an anthropological, theological and spiritual nature such things like charity, justice and peace are inseparable in a Christian promotion of the freedom of human person." This theological nature regarding common good and the society concerns is with the Church's three-fold tasks in every age, situation and society, thus:

a) Announcement of the truth about human dignity and rights.
b) Announcement of unjust situations.
c) Contribution to positive changes in the society and real human purposes.[194]

Pius XII here said that philosophically speaking, the "common good" is higher than private interest although it is inseparable from the good of human person. It commits public authorities to recognise, respect, protect and promote human rights and facilitate the fulfilment of the respective duties.[195]

In fact, public authorities and the state itself exist to fulfil the demands of the common good. The church considers the common good as a special value in the service and organisation of social life and of the new order of human existence of how man should behave and relate to one another.

Following the meaning of Aquinas Thoughts and the United Nations Delcaration of Human Rights; the propositions or yardsticks with which peoples of all lands could look to, UNDR provided people with the international accepted moral, and standard of rights to which nationalists could

---

193 Cf. The Medieval Period of Aquinas, cited by Stumpf. S. E., ind his Book, Philosophy and Problems, op. cit., p. 183ff.

194 Cf. Vat.II, Gaudium et Spes, nr. 12 and also John Paul II, Laborens Exercens, nr.1.

195 Cf. Pius XII, Christmas Message – con sempre nuova, Roma 1942, AAS 35, 1943, p. 43, p. 13- Emphasis on Human Existence Guidelines p. 40. He stresses its human meaning and ability to animate social structures in their globality and in their particular sectors. The Church encourages indepth transformations according to the criterion of social justice. in their particular sectors. The Church encourages indepth transformations according to the criterion of social Justice according to the criterion of social justice. according to the criterion of social justice.

appeal in their demands for independence from European colonial powers. However, no man is an island, people say.

Human beings need interdependence among one another and to respect freedom of each other because one is limited and no body knows everything or have everything and so we are dependent to one another in one way or another by natural inclination for our survivals.

We need each other often for helps and interactions and for our general livelihood. A wise person should build on the consensus which lies in the fact that society is necessary for the good of man. This necessity therefore, derives from the very nature of man.

He needs to interact because he is by nature out reaching as *'anima socialis.'* Man besides contains or that have certain qualities as well as physical characteristics that set him apart from other higher animals with certain social and intellectual traits which man possesses exclusively at least in certain marked degrees of his subsistence.

The articulated speed and the use of symbols as the principle vehicle of culture, for man's initiative alone is a good inventive. That man as a social being above all things should be freely manifested in his use of human language for interaction. Man is the only being that uses language freely of speech, in full liberty where he is; with his personality as an intelligible being and he remains communicative.

Language being a deliberate signification presupposes knowledge as St. Thomas Aquinas logically remarked: "Speech is itself an act and a peculiar thing to a rational nature."[196]

Other social philosophers also regard language as a distinctive feature of human mind which is always being closely associated with, if not identical to the level of reasoning. It is also in the knowledge of St.Thomas Aquinas who said: "To speak to another is nothing other than to make known to oneself the concept which one has in mind."[197]

To butress freely this point concretely he further said that speech is properly that by which one righteously leads another to the knowledge of something hithertho unknown to him so that, what was formally absent becomes present to him.

---

[196] Cf. T.Aquinas., De Veritate, q 9, a 5c.

[197] Cf T., Aquinas., Summa theologica, 1a q109, a, 1c.

In this aspect, Martin Buber posited his own ideology when he said that what is particularly characteristic of the human world is above all, that something takes place between one being and another, like that of which one can be found in no where in nature.[198]

Language is seen here not only for communication or normal interactions but as mediate and immediate dialogue between two persons, each of whom recognises himself as a person for a harmonious living of purpose.

Thus, it is the only way of dialectical thought that we can approach the knowledge of human nature, and Cassire said that truth is by nature the offering of dialectical thought.[199]

Man being a rational animal means that as an individual, he does have the essence of man in himself because man's essence is contained in the unity of man with man in his continued existence. Buber also articulated his mind saying:

"The human person tends to overflow into social communications in response rightly to the law of super-abundance inscribed in the depth of his being, intelligent and actively alive."[200]

In our modern society, this human relationship or interaction process, cannot but have the purview of what socialization cum relationship is dealing with. In broad terms, socialization or human relation is the process by which intelligent beings who are biologically human become socially human. It is the process by which man acquires his social behavioural patterns. Seeing this as an interactional process whereby a person's behaviour is modified to conform with expectations as held by members of the group to which one belongs.

This in a broad term too, touches other forms of communication such as mass communication other than only the personal type. Naturally then, man is a social being and requires others around him for his actualization. As Buber remarked that I become through my relation to the Thou; as I become I; I say Thou.[201]

---

[198] M. Buber., Between Man and Man, Great Britain, p. 244.

[199] Cf. E. Cassire., An Essay on Man, USA 1988, p. 13.

[200] Cf. M. Buber., Between Man and Man, p. 244.

[201] M. Buber., I and Thou, New York, 1968, p. 11.

This type of relation is essentially for one's right and self awareness of self-realization. In such a case, living together is sought for its own sake, as social communication and mutual enrichment.

One sees clearly from the point of view of human relations and communications that man could be happily living well with others and doing one's best in keeping to the rules and regulations of the State. It is factually spreading good news about good life by himself the message of peaceful co-existence in respect to people's rights.

The dealing with others or for a better interaction with others does not only focus on truthfulness, honesty, co-operation, being with others for a sincerity of purpose, it rather entails also often on creating or joining an enlightenment, periods or recreational time for cheerfulness, jokes and humours which ushers in peaceful and harmonious living.

These keep the individual groups more alive because such times are valid for cheers and smiles in enrichment for good health, wealth and happiness.

The fact speaks for itself, regarding peace of mind and cheerfulness, a smile a day, they say 'keeps the doctor away.' nay more, 'smile and the world will smile with you'weep and you weep alone.

The human relation has majorly its ultimate in human happiness which everyman has right to in all justice.

In our modern world today, one's happiness as far as human rights are concerned are freely acts of links purposefully gratification of any thirst with ultimate beatitude. However, this locus of man's craving is the realm of the mind as it touches man's acting and self realization. In this sense, S. Perry rightly said: "a smile radiates joys with one another." It radiates joy; it spreads sunshine where there is gloom; it makes the world a better place to live in. When a man cannot contain himself with a smile, he bursts into laughter. And there are occasions when we laughed till we cried. Why?, if I sincerely and righteously laugh at myself, I feel to cry."[202]

---

202 S. Perry., How to Enrich Yourself; Human Freedom, Bombay 1995, p. 51. However, as we grow older our smiles become rarer. We can no longer smile for being alive, May be, some of us altogether forget to smile. But everything in this world has its uses and abuses- even smile and laughter. Nero laughed when Rome burnt. In the same way, may be we have some people around us who laugh when our home burns. Ibid. We remember the Chinese proverb, which says: "A leaf on the tree 'laughs'at the other leaf that is following, but poor thing, does not know when itself will be blown off." In the

The diverse human nature affects all manner of human relationships at all levels either singly or collectively, but singly wise, it is the meaning between one human and another.[203] In general, man has all along, and still requires from his fellowmen good-will, acceptance and recognition. In particular, his requirements have depended, and still depends on and requires from children and adults; the obedience and respect from children, and in turn from their parents understanding and security. Getting along with others in man's freedom and righteousness is very important and rewarding.

Let us now delve more on the issue of co-operation in the human interaction and exercise of Human Rights. In today's society, there is the fear of opening our hearts to the other; this is because we keep our vulnerability and fragility hidden. Some have the difficulties in using well certain chance of freedom on forming relationships because of the fear of the unknown.

The State government and the church religious leaders have also their obligatory roles to play regarding justice and human rights and man's freedom for a new better society for all and sundry especially focusing on Aquinas Thoughts of justice and fair-play. The states are to see that justice is maintained and human dignity upheld and protected.

The government being an institution set by every society should direct its affairs righteously as representative of God in all their undertakings; and also harmonize individual desires, assign duties and obligations to members, to see that these are fulfilled for the protection of the right of the citizens.

Additionally, it should provide or direct the provision of goods and services and to see to their adequate and equitable distributions. For any society to be worth-while and smooth sailing, its government should take its task seriously as it should be responsibly and righteously handled. The gov-

---

Bible we read also an abusive laughter, "Abraham fell upon his face and laughed saying in his heart: shall a son thinkest though, be born to him that is a hundred year old? (cf. Gen 17, 17), which when Sara heard she laughed behind the door of the tent. (cf. Gen 18, 12). Keep smiling. We admire more those who in spite of their misfortunes seems to own a fortune. Lin Yutang, in his write-up. The Importance of Living'said that if all men have a large sense of humor, there will be no more trouble in this world; and if all the countries are to be represented at foreign conferences by their best humorists, there will be no more wars." (cf. S. Perry., quoting Lin Yutang in his book 'How to enrich Yourself, p. 53).

[203] Cf. Maurus. J., It is Human Raltion that Counts, Better Yourself Books, Bombay, 1997, p. 21ff.

ernment should be there to organise things in such a way by which people will compliment the work of each other for the better life of all the citizenry. The society through its agencies and policies also should orientate and direct individual ambitions, actions or desires to avoid clashes of interest that can result in chaos.

This could be workable if the society through the government of the state, assigns certain duties with obligations to each member of the society.

It is the general role of all in the society to carry out our duties and fulfil the obligations imposed on us by the society provided they are profitably sound enough on the things which will lead the people to the fulfilment of their purpose on this earthly hemisphere.

The righteousness regarding good human relations the society could be well restored, but the people should with wisdom and tenacity of purpose and clarity of vision strive righteously to be conscious and sincere to what should benefit all in the society. We shall now see the next topic on Justice on human rights in the Nigerian nation and the application and relevancy of Aquinas Thoughts.

Chapter Four: Aquinas Philosophy of Justice and Human Rights as a Panacea for the Africa-Nigerian Cultural Conflicting Society in 21.Century

4.1

Freedom of Rights and Human Acts and Africa's Own Human Rights Declaration and Objectives

The freedom of rights and human acts and African's own Human Rights Declaration buttress the fact that this is based on the fact that Africa's own Human Rights Declaration did prove its own might and effectiveness for the people. The declarations were in the following ways as stipulated here below.

The African Charter and Peoples'Rights was adopted by the African Union predecessor, the Organization of African Unity, in 1981, as the continent's primary human rights instrument[204] and these rights and duties include:

a) The Right of Equality with other peoples and to be free of domination.
b) The Right to international peace and security.
c) The Right of oppressed peoples to free themselves by " any means recognized by international community.
d) The Right to control national wealth and resources in the exclusive interest of the people.
e) The Right to economic, social and cultural development
f) The Duty to promote and strengthen national unity and the state.
g) The Duty to preserve positive African cultural values.
h) The Duty to contribute to the achievement of African unity.

One can say in this meaning that a major element or aspect of justice considered as highly important in this relation is the idea of equality- in the various senses of equal treatment, equal categorisation *(Gleichstellungsproblem)*, and this regards equal distribution.

[204] Cf. African Renewal, Gazette, Vol. 18 nr.2, July 2004

Indeed, factual and normative type of assertions of equality of different kinds in human societies usually generates claims about distributive justice, which itself is one aspect of the three categories of justice that Aristotle subordinates to the general justice.[205]

Factually speaking, this plays a crucial role in determining the proper connection between Justice and fairness as ethical principles of social relations. There is a common agreement in this connection that fairness itself seems at least to require some kind of equality.[206]

Here responsibility and freedom of the will plays its own role, we human beings know what is good and what goodness and freewill of achieving or arriving at Excellencies for happy life is all about. For Chambers dictionary, it trust or charge for which one is responsible, liable to be called to account as being in charge or in control; thus answerable to a person or for something. It is one deserving the blame or credit of a sense of responsibility; being a free moral agent, morally accountable for one's action. Then, coupled with the liberty and willingness, volition, inclination, determination choice and the disposition to be acting accordingly. Schwarz and his intellectual groups will put it that, as far as life is concerned, a force in human being which propels all our being and actions, feelings, desires, aspiration, loving self, preservation, emotions of good and evil, God the architect and giver of life; calls and expects to live in a certain responsible way.[207] Every act that denies life to the full can be termed irresponsible.

We should also at this juncture consider the right to health as part of the concept of a right to an adequate standard of living in article 25 of the Universal Declaration of Human Rights (UDHR). This right is also provided for in section 17 (23) (d) of the Constitution of the Federal Republic of Nigeria, 1999. Thus, the Nigerian "States shall direct its policy towards ensuring that there are adequate medical and health facilities for all persons. "The right to the enjoyment of the highest attainable standard of physical

---

205 I. Mcclean., 9 (ed. The Concise oxford Dictionary of Politics, Oxford, New York 1996, p. 161, Aristotle distinquishes between distributive Justice, Legal Justice and Commtutative Justice, all of which he subordinates to the general Justice of 'given every one his due according to law.' Cf. Aristotle, Ethics, Bk. V. 1129 al- 1138b22

206 Cf. K. Nielson., Conceptions of Justice, in: Hawkesworth, M/Kogan M., (eds.), Enyclopaedia of Government and Politics, Vol.1 London, New York 1992, p. 80.

207 Cfr. C. Schwarz., Davidson, G., etal., Chambers 20th Dictionary, Edinburgh, new (ed.), of 1993, p. 1467.

and mental health is also codified in article 12 of the ESC Right Covenant to which Nigeria is a signatory.

Article 16 of the African Charter on Human and Peoples Rights provides to the same effect and enjoins States and parties to the Charter to take necessary measures to protect the health of their people and ensure that they receive medical attention when they are sick. It is happy to note that the African Charter has long since been domesticated as part of Nigerian body of laws with its attendant justice able implications.

Enjoyment of this right will include access to health supporting conditions, primary, secondary and tertiary healthcare, access to immunization and general child care, support for maternal health, health insurance, etc., will also include access to clean water, the prevention, treatment and control of epidemic, occupational and other diseases.

On the meaningfulness of this responsibility and rigths, Epithets once explained that God entrusted me with myself. The fact and claim that life is a gift entails a clarity and responsibility. Responsibility in this meaning includes love for self and love for our fellow human beings.

The judgment which ethics makes and values concerning any issues is often referred to as 'value judgment.' Such judgment are made with the parameter of moral values, as opposed to legal values or religious values. Sometimes, 'values' are distinguished from 'facts' what then is the meaning of value? Like the "good", value is "an elusive term but in general value is regarded as good, as desirable, as worthwhile, a course worthy of pursuit, worth living for and dying for. Value provides the motivation for deliberate human action. The assessment of the content of the value could be made by a person, or a group of persons, or the society. Thus, "a value can be individual or social, something considered good for, and by individual or for, and by a group.

Hence, a value could be subjective or objective. In reference to the individual, a value could be subjective arising form his 'personal participation, in making a decision concerning the perceived worth of a thing. It is objective value, when it possesses foundation independent of the perceiving subject. A value, whether it is subjective or objective, is essentially referential; having a basis from a given point of view, and context. Many customary values taboos, norms have their foundations and raison d'étre from their cultural backgrounds. Some cultures abhor the killing of pythons because of the perceived values they have in the community.

Other areas attach such importance, rather to 'tortoise', or crocodile. In other words, every value is a value for someone or some group of people.

Value can be instrumental, or intrinsic value. An instrumental value is one which serves as an instrument (or means) for bringing about or maintain an intrinsic value. An intrinsic value is one that is independent of any other value, as its means. The relationship between the 'means' and the 'end' values; for instance the wood, is the instrumental value to the production of a cushion furniture. (Human) self can exhibit both instrumental and intrinsic value. He is instrumental value, when he is considered in relation to the assistance he renders to others, and to his society. But man has not only an instrumental quality, he possesses also an intrinsic value.

His existence is an-end-in-itself. Man has also an intrinsic value which does not depend on any other considerations. Man's intrinsic value (the bedrock of ethics) is rooted on the very fact that he is a 'self', a 'person."

The consideration is based on Aristotle's 'man-as-such. The Igbo conveys man's intrinsic value by the concept, '*mma-ndu*',(a human being) 'the beauty of life 'the summary of existence', as we shall consider in the course of our terminology and equity.

The expectation of human beings should be to answer or respond with a sincere and open hearted appreciation. That is why Blessed Mother Theresa of Calcutta, told us that responsibility in life entails that we too must live to give to one another until it hurts.

Unity of purpose taking care and cognisance of all that are emanating from human acts could yield better fruits. The European Union, and all the Organisation of American States had attempted to lay their separate individual standards for their members, hoping by such things as the African Charter on Human Rights, and so on not only to supplement the efforts of the Universal Declaration, but to also bring to the every doorsteps to every government and individual, the responsibility of implementing them. But Despite this, Africa is still far behind in Human Rights questions.

Nevertheless, any genuine efforts for development will find fundamental Human Rights in full accord with itself.

For, in the same way that economic development can succeed only when undertaken along with political development, any serious new State must uphold fundamental Human Rights not only in theory but along with the political atmosphere, and the socio-economic and legal conditions that will make them possible and practicable.

Those in the 3rd World who had lived under reactionary military regimes would easily appreciate the necessity for a free valuable and open society that the fundamental Human Rights guarantee. The right to life, in particular, and the freedom of information, thought, expression and association, have now become some of the most important hallmarks of the modern nation-state, and indispensable for attaining the scientific and technological revolution which every African and other 3rd World nation need as the foundation for her development.

Indeed, the concept of fundamental Human Rights embodies and represents the elevated ideals of progress and the universal needs of man and, as such their objectifications remains an indispensable element of civilized existence, and accords with the aims of good government.

And from whatever perspective the fundamental rights are viewed, be it social, moral or philosophical, economic, legal or ecclesiastical, especially the political, all men seem to agree that a democratic form or instrument of collective life, the best chance of guaranteeing the rational achievement and practical exercise of these rights. Hence, fundamental Human Rights work best in societies where the levels of political consciousness are very high, such that citizens associate the rights and freedoms they enjoy with duties and responsibilities they discharge to the State and civil society.

It is both an implicit and explicit recommendation of the Universal Declarations that nations and peoples work towards this noble objective, of living peacefully and practising justice and fair play and observing natural and fundamental Human Rights of each other.

There are also conditions for the practical achievement of Human Rights in the Africa- Nigeria Society and elsewhere. The most important condition is raising the level of knowledge about and popular consciousness on Human Rights, and these are only through a system of patriotic universal and free education. For, even though Human Rights are applicable to all citizens, they are most consequential for weaker members of society who because of poverty and other disabilities are unable to sufficiently help themselves or have access to education and knowledge. Human Rights do not come easy in society, for they are often seen by ruling classes as a privileged concession to the masses, making the struggle for their achievement and sustenance the only viable option left for the later. A democratic and just government is also essential, but this is tied to struggle, the subjective consciousness that can build upon the objective conditions for change, and the patriotic education that most governments in Africa are corrupt and unpatriotic.

It means that in addition to perfunctory demand upon official public institutions of civil society, non-governmental organisations and conscious individuals that can lead a successful struggle in its favour. This ties the recognition of an objective reality, to a call for positive action.

Problem only arises in determining what kind of equality that fairness requires and what extent it would be for justice to be achieve in social practices. That is, whether Justice practically requires a 'fair equality of opportunity', 'equality of condition' or 'equality of certain kind and extent constitutes a basic criterion of justice in social relations.

4.2

Human Dignity and Rights of Man in Vatican II

From time immemorial, the Church has always strived through many avenues to be steadfast and to remain faithful to her moral responsibility of active engagement for the realization of the rights and dignity of man at all places, after the example of her Lord Jesus Christ.

In our own time, one of the ways through which the Church bears witness to Jesus, defence of the right of the poor is through her numerous social instructions concerning the dignity of the human person as reason for his basic rights. The world body, international communities cry out concerning the millions of children are in few years displaced by conflict globally. The United Nations Children's Fund (UNICEF), yesterday, said more than 28 million children have been driven out of their homes by conflicts and violence world wide. UNICEF Executive Director, who made the revelation, also stated that the report found that a total of 50million children were either refugees, internally displaced inside their countries or migrants in search of better life abroad due to gang violence and poverty.

The international body urged countries affected by the report to look at underage refugees and migrants as children " first and foremost,"who are especially vulnerable to violence and exploitation. He reiterated that about 20 million of them have been classified as child migrants who left their homes because of poverty and gang violence, often travelling without legal documents and lacking legal status. While lamenting that children living as refugees also face increasing xenophobia and were five-times more likely to be out of school than their non-refugee peers, he also noted that children made up about half of the world's refugees seeking shelter abroad in 2015, with 45 per cent of child refugees under the UN's care coming from Syria and Afghanistan.

Elaboratively wise, these have been eloquently expressed in many important social documents of Second Vatican Council.

Two of these deserve special mention here, namely the documents on the "Declaration on Religious Liberty," *Dignitatis Humanae* and the "Pastoral Constitution of the Church in the Modern World," and *Gaudium et Spes.*[208]

The introductory statement of *Dignitatis Humanae* begins with an evaluative assessment of the implications of the growing universal awareness of the dignity of the person, for the respect for his freedom and duties.

It states: Contemporary, man is becoming increasingly conscious of the dignity of the human person; more and more people are demanding that men should exercise fully their own judgement and a responsible freedom in their actions and should not be subject to the pressure of coercion but be inspired by a sense of duty. As can be seen, a central point in this statement is the acknowledgement and defence of the right of the person and communities to religious liberty in appreciation of man's spiritual values as religious being.[209]

In a similar way, *Gaudium et Spes equally* stresses on the respect for the human person. To achieve its aim, it admonishes not just on respect for human life but also emphases the provision for the "means necessary for living it in a dignified manner. Respect for life involves not just love of neighbours, but also respect and love for those we do not cherish, because the personal dignity of the human being is never lost, even when he is in error.[210] This is true expression and affirmation of the universal character of human dignity.

---

208 http://www.newsjs.com/ng/unicef-50-million-children-displaced-worldwide/DailySun Newspaper, Nigeria, Africa p. 13.

209 Vatican Council II, Declaration on Religious Liebrty, Dignitatis Humanae, in: A. Flannery., (Gen. Ed.) Conciliar and Post Conciliar Documents, p. 799.

210 Gaudium et Spes, no. 28.

4.3

SOCIAL TEACHING OF THE CHURCH AND HUMAN DIGNITY

The social teaching of the Church is very important and unavoidable as far as human dignity and Human Rights are concerned, Aquinas harped positively on this issue for the good of man and his society.

The Catholic teaching also do consider equal dignity of all men as the very first authoritative source of the truth concerning human behaviours and fair treatments for common interest and common good of all the societal practices and schemes of all the citizenry. In all ramifications, this enormous responsibility involves majorly finding a way of protecting the dignity and right of individual citizen. In a special way, Catholic Social Teachings also consider the equal dignity of all men as the very first authoritative source of the truth that minority groups all over the world deserve the same fair treatment, as other people in all societal practices and schemes.

The prophetic mission of the Church in the modern world essentially includes her moral responsibility to ensure justice and peace.

In many occasions, this enormous responsibility involves finding a way of protecting the rights of minorities, while at the same time encouraging the peaceful co-existence of both minority and majority groups in one society.

The Church as an institution as well as Christians as a whole has a duty of bringing the ideas of forgiveness, truth, love justice and fairness as foundations of a peaceful social order to the consciousness of the world. On this note, the Church has in different social documents sought to defend the equal dignity and rights of minorities in their different aspects. Significantly, it has been established that so far the social documents of the Church has clearly gone far more than documents of other international organisations such as those of the United Nations, in considering minority rights not only in their individual contexts but also in their essentially collective contexts as group rights.[211]

In some of the documents, the Church unmistakably stresses the protection of different rights and duties of minorities in the society. An instance of this is thus; The Message of John Paul II on World Peace Day also strongly recognises the fundamental right of national minorities to existence as distinctive group. It condemns the abuse of this right, which takes different forms, even up to the extreme cases of denial through genocide against minority groups.

Historically, the rise of the 'social realm'in western society since the 18th century equally corresponds with the rise of private sphere of human affairs, originally restricted to the domain of the family and the household economic activities (oika), into the public realm of political activities (polis). This results in what is now known as the modern society. Modern society thus becomes the platform for both socio-economic and political activities. With this, the term society equally begins to acquire more specific meanings, referring to specific things according to its respectively intended objects. Two of these are worth highlighting here; (a) The State as political society. A major interpretation of society in its modern sense is found in its usage as subject of political analysis, in which society is usually connoted with shared political relations in a defined territory. Society is thus used as a term for the State, as political society, what I may personally refer to as 'State-Society.'

This is most frequently used to refer to the population of a nation-State.

Yet, society needs, not necessarily coincide with boundaries of a State.

For example, tribal society may exist without subjecting themselves to State power. This later idea of society rather refers more usually to a 'nation' or ' culture': (b) Civil society as opposed to the State. In its modern usage, society, as civil society, is counter posed to the sovereign power of the political State. Here the word society significantly denotes two things at the same time, though in relatively varying degrees.[212] It primarily denotes the smaller associations and groups in the social order, which include a variety of reasonably independent religious, cultural, educational, professional, and economic associations, which are voluntary in nature, and

[211] Cf. K. Egger., (ed.), Kirche und Ethnische Minderheiten, pp. 13ff.

[212] Cf. K. Egger., (ed.), Kirche und Ethnische Minderheiten, pp. 13ff.

equally complements one another. Encouraging the peaceful co-existence of all people of God is the onerous duty of both the Church and the State.

The Church and the State as a known strong institutions coupled with their inhabitants have the duty of bringing the ideas of forgiveness, truth, love, justice and fairness as foundations of peaceful social order to the consciousness of the world.

The Church as an institution has in different social documents sought to defend the equal dignity and rights of man.

Significantly, the message of John Paul II on the World Peace Day (01.January 1989), was dedicated exclusively to the defence and rights and dignity of man. This document on World Peace clearly, expresses the Church's belief that solution to the problem of injustice and unfairly treated persons does not benefit the society rather categorised as a due justification and respect for the dignity and rights of marginalised and the down trodden equally contributes to the preservation and restoration of peace in the world.[213] Twentieth century socio-political thought focuses on this aspect of the necessity of differentiation between the sovereign State and the society as a way of guaranteeing the freedom of the associations as a sphere of society distinct from the State.

This distinctive sphere, the realm of civil society, is first presented in its very modern meaning in Hegel's earlier conceptualization of society in the ' Philosophy of Rights'as the sphere of ethical life interposed between the family and the State.

Thus, variously deriving from the work of Hegel, Marx and Gramsci civil society represents:"those relations which are part neither purely of the private sphere of the family, nor purely of the public sphere of the State, particularly the relations within voluntary associations of the time."[214]

The social documents of the Church have clearly gone far more than documents of the other international organisations such as those of the United Nations in considering rights not only in their individual contexts but also in their essentially collective contexts group rights.

It also recognised, that in some documents, the Church unmistakably stresses the protection of different rights and duties of the marginalised and minorities in the society. More so, the message of John Paul II on World

---

213 Cf. GS, no. 73.

214 Cf. K. Kumar., "Civil society", in: BDTCST., pp. 75/76.

Peace Day strongly recognises those fundamental rights of national minorities in existences as a distinctive group. It condemns abruptly, the abuse of this right, which takes different forms, even up to the extreme cases of denial through genocide against the great-suffering minority groups.

In Gaudium et Spes, this particular forms of violation of minority rights received outright condemnation in these words:

> The most infamous among these are those designed for the reasoned and methodical extermination of an entire races, nation, or ethnic minority. This must be condemned as frightful crimes, and we cannot comment too highly the courage of the men who openly and fearlessly resist those who issue orders of this kind.[215]

Thus affirming strongly the inviolability of the right to life, the Pope's message, which is cited above, warns that any State that either undertakes or condones any action directed at endangering the life of members of its minority groups violates the most elementary right that regulates the social order. To build a new world to actualize authentic human development and to construct a world of peace, we have something positive to do.[216]

The Supreme Pontiff John Paul II says that all people, the youths inclusive, must at least agree to place their trust in few elementary but firm principles, such as the followings: "The Human affairs must be dealt with humanely, not with violence. Tension, rivalries and conflicts must be settled by reasonable negotiations and not by force. Opposing ideologies must confront each other in a climate of dialogue and free discussion.

The legitimate interest of particular groups must also take into account the legitimate interests of the other groups involved and of the demands of the higher common good. Recourse to arms cannot be considered the right means for settling conflicts in the society.

The inalienable human rights must be safeguarded in every circumstance. Flynn Brennan tells the youths: "It is not permissible to kill in order to arrive at a solution."[217]

The *Pacem in Terris (*Peace on earth) John XXIII also condemned such heinous extermination of minorities as the violation of the rule of justice.

---

215 GS, no 79.

216 S. O. Flynn Brennan., (Art. Nature), in: New Catholic Encyclopedia, vol. 10, 1967. p. 279.

217 John Paul II, Address to the Members of Diplomatic Corps, 26 January 1979, Insegnamenti, vol. 2, 1979, p. 157.

The document of the world peace of 1989 also points out that the right of minorities to existence can be violated in a subtle manner such as through denial of rights of group to land-ownership.

On one hand, the social documents of the Church generally consider all the rights mentioned above including many similar ones as inviolable rights of minorities. On another hand, however, the teaching documents did not fail to equally emphasis the duty of minority groups in contributing to the common good of the society, which they are found in and their moral duty to always take the rights of other members of the majority into consideration. But in this *Pacem Interris,* peace on earth of John XXIII, sternly warns against member of minority groups over-emphasising the special nature of their own group, so much that it tends to diminish the value of the common humanity, as if the well-being of the entire human family must be subjected to the well being of their own group for the general good.

It cites the example of certain cases where aboriginal or indigenous minority populations are denied the right to their traditional lands, with which they have developed a deep-rooted cultural and religious tie through the ages of this period. This has also contributed significantly to the growth of local Churches in developing countries by supporting, among other things, the continuing formation of their clergy and religious, the provision of shelter, medical assistance and care to the poor and needy, and creation of much- needed educational and employment opportunities.

This encyclical document remains forever an opportunity which stood the test of time and has served as an incentive for our commitment to promoting reconciliation and peace at every level of our society.

Chapter Five: Recommendations

Before embarking on this immediate topic, we should first and foremost mention or posit certain current situational problems in the country which concerns violation of justice and Human Rights in the Nigerian nation. This boarders mainly too, on the level of confidence in handling some sensitive issues, like the escalating ethnic/religious tensions in certain parts of the country. The nation is also not fulfilling the expectation of raison d'etre that could stabilize the government both in efficiency and proficiency. Some other problems include, reminding the federal government on the routinely disobeying the courts of law, violation of the human rights and the rule of law. The consolidation of Nigeria's transition to democracy after decades of military dictatorship and the necessity of avoiding crises of logistics envisaged in our society. This will help putting in order the image crises of Nigerian nation and her citizens. There should be that spirit of global serious effort to promote dialogue between cultures. The nation should often share their some common experiences in terms of culture, multi-religious and linguistics heritage for their general welfare.

The perennial problem of assaults on the oil installations and general collapse of social infrastructure as well as the disappearance of faith in the Nigeria ideologies which necessitates a good mission for Nigerian expectation to regain an admirable great nation is here with us. The issue concerning religious politics should be well controlled if various denominations see themselves as being created from one God as that could or should make us work neutrally and without any biased mind or being unfair to giving any person his due or merit. That is reflecting the biblical maxim in (Matt7:12) regarding the golden rule for threating others as you, yourself will like to be treated for the expected peace and harmonious co-existence.

In order to have a renaissance, Nigeria is in need of a messiah and liberator for the increment of stability for the nation's growth; a zero tolerance for corruption is always adrem and needed in the country, so that reasonable progress is achieved and more so, in order that, the dragon of poverty would be slaughtered. Although the government did introduce poverty alleviation programmes, but the effect of whatever the alleviation that was going on could not be felt.

The corrective measure or intervention of the judiciary and the government in power for justice and good governance should be strengthened.

When the situation is bizarre, it will then be a shame and charade of the Nigeria government for not initiating contempt proceedings on crucial problems on the matters of justice. As Justice is the act of God (a virtue), dispensing justice then, demands a high level of ethical conduct and decorum.

The judiciary should be more active and always to emerge and remain truly as the last hope of common man. The availability of power (electricity)- the energy question better education in the country, both in the colleges and tertiary institutions, extractive industry, health, bad roads and unemployment crisis and financial sector to be hailed as revolutionary, so that personal interest could stop obstructing the common good.

There is also the problem of infiltration of prejudice and undermined the confidence of Nigerians in constitutionalism and the rule of law.

The stand point here is rather how we can present a model formulation of the ideal image of justice to country like Nigeria, redeveloping it as a concept and bringing it face to face with our contemporary world.

What holds strong as the good and right of man today in the nation is no longer maintained or actually cherished substantially.

The problems of Nigerian as far as equity or egalitarianism is concerned is fundamentally the problem of justice and good administration upholding of rights of man and dignity and freedom and bringing to an end, the flagrant delinquency to the rule of law. Another good recommendation and suggestion is that we need a serious Re-think or recapitulation on the condition and the situation of the country presently.

Our greatest burden should be instead of correcting, learning from our past mistakes, we unwisely and ignorantly degenerate and repeat unceasingly those things that militate against our progressions and economic development. The issue of justice and Human Rights are very important in every society and this is all the more needed in the Nigerian nation of today. Justice and equal rights for the citizen then may not have any clearer meaning without adhering to the moral habits which the law define.

In the words of Higgins, it is the moral habit which regulates our conduct towards other men.[218] He sees justice for all as a kind of virtue which makes one to seek the good of another as well as his own good.

[218] Cf. T. J. Higgins., Man as Man, London 1949, p. 152.

In a more precise form, justice is 'another good"'*bonum alterius"* for Aristotle in this sense it applies to equality since it is concerned with another's good. Justice as regards to equity for Aquinas is, "a kind of equality and hence absolutely, justice is between those that are absolutely, but where there is no absolute equality between them neither is there is an absolute justice."[219] Nigeria should then think –thought in what is lacking in her own side in this situation. If justice is the constant will to render to every one his due, this

goes to mean as already said and emphasized, recognizing and giving each person his deserved right as enshrined in the natural law.

This notion of justice as giving to every person his due remains a more plausible one, and according to Aquinas it is the perpetual and constant will of giving every person his due.[220] The proper objects of justice consist in giving others their right and those things belonging to them as theirs (rightfully). It is an act of the will and so must be firm and stable that is why it is and should be perpetual and constant. It is that virtue which results in each person receiving his due.

In Nigeria, nationalist leaders were cautiously optimistic about the impact of the Declaration of the Human Rights, challenging them to be more serious on this issue on their aspirations for independence and self-rule.

With independence, rights talk began to assume new meanings and significance for the nationalist elite who now constituted the ruling class. This shifted from being mainly a means or challenging the colonial state to becoming a means of validating postcolonial nationalist projects such as redressing the distortions of colonialism and promoting traditional African family values. Much time and efforts was spent articulating vague ideals such as the constitutional right to family life, while more important human rights issues, such as institutionalized discrimination against women and

"Illegitimate" children were overlooked as part of class-centred political compromises. The promising adaptation of right ideas by Nigeria elites as a means of moderating State power during the colonial period completely fell apart after independence.

---

219 T. Aquinas., Summa Theologiae, Ia- IIae 114, 370c- 371c.in the Great Books vol. 20, USA: 195, p. 271.

220 Cf. T. Aquinas., Summa Theologiae, IIa- IIae Qt. 58 Art.

Rights talks that once wielded effectively by the elites to challenge colonial power was thrust aside once they attained power.

It can be recommended too that social studies organization, social studies Association of Nigeria practitioners should provide forums for more seminars, conferences and workshops for peoples so as to continue to conscientize the masses on those positive values that promote peaceful coexistence, national integration, national unity and ethnic tolerance.

Social studies should be taught and made a compulsory subject at the senior secondary school.

Further more, in the nation one should see this as the basic value underlying systems of law or the objective whose systems seeks to attain its objective. The true practice of justice is all the more important and this made St. Augustine of Hippo to have often times described any state without justice and recognition of human right, and dignity of man as no better than a band of armed robbers.[221]

In Nigeria, the important principle governing social life is subsidiary which is to be considered as the complement of solidarity for the good of all people. There has also been an additional Presidential Committee set up on Dialogue and Peaceful Resolution on security challenges in Northern Nigeria. These group work hand in hand with the Minister of Special Duties and Inter Governmental Affairs to be in settling matters, be it general insecurity, boundary or ethnic problems in the areas where confusions or misunderstanding happened to ensue.

On this ground, solidarity and righteousness on the part of the government and citizenry is involved. Pope John Paul II in his Encyclical letter *'Solicitudo rei Socialis'(the Church's social concerns,)* has particularly underlined the importance of the principle of solidarity, identifying it as a human and Christian virtue.[222] Based on this principle of solidarity each person, as a member of the society, is indissolubly linked to the destiny of society itself and by dint of Gospel, to the destiny of all men's salvation.[223] However, the principle of subsidiarity follows suite here in maintaining that the state or any other authority should not prevent or take over the responsibility from a person, group of community or the other former levels of

221 Cf. St. Augustine, Concerning the City of God against the Pagans, p. 881f.

222 Cf. John Paul II Solitudo rei Socialis, nr. 39-40, 1987, AAS 80, 1988, p. 513.

223 Cf. John Paul II Solicitudo Rei Socialis, Introductory Guidelines, p. 40.

action where we have competence and ability to carry out such activities and achieve the expected results on their own level of competence.[224]

This issue of competency should be well observed in the Nigerian nation as it enlightens the equal rights meaning and action.

Plato in his own view wrote: "We thought that in a State which is ordered with a view to the good of the whole should be most likely to find justice and the ill- ordered State of injustice."[225] In Plato's idea, justice in the direction of Human Rights means here moral justice.

There will be no effective management of the state without the virtue of justice. On this aspect Aristotle also remarked:"Whereas without free population and wealth, there cannot be a State at all, without justice and without justice and virtue, it cannot be managed well."[226]

The Vatican II document on the pastoral constitution on the Church in the Modern World has clarified this well with the ethical demands regarding justice, man's freedom, equal right and urges all men, groups and local communities, associations and organisations, nations and continents to strive to participate in the management of all the activities pertaining to economic, political and cultural life while overcoming any purely individualistic conception.[227]

The United Nations Charter also in their rulings in the Universal Declaration on Human Rights (UNDR), have time without number cautioned the various nations Nigeria inclusive on the danger and abuse of Human Rights and human dignity when they emphatically said:

> Whereas disregard and contempt for human rights have resulted in babarious acts which have outraged the conscience of mankind, and the advent of a world in which human beings shall enjoy freedom of speech and belief and freedom from fear and want which has been proclaimed as the highest aspiration of the common people. All human beings are born free in dignity and rights.[228]

---

224 Cf. Pius XI, Quadragesimo Anno, ASS, 23, p. 203.

225 Plato, The Republic, trans by B. Jowett., New York 1974, p. 129.

226 Aristotle, the Politics , trans by T. A., Sinclair, England 1962, p. 209.

227 Cf. Vat.II., Gaudium et Spes, Nr. 30- 32, see also John PaulII Discourse at the 68th Session of the International Labour Organisation. (ILO) United Nations, June 15, 1982, AAS 74.

228 United Nations Charter and Universal Declaration of Human Rights, Department of Public Information: Preamble, Art. I, The General Assembly, Research Approaches, New York 2006. of Public Information: Preamble, Art. I, The General Assembly, Re-

They are endowed with reason and conscience and should act towards one another in a spirit of brotherhood.

The good understanding of these rights and freedom is of the greatest importance for the full realization of dignity of human person.

The United Nations Charter also should steadily reaffirm their faith in fundamental Human Rights, in the dignity and worth of human person and the equal rights of men and women which is determined to promote social progress and better standards of life in larger freedom.[229]

It protects the human person, local communities and intermediary bodies from the danger of losing their legitimate autonomy and competence.

Pius XI also remarked: "The Church fights for subsidiary in so far as this principle by reason of man's dignity, respect for what is most human in the organisation of social life and safe-guiding of the rights of people in relations between individual society and universal society."[230] The human structures and the communities of persons are here involved.

This concerns the modern day societies and the danger caused by technical and mechanism of the livelihood of the people. Such structural threats do not leave room for the development of a true humanism.

In many capitalistic nations like Nigeria, the State is transformed into a huge, administrative machine which invades all areas of life and drags man into a state of fear and anxiety causing his depersonalisation, threatening his dignity as a person reducing his personal and social freedom among others. Associations, structures, private co-operations, public and state apparatus are legitimate in so far as they reserve proper space for the person, and encourage the growth of collaboration under the common good.

---

search Approaches, New York 2006. Approaches, New York 2006.of Public Information: Preamble, Art. I, The General Assembly, Research Approaches, New York 2006.

229 The Charter equally determined to focus on the purpose and Principles, in Chap. I, of the Charter, Art. I, (i and ii) is to maintain international peace and security, and to that end: to take effective collective measures for the prevention and removal of threats to the peace 'and for the suppression of acts of aggression or other breaches of the peace, and to bring about peace means, and in conformity with the principles of justice and international law, adjustment of international disputes or situations which might lead to breach of peace, to develop friendly relation among nations based on respect for the principle of equal rights and self-determination of peoples, and to take other appropriate measures to strengthen universal peace.

230 (Guidelines), p. 41 see also John XXIII, Pacem in Terris, AAS, p. 294, and John Paul II, Laboren Exercens, AAS, 76, p. 616.

In such a pluralistic States, the organs of the human structures approach persons and invite them to participate in the common talks of promoting peace, economy, forming or creating intermediates bodies cum labour or capital unions. Terrorism poses much concerns these days in the nation especially the dreadful Islamic Sect called Boko Haram.

The insurgents seem to be tricky as they simply adapt the strategy of striking and seeking refuge in neighboring countries or mingling with other people in the community.

It may be impossible for the soldiers to fight the sects across the border. The international convention laws also restrict them from chasing the insurgents into foreign territories.

While the fight against terrorism is being hampered by the presence of civilians in areas being used by members of the insurgency as hideouts, there is the need to devise fresh strategies, if the war on terror is to be won.

Nevertheless, the government, the media and the citizens must realise that there is no more time to be wasted in blame games.

The military needs all the support and encouragement to wipe the tears of those innocent widows and widowers, fatherless, motherless and deserted communities in the north-east.

I strongly support the call by the Senate committee on Defence on the relocation of the Chief of Army Staff, Lt.Gen Minimah, to the states facing the onslaught. In this vein, more security men will naturally be deployed to flash points where these heinous, inhuman activities can be checkmated.

Although the sect is taking leverage of territorial border laws to perpetrate its crime, the government can seek the cooperation of neighbouring countries on border control. There is therefore the urgent need for the government to explore bilateral security arrangements with its neighbours, especially Chad, Niger-Republic and Cameroon on how to tackle the activities of the insurgents around the border areas. As we continue to pray for an end to this senseless carnage, we sympathise with the victims and their families and the personnel in the volatile region. The media, too, has a role to play, to control unnecessary giving of cheap publicity to the insurgents. The implementation of these principles would be relating to persons and structures in order to enable the overcoming of any tensions between socialisation and patronisation for such things to come to a good end with a better approach.

All these refer to the communal obligations of man especially the government of the day and also the expected righteousness in the execution of one's duties among his fellow men in the State. A recapitulation of Aquinas Thoughts as concerns Nigeria and Africa generally is that it touches the problems of development and the problems of justice and right of man human which include corruption, insecurity, economic imbalance, partiality unjust distribution of wages between professions, joblessness, tribalism and despotism and other basic grounds which are also more challenging like the problems of justice which focuses on the problems of under development, inadequate material and human resources, false priority and indiscipline.[231]

Of importance is the inability to realize the need for prima-faciae duty which operates with these principles.

a) The obligation to improve ourselves in respect of virtue and intelligence.
b) The obligation to do good to others.
c) The obligation to distribute rewards or punishment in the accordance with merit.
d) The obligation to make restitution for the things done.
e) The obligation to keep promise.
f) The obligation of gratitude.

Equally, is the obligation to abstain from injuring others. Although, some of these obligationsfall under utilitarianism but they are necessary principles for justice.[232]

The issues of human freedom and dignity draws attention to the multi-layered discourse about rights and liberties employed by both the colonial state and its African subjects. It focuses on the complex dynamics engendered by the intersection between existing African notions of rights and the more formal regimes of rights introduced within European Christian humanism, colonial customary law, and the imported English common law

[231] For the honour and dignity of man: The big question that remains are on these people in the different areas of the country to be forgotten and then be abandoned in their poverty? But we proclaim that opportunity and favours are not equal. This group of people deserve pity, don't they? Are they not meant to be enjoying the natural resources and blessing of the nation like: money and food or what people call "national cake"Focusing on the man: Christian and Politics, we should then reflect more on the meaning and our understanding of justices and equal rights. loc.cit., referring to all especially the less privileged in the society.

[232] Cf. B.O.Dike., Man With Man, (Political Psychology), Owerri- Nigeria 1988. p. 7.

systems. It seeks to examine how diverse interest groups within this African society-including colonial officials, missionaries, African elites, women's group, and later, nationalist activists- employed the language of rights and liberty to serve varied social and political ends.

Part of the objective is to connect the significance of the evolution of the rights discourse within colonial African contexts to the quest for a viable Human Rights regime in the continent.

All good and beautiful constitutions setting out noble principles in the country like Nigeria should be established and geared towards a steady restoration of the dignity of man in the nation.

The government should directly or through some of its top execution and actions bring to prove beyond reasonable doubt that might is really might.

That which is to be only the advantage of the stronger (rule) is not justice but injustice. Justice and equity cum fairness is for the common good of the people in the society.

This is a moral and social virtue and according to Plato and Aristotle, justice and equity in this meaning is the foundation of the state in terms of unity, tolerance, and accommodation.

It means that any state where justice is overlooked is heading to its ultimate ruin with the passage of time.

In the thought of W.Vossenkuhl; we should acknowledge meaningfully these words from his propositions:

"What Aristotle has in mind about moral excellence of virtues in the society, Kant about the good will and the quint essence of morality, and the law of contract- theorists regarding the cooperation and the usefulness of the ultilitarian thinkings.There should be in ethics and customs a good corresponding normality."[233]

That means, our cognisance of morality as being the standard of behaviour is based on the principles of right and wrong. Aristotle in this issue came in with this concrete point when he said: "Justice is a vital virtue of the State without which the State cannot be managed well."[234] However, the exercise of justice and equity is equally practiced sometimes better in many countries today like in Europe, and America that in some many countries in African and Asian continents.

---

[233] Cf. W. Vossenkuhl., Die Möglichekeit des Guten Ethik im 21 Jahrhundert. p. 119.

[234] Aristotle, loc. cit., p. 209.

Society gains and progresses more when justice is really upheld for all in all objectivity.

Nevertheless, dishonest people could be found anywhere; and good and honest people, and also, those who jeopardizes and waters down the efforts of others and by so doing could in this way harm the society at large; so the people concerned or involved in the problem should always be

apprehended for a corrective measure. On the side of Thyrasmachus ideology, Justice is what is to the interest or advantage of the stronger.[235] This is what is obtained in some states in Nigeria today.

This is equivalent to the expression "might is right"but only when the judiciary allows it because it is the main organ of justice.

It is more manifested in the government which operates under the rule of law, where our rulers often suspend the provisions of the constitution at will and the rule of law which advocates what the rule decrees.

The administration also in Nigerian States should do their best to be meeting its obligations in justifying matters. According to Athenian philosopher, a stranger in "The Laws" injustice arises when one is mastered by passion and desires, which is by fear and anger, pleasure and pain, etc.[236]

In the state justice means equality and inequality before the law. Plato confirms this in his book, "The Laws" when he said:

> For that state in which law is, their subject has no authority, one perceives to be on the high way to ruin; but I see that the state in which the law is above the rulers, and the rulers are inferiors of the Law, but should have salvation and every blessing which the gods can confer."[237]

To integrate the Aquinas doctrine on Justice, human rights and fair-play into the nation's systems of administration, is that, the human dignity and freedom for all persons is what the law guarantees and protects. This is because everybody is born equal before God and therefore has a right to freedom of expression, association, religion and worship; others have a duty to respect these laws in the state which are made to guarantee these rights.

Be this as it is, only where there is equality of human recognition in a society, then there is a free society, each man sees a reflection of himself

---

235 Cf. Plato, the Republic, op. cit., Bk.1, nr. 338.

236 Cf. Plato, the Collected Dialogue, (ed.) by Hamilton and Coins, New York 1966, p. 487.

237 Plato, the Dialogue, trans., by B. Jowett Vol. II. New York Press, USA 1975, p. 609.

in each other and so fulfil the golden rule which states 'do to others as you would like to be done on to you'(cf.Mt.7,12). And this is actually the aim of justice and equal rights.

A society is not free when one man or group of individuals are supposedly free while others are treated as slaves.

The root cause of indiscipline and lawlessness in any nation could be curbed or checked by the government of the day.

While the politicians and public commentators may continue to condemn the security personnel and others for insensitivity, they should be mindful of their wordings that could discourage the military officials risking their lives to protect us.

It is obvious that the military may have been facing some constraints, but, by their orientation they don't go to public to expose any sign of weaknesses even when they courageously challenge criminal elements and terrorists.

The individuals in the society should see the law as something meant for their own good and not in the interest of rulers and the rulers should in turn manifest this notions in their actions by abiding by the rule of law. If this is to materialize well, it depends on both the rulers and the populace being ruled. We are to continue to yearn and question the root causes of human sufferings and abuses in ones sphere of life on earth. To hold strongly well to the maintenance of justice and equal rights, the government of the day should jointly be contributing to the welfare and developments of humanity. This is because the vehicle or means for actualizing the happiness and development of humanity is through justice and peace, respect for human dignity, respect for the laws of the land or the constitution. And equally the religions orientation and ethical re-orientation, the biblical principle of love; love of God and love of man is to be held.

We shall now at this juncture, integrate or apply the Aquinas thoughts and teachings on justice and Human Rights to the Nigerian system of government as this would be suitable and be of great relevance to the Nigerian multi-cultural nation. This will go a long way to adjusting the nations systems of government cum execution of laws, thereby gradually changing their modus operandi for her greater advancement. It is no more rumour in the Nigeria of today, that what justice and human right mean is often rejected and banished from the natural and legal jurisdiction to the sphere of weak manipulation of the State with crazy egotists.

When the people break the law with wanton impunity, they should be punished, the grass root citizens and the poor should not be denied justice because they might suffer more on certain occasion if they have no body to intercede for them judicially wise. The problems are because of the wrong administrative acumen and undue application and execution of laws in the State. Aquinas advocates that in a state like Nigeria, the sovereign has all the legislatives and judicial powers to act well and promptly for the welfare of the people.

Aquinas after his fully entering the teaching career in 1252 in his record time and popularity made it clear in his method of scientific investigation and synthesis with developed proofs that justice could always be held for all and sundry, and even for those in the grass root of the society.[238]

The government being the force of the people should represent well the common interest of the State.

In a country like Nigeria, the good application of the Aquinas Philosophy would help the nation to focus better in continuing to fight injustice to enhance authenticate existence. Aquinas showed us that the inalienable right of all people in a society is a sine-qua-non for man's existence. For the societal welfares regarding justice Fagothey expressed his view: "Justice is love limited to the absolute requirements of basic human equality as the love that is expanded to the fullest scope of the human person's dignity."[239]

As stressed above on the better administration of justice, the government should have to curtail or abridge the much injustice done to the cit-

---

[238] Cf. Adler. J.M., Aquinas 1, nr. 17, Great Books, op. cit., p. v.

[239] Fagothey. A., Right and Reason, London 1971, p. 267. A theological understanding in Nigeria-and Africal as a whole may conclude with this insistence on a positive image of a man where suffering endured in resisting oppression is seen as part of man's involvement in his universe in order to transform it. The aim of the struggle is not simply the destitution of oppressor who creates a hostile enviroment for the masses- this may only reproduce the hates, the violence, and the corruption of the opressor. Rather the empowerment of the poor is to transform, and thus to humanize, the earth. Christian theology needs to provide for the freedom movements a spirituality which integrates the cosmos into its orbit. This is based not on the anger aroused by the inventory of wounds inflicted but on the hope of the realisation of a new humanity which emerges in the struggle.Cf. O: Ike and U. Ogboaja (ed.), Human Right, Human Dignity and Cath. Social Teaching, Lessons for the Church in Nigeria, Enugu 1992.

izens in the state, any power that must be, must act within the rule of law what constitute a bad government either due to ineptitudeness, non-challancy, ignorance, jealousy or malice both to the ruler and the ruled. So with caveat from the Federal government, any aspect of terror or corruption challenged and stopped should be returned under any circumstances. What a Herculean task to address the malaise of corruption in some part of Africa.

How can one curb both the impunity and intolerance prevalence of corruption in today's society? The politicians concerned should always know that corruption is a short-cut to the mortuary.

Corruption today would become more deadly than AIDS and Cancer. It would be a disincentive for rigging elections. What would be the point if public office only gives you a visa to go to see your ancestors prematurely. The challenging question is, could there be in the state a constant room for proper peace and stability in every circumstance?

Why do many people suffer unjustly in the State? Why is it that the government does not really apply the rules of fairness, and does not often acknowledge human dignity?

The summary answers to the above questions should be reflection on the olden days when the Almighty God even applied the rule of freedom, justice and fair hearing in the garden of Eden and if so why should that be lacking in our mundane world of today? The citizenry should not suffer ill-treatment, deprivation, violation, and abuses of their rights plus increasing cases of torture behind bars or in the police cells.

On certain cases of injustices and inhuman treatment, the African Concord noted: "Catalogues of human rights atrocities were harrowing experiences through such a prison system where over crowding diseases, starvations and death rate constantly rises."[240] In every society (state) right comes before justice. If something is due to man as his own, the fact of its being due to him first and foremost, has not come into existence through justice. What is due to a person and obligatory in the state could be equally be ascertained objectively depending on the circumstantial situation of things reasonably before embarking on any action. For example meritoriously a

[240] African Concord Magazine, The Inhuman Abuses, Vol. 2, nr. 38, Lagos Dec. 19th 1988, p. 10.

labourer by reason of something he has done as required, then, righteously something should be due to him and his deserved right.

Aquinas explained it well in his answers that, a thing might be due to a man on the basis of certain agreements treaties or legal decision and so on.

The implication to reckon with basis by right and licence and judicial obligation is when we have a concept of a man in consideration of human

nature. A reasonable nation should also know that any law which lacks defensibility lacks the characters of law raising the question whether such law should be obeyed. A State like Nigeria should love and obey the law for both orderliness and for moral enlightenments of the nation.

Sometimes there exist a serious injustice, building up around the State like a network of domination, oppression and abuses which keep the greater part of humanity in such a continent from sharing in the building up enjoyment of a more just and fraternal world.

In the Nigeria nation, we should have the right to seek and accede the truth and to protect life of man even from the baneful consequences of ignorance.

However, a cursory look at the right to life is most fundamental of all Human Rights, as right to live, both for the already born and unborn child or infant. The right springs directly and immediately from the very nature of man, such rights which a man-human beings enjoy fundamentally because he is a human person not a mere animal.

T. Wood here remarked: "Man's right to life, grounded in his divine origin is the basis of all other human rights and foundation of civilized society."[241]

The instability of the country's problems could destroy the legal systems and undermines the trust needed in order for a society and economic activity to function well. The Vatican note expresses concern over advanced democratic societies that suffer the break-down in moral standard. An excessive pluralism in modern democratic societies like Nigeria can lead to lack of consensus on ethical standards.

The excellent collaboration for the purpose of communitarian harmony in the state is praise worthy for the nation and for the awareness of all. In considering the scope of justification of the right of individual in the country, we see that each person has the natural right to live and to act rationally

[241] Wood, T., Life Sacredness, Dictionary of Christian Ethics, London 1980, p. 196.

with his fellow man in the attainment of his peace and happiness. Aquinas is of the opinion that for Nigeria to be an ordered society the citizens should be living and acting and integrating, communicating with one another for better co-operation, and avoiding untold hindrances and intimidating the less privileged in the State.

The nation should be goal oriented for the orderliness in keeping to the law and avoid any unnecessary assumption and presumptions act.

The Papal documents enunciating rights often placed right to life in the first place in the society. Human life is the sacred gift of God; it is directly from God alone and should be protected.[242]

On the categorical scriptural injunctions and insights on the aspects of Human Rights in the society, it meant that we should here refer to the fact that Christ showed that He is always attentive to the needs of His people, especially those suffering injustice, maltreatment and the down-trodden in the society. If Nigeria nation adopt well the tenets and meaning of Aquinas meaning of human rights justice and fairness under the rule of law, the country can in this sense plan well and progress accordingly based on the fact that the intention should be made for the general good of the state and its populace. The justice of any state without laws is not qualified in the real sense of it to be called a State.

Laws guarantees and protects human dignity and freedom in the State, and so, to be law abiding citizens is very necessary even if man exists in a state of innocence as opposed to the state of nature.

This means that the citizenry in the state should recognise this meaning as meant for the welfare of every citizen and never to be seen as a punitive measure otherwise it denies its raison d'étre. There is divine intelligence-the Almighty creator that leads and guides man towards perfection. Scruton in his philosophical realm summarized this well by saying that God created man and put into him a political consciousness and freedom for a reasonable goal thereby taking the purpose of a state at heart. This is the more reason why we have terms like ' nation-state'that means that it could be organised for the government of a nation (or a more closely related nations)

[242] Cf. Pope Pius XII, Discourse on the Dangers of the Technological Conception of Social, Anniversary of the Rerum Novarum, Rome, 1956, p. 231.

whose territory is determined at least in the part by national customs and expectations.[243]

The Aquinas characterization of his various works are free of corruptions between 1256-1269 on religion, Metaphysics, Ethics, Politics and the Posterior-analytics which made us to know that the end of the state is intended to make its members live well for the good of all.[244]

This means that the state is a means to an end-the good life of man, and this good life is the life of happiness according to his master Aristotle.

This is so to say that Nigeria as a nation, has the onerous duty and authority in the distribution and maintenance of power; upholding the moral justification of the state and the authority as traditionally conceived but should also be more of legitimizing power in the de-facto political situation. The government and the Church can help also through communicating its social doctrine. The application of principles such as the dignity of the human person, the common good, and solidarity can be of great assistance in struggling against corruption.

The Vatican recommends more attention to the moral struggle that takes place within each person.

Reducing corruption will be easier if citizens cultivate virtuous behaviour and see the fight against bribery and other corrupt practices should be part of immediate task for every country. These are what Nigeria nation and the church in her country would put into practise for the smooth running of the country.

From all we have seen here so far in the philosophy of Aquinas, it makes us understand and to know then, that idyllic happiness, good administration and progression for a hopeful nation is very necessary and worth-while.

The state being the combination of both the government and the governed; it is the machinery through which the purposes of the state are sought to be realised, and this could usher in perfect ordering of things.

Thus Eze, put across his opinion for the application of Aquinas tenets of political philosophy for Nigerians government policies when he commented on the perfection of a state and said: "A perfect of self-sufficing

---

243 Cf. Scuton. R. A., Ditionary of Political Thought, op.cit., 1982, p. 313ff.

244 Aristotle, The politics, trans. by T. A.Sinclair, New York 1962, p. 168.

natural society constitute of many individuals and families of a united common authority for the realisation of their temporal welfare."[245]

Suitable for Nigerian nation therefore is to imbibe well and to put into action the Aquinas ideas for the Nigerian government and to recognise that every state is and should be for the welfare of its citizens.

In any case where the government by its action overtly or otherwise indicates favours on some citizens to the detriment of others, then it could fail in its duties and zeal and the situation could worsen.

The good executive of laws should carry out well the judiciary which interprets them and decide upon their application in individual cases.

This means that a nice enforcement of law cum reasonable adjustment is expected for the progress and better development of the nation.

It is good to mention the general observations and Suggestions for the Identified Problem before we bring this work to the expected good end.

The rule of law is so fundamental for sustainable progress of any nation, and Nigeria is indeed on this issue not an exception.

Actually, one of the most pertinent and fundamental problem facing the Nigerian nation is the political crisis which needs to be rectified and resolved, in order to give room for peace and stability in the country.

It is clear that after few years of implementing certain economic growths seemed to have proved elusive. It is also envisaged that some foreign countries like Europe and America where many policies have worked

245 O. Eze., Society and the Rule of Law, (ed.), Nigeria 1987, p. 89., Jean Vanier on the complex society of our time said that to be really integrated, people need to be trained in order to be competent enough to handle matters... This is because life in the society is governed by the laws of competition at the top of the social hierarchy the ' winners', who are strong and capable . At the bottom or base level are the 'losers,'the weak who need helps. Everyone seeks to climb up the ladder of human promotion so as to have more priviledges and money; those who cannot climb up tend to sink into despondency. Naturally communities in the various enclaves of the state, such as the family, have been contributed to the weakening by constantly offering new and powerful experiences, this is also typical of Nigerian nation. Cf. Vanier, J., Our journey Home, Rediscovering A common Humanity Beyond Our Differences., op. cit., p. 178.climb up the ladder of human promotion so as to have more privileges and money; those who cannot climb up tend to sink into despondency. Naturally communities in the various enclaves of the state, such as the family, have been contributed to the weakening by constantly offering new and powerful experiences, this is also typical of Nigerian nation. Cf. Vanier, J., Our journey Home, Rediscovering A common Humanity Beyond Our Differences., p. 178.

out well; are working constantly to maintain their clear goals and strategies for achieving their purposes. No doubts, the little sacrifices, failures and denials of addressing the problems past and present properly well resulted in economic instability and political upheavals.[246] Having insights into human behaviour is also an enormous valuable skill for the nation to take into cognisance of reaching the expectations. In any case, avoiding ethnic or boundary conflicts could always keep the country in progressions advancing than what was the case in the recent past years in the Nigerian populace.

In Nigeria, vocal elites were no longer contented with their status as colonial subjects and British-protected persons. They demanded their rights as "full citizens of the empire"

The emergence of the contemporary human rights movement has been linked to certain outcomes of war, particularly the UNDR, which has become central to the definition of human rights. In Nigeria, as the case elsewhere in the colonized world, the language of universal rights in the Atlantic Charter and the UNDR became an important part of the nationalist rhetoric and a model for the constitutional rights regime introduced at independence.

Much of these debates centred on two issues. The first was the concern of African chiefs and their supporters among the Western-educated elite about the erosion of their political power under British rule. The educated elites opposed British intervention in local politics and sought to defend the political rights of chiefs and their subjects against colonial excesses. Putting aside their sometimes-acrimonious differences, Western-educated Africans allied with local kings and chiefs to promote what they construed as the political rights of Africans as the reach of British power expanded.

With the growing regional sentiments among dominant ethnic groups, leaders of minority ethnic groups should continue to demand either for separate states of their own or for constitutional safeguards to prevent their domination by majority ethnic groups in an independent Nigeria.

These concerns should be based on the leaders of the numerically dominant ethnic and cultural groups-the Hausa-Fulani, the Yoruba, and the Igbo. These ethnic groups more often effectively controlled the major political

[246] J.B.C. Abba., The Contemporary Nigeria, Our Fate, Glories, Woes and Prospects, Independent Series Vol. I, Enugu, Nigeria 1997, p. 33.

parties. Minority groups were based justification; on the fact that the independence from British colonial rule would only be replaced by permanent Hausa, Yoruba, or Igbo domination. Don Richard Riso also observed that nations living in peace and in good relationships will benefit from great understanding and could have more from themselves and their partners, since good relationships depend among other things on harmony, honesty and trust.[247]

However, it is also observed, that, no good relationship can work better unless both parties, the countries concerned, brings sensitivity and insight to it, particularly when conflicts and misunderstanding arise.

Creating of self-knowledge, freeing ourselves from conflicts and neuroses would be virtually impossible. Once we have been drawn into neuroses, we find it increasingly difficult to choose what is best for us in the state, thereby seeing things as more difficult to work out to overcome these problems. We can reverse the vicious circle created by not being trapped in our typical fixations but by fully acknowledging and releasing our fears and habitual tendencies. If we do so, we could find out, then, that life for each member in the state would becomes easier because our time and energy can be used for living creatively rather than being wasted in internal conflicts and squabbles of any kind.

This is no wisdom or joy but a blatant stupidity or so to say as, one living in a fool's paradise. Equally noticed is that a reasonable lasting patience, justice and wisdom should be a sine-qua-non to bring things to normality and in the right place, and to work together for a secured atmosphere as Aquinas pinpointed out in his notion of justice and fairness.

Governance in Nigeria has gone awry, and there is not a more compelling evidence of this other than the growing phenomenon of carelessness and taking the rule of law for granted.

When the governance accepts both the principle and operation of true federalism many problems could be solved. What has obtained in the Nigerian nation since the so-called return to democratic rule and the adoption of a federal constitution has been a sham of both democracy and federalism.

The so-called constitution of the Nigerian nation is itself a bequest of the military and its centralist mentality that derives from the corruptly na-

[247] Riso. R. D., On Justice and Fair-play; Discovering Your Personality Type, Boston 1995, p. 4.

ture of absolutist power. It is painful to hear this effects badly and attacks-political psychological and physical-on our judges, which in every instance amounts to a violation of the sovereignty of the courts as articulated in section 6 of the 1999 Nigerian constitution. Mob attacks on courts such as we observed in the recent past, erodes the confidence of the community in the judiciary and may lead to the emergence of supine judges.[248]

Most of the case of human rights violation in Nigeria result to a greater extent from this spread of self-help.

On this inviting urgent situation, the protection of the rule of law is self-evident. For instance, it is the onerous duty of judges to interpret and protect the law. The court-room and their work-place, should be a hallowed space, where reason defeat emotions.

Disobedient of court orders and physical attacks of judges or their intimidation by authority figures are all unconscionable attempts to reduce the scope of the court's exercise of authority and the country's growth will not advance with such ulterior-motives.[249] The nation should always know that the decision of the courts needs not conform to public opinion although judges themselves as human beings are not impeccable or unmistakeable.

The impetus of nation's jury should always be acknowledged and respected.

So, justice should remain the will of man's power to choose the good for which the sense desires are concerned. Justice has its origin in natural force, the mind and reason with which the intelligent man measures justice and injustice. Suffice it to say, that justice undoubtedly does pertains to man's righteousness not only to do the just thing but to be just as well.

The independence of the judiciary is a pre-requisite for social order of the nation. Public education for the good understanding of the masses is also necessary in certain situations; some judges suffer double jeopardy often; they neither cannot answer back nor can they recruit their own thugs, to take up issues physically with the thugs that have sometimes invaded the open court. The judges cannot but as their primary duty protect the rule of

---

248 Cf. W. Soyinka., R. Abati., Commentaries on the" Nigeria World and Pertinent Issues." May 18 and June 7, 2007.

249 Cf. W. Soyinka., R. Abati., Commentaries on the" Nigeria World and Pertinent Issues" .May 18 and June 7, 2007.

law, no matter whose ox is gored for the stability and greater advancement of the country in order to conform to the proceedings of Human Rights.

They should be up against the mischief of both government and litigants.

On salient advice, the church puts across these suiting statements:

"Trust transforms people and gives them a challenge for self-respect and a willingness to show that they are worthy of the trust put in them This attitude is often lacking among the development policy makers and their expert implementers."[250]

This being the case, it is always the best way to keep the citizens psyches healthy and well nourished. Another good observation is the lack of consciousness for a better development of the country.

In a every human community of any nation, a nice human interaction environment should be a thing of paramount importance for the opportunity in having dialogues on certain sensitive matters arising, sharing of ideas and the openness for the true concern for others and their way of living and survival.[251] There should be the constant need to reduce the rate of human rights abuses, violence and the work towards the eventual obliteration especially those things contrary to natural justice, equity, and good conscience. The family has a role to play in the promotion of Human Rights because justice remains efficaciously a sine-qua-non for the good of all. This is because; in the reality of human existence, the acceptance of common good will always help us to check our progressions, retrogressions and backwardness.

On this ground, St. Paul in his works made us to know that it is in God that we live and move and have our being (Acts 20:28), which can be compared to the issues of nature, justice and rights. One notices also that as regards human reasoning, the social nature of man with its consequential problems among human beings are often times confusing seemingly complexity and sceptic. This means that the recognition and cherishing more, the natural laws as foundation of Human Rights is very importance. In these entire scenarios, people have tried to put up some defences albeit weak. What is left for the society to do in order to recover the vast heritage to humanity wastage.

---

250 Vat. II., The Church Today, nr. 22.

251 Cf. J. Vanier., Righteous Living and Our Journey Home, Discovering A Common Humanity Beyond Our Differences, p. 187.

More so, well noticed is listening to one another, or allowing others to chirp in their own views and objectives, needs and expectations which could also bring in calmly peace and serene atmosphere for the country.

A respite then could come into focus to certain happenings or a chaotic situation at the availability of competent facilitators or peace-maker or moderators to be accepted by all in the time of need.

In order to minimise the exhibited transparency of our over simplicity or that of complexity our strong cure of our being, the nation need to prove herself and to see any commitment or challenge as a special responsibility gearing towards human maturity as a nation. This however, needs sometimes more incessant efforts and extra-charisma to come up to the expected fulfilment. The availability of a greater needed reasonable technology is not yet there in the nation if the country should advance more both economically and otherwise.

The respect for Human Dignity and Human Rights should be held in high esteem, but there could be a good stop and a necessary urgent stop or break by the government imposition of certain laws with actions on the assassination of a person that sometimes occur in the country.

There is a loud cry for life and liberty, a desire for pro-life, to suppress any oppressor and those perceived as oppressors. The existing walls of hatred or walls of depression and the refusal of life should be shunned promptly by the government of the day.

On Human Dignity and protection of life per se, the Vatican II Council documents equally reminded us of our acceptance of each other and to rightly and anticipatively know that human person is a creature of God, made in his own image and elevated to supernatural destiny transcending earthly life. Man therefore as an intelligent and free being, subject of rights and of duties, is the primary principle and one can say the heart and soul of the social teaching of the Church.[252]

The basic rights guaranteed in the country's constitution should always strongly include the right to life, freedom from inhuman treatments, freedom from slavery and forced labour, the right to personal liberty, the right to fair hearing, freedom of peaceful assembly and association, freedom of movement and residence; freedom from discrimination, which we have examined in the previous chapters. Although most Nigerians welcomed the

[252] Cf. Vat. II, Gaudium et Spes, nr. 17.

inclusion of a bill of rights in the constitution, some criticized its theoretical and practical limitations on two main grounds.

Firstly, the bill was only a statement of civil and political rights; it did not make sufficient provision for social and economic rights such as the right to education and work which we thought the state should also protect.

There are some additional further challenging thoughts not be left out regarding justice and human rights in African continents and these are the urgent problems of today in most African countries.

Such as the required steady serious attentiveness to African Human Rights Charter Declaration 1981 for a New Nigeria.

The need to imbibe the quantum of equilibrium through intelligent with better administrative acumen as the touchstone-*(recta ratio)* right reason of any rational being is important. This is to do with the gift of intelligence instead of emotional intelligence and be avoiding utopia issues, narcissism and machevellianistic (end justified the means philosophy), ways of livelihood.

The cherishing of constant discursive dialog-orientations for a *"Live and Let Others Live"* Maxim should always be reflected. To be law abiding, duty-consciousness, dedication and sincerity in *Vita-Communis* is needed. The necessity of the African unity and dispensing Justice with Human Face should always be observed.

What then could be other further possible propositions to solve the Seemingly Africans-Nigeria perennial problems? It is by having the listening ear and the lust to be imitating the Western World's *modus operandi* and Objective Norms. The importance of curbing and abating, ignorance and naivety, illusions, mayhems and wild temperament for the nation's youths for the sole reason of their welfare: motivational formation and the right to Education for everybody.

Knowing and clamoring for the renaissance, knowing and realizing myriads of African problems to avoid strictly those systems which always draws us back stuntedly for progressive developments is a necessity.

Be that as it may, man remains an ethico-moral being of the creator; an average-Africa- Nigerian persons, should have the basic education, objective reasoning to live in our society. This is because, an ideal man or person need not only moral virtue to survive and mature but should equally acquaint oneself intellectually.The understanding for togetherness regarding the Pan-African Way to a better future comes to the fore.

This is the sole purpose the Africans need for a' 'Political Messiah"and Ideal Philosopher Kings to lead Africans to the promised Land of lasting peace, authentic existence promotion of negritude. So the re-Thinking of the status quo par excellence and the advice of the International Community to come out of our shackles of mundane policies vis-à-vis conscience and "inferiority" of Third World Countries Palaver for neo-welfarism, concept of New Africa Liberalism will evermore be hearken to. Nigeria being one of the most populous country and rich nation would work harder all for the needed progressive developments and to be an exemplary to other African nations. On this terrain therefore, the leading figures of Modern Africa continents concerning the reviewing of Pan-Africanism, African Union (AU), Our African Theorists, both their dead and living, Great Patriots should be cherished coupled with their salient roles they played, to mention but a few here:

a) Nnamdi Azikiwe (Zik of Africa), Nigeria, 1904-1996-on neo-welfarism and justice.
b) Julius Nyerere of Tanzania, 1922-1999- on Ujamaa, (neighborhood), and common good for mutual existence.
c) Kwame Nkrumah of Ghana, 1909-1972-on Pan-Africanism and Promotion of Negritude.
d) Leopold Senghor of Senegal, 1906-2001-on Nationhood and Socialism.
e) Nelson Mandela of South Africa, 1918-2013-on Apartheid and Human Rights.
f) Wole Sonyinka of Nigeria, 1934- (Litr.Noble Intertnl.Price Laureate Winner!), also harped more on the right of educational right and justice for all. What the nation needs urgently or the way out is an active operative remedy. No matter the greatness or wretchedness of the citizens, our life ambition and expectations, dynamism and the true consciousness are also good material for a viable, renewed Nigeria and Nigerians.

The UNO and NATO should watch constantly and regularly the activities of the Boko Haram from the Islamic States Insurgents the Fulani Herdsmen-Nomads, in Nigeria and any other African nations or elsewhere in the world having such problems of Islamic-Muslim Terrorisms.

Secondly, all the rights provided for were so limited by provisions that they were made nugatory for all practical purposes. For example, while the constitution guaranteed the right to "dignity of the human person," and "freedom from tortures, inhuman or degrading treatments;" it exempted them from these guarantees any punishment that was lawful and customary in any part of the country since November 1.1959.[253]

These identified problems and observations mean that dynamism and meaningful adjustment of situations could make ends meet the watch-word for good adaptation of the individual personality in the State.

The Nigeria nation after a torrid years of uncertainty, dilemma, confusion of endless, Islamic State Terror-Networks; Al Qaeda terror Networks, Boko Haram, Taliban, the abuse of human life and human life and human rights and injustice and high rate of corruption, backwardness is urgent need to wake-up now from our long-sleep hours for the peak for renaissance to commence a new African, Nigeria populace.

The workability of the nation's constitution is also noteworthy in order to eschew certain misnomers in the government administrative circles. Nonetheless, the Nigeria nation cannot but continue to gradually, carefully and wisely muster courage for more advancements and progressions.

Every crisis has a history no matter the eventualities and happenstances; and also let us not repeat our past mistakes in the present epoch.

What our country needs urgently or the way out as a pro-active operative remedy to put the nation expectantly superbly organised for the better growth for peaceful, harmonious and progressively moving ahead for stability and for a true dynamism.

The nation should therefore, acknowledge strongly that the rule of law. Which guarantees a good degrees of objectivity in dispensing justice, assurance of Human Rights, defending of life and human freedom, promotion of peaceful atmosphere and prosperity in the society should always be highly cherished and upheld.

---

[253] Cf. A.T. Aguda., The Judiciary and the System of Laws in Nigeria Since Independence. The First 25 Years, Vol. 4. Ibadan- Nigeria 1989, p. 117.

Chapter Six: Evaluation and Conclusion

6.1

Evaluation

For the African-Nigerian nation to partake in the human flourishing and universal justice, all hands should be on deck for this to come to reality. Where lies the problems and the nation's setbacks? It is the abuse of trust of the nation, the corrupt political process which erodes the very condition of the nation's being. From all we have said so far, Nigeria needs a re-think of their cultural-political conflicting situational problems. The strength of any progressive nation like Nigeria is the strong will of its inhabitants to live more godly, dedicated and focused; and to always conscious of her problems and strives daily on how to abate it. There is every hope that Nigeria nation will still blossom and be great again. There is the need for all the citizens to value democracy and advocate the dignity of peoples as manifested both in the right to choose their leaders painlessly and in peaceful conditions.

Man as a human person should be human enough in acceptance of another personality and the test of the truth which lies in nurturing the environment and justifying the condition of things and their livelihood. This means that we need in this nation a holistic understanding of how the living conditions of persons are to be shaped through the interplay of various institutional regimes, which influences one another and intermingle in their effects.

A reasonable cooperation is very important in a multi-cultural ethnic State like Nigeria. The neglect of justice and peoples right has been a thorn in the flesh and a can-worm in our flesh and this has eaten deep into the fabric of our society. The freedom of right and human acts then comes into play.

We did also look into the aspect of Nigerian human problems and conflicts on the ground as an exchange or inter-play of the expected purposeful peace to reign.

The queer or undue mentality of an individual or groups undercuts any systematic co-relation between categories of Human Rights and ways of fulfilling them. The Nigerian problem is based more on the Nigeria people's consciences; many people never listen to what their consciences are saying to their heart. Many people seem to be having dead consciences and might have allowed even their conscientious heart to grow mucous or fungi.

Modern Cognitive Psychologist opined that treating people maliciously and unjustly like a beast might lead them to become beast in the process and this buttresses the words of Aristotle's Nichomean Ethics we treated in the fore-going chapters above that the standard of behavior should always be based on the one principle of rights and wrong justifiably.

The interdependence are of great significance, and this nonetheless is initially clarified in this work; and should not be overlooked at either by any moral philosopher, social scientist or by a politician and other educated elites who have great lust in the development of the nation as it should be.

On this regard, R.Pogge said that we tend to assess a country's domestic institutional level, and also the policies of its rulers, by reference to how they treat its citizens."[254]

The congregation for the doctrine of faith equally in *"Introductio Libertatis Conscientia"* on the Christian freedom and liberation remarked

that the Church will never be tired of protecting human right and fighting injustice but will ever more insist on the dignity of all persons, against all slavery, exploitations, and manipulations perpetrated to the harm of people, not only into the field of politics and enormous economics results, but also in the cultural ideological fields.[255]

The most fundamental problems facing this country are lawlessness, corruption, the frequent political crisis, ethnic, cultural differences, security and power tussles which need to be resolved to give room for peace and stability in the country. Since first of October, Nigeria has the largest size on the West Coast of Africa with now over 165 million people according to the (NPCS), the National Population Commission Statistics. Since independent many of our national self-respect is still lacking. Independence is not an end in itself, but only a means for the country's own survival and

---

254 T. Pogge., World Poverty and Human Rights, On Human Flooring and Universal Justice, p. 33.

255 Cf. AAS 79, 1987, p. 586.

self-awareness; to find our feet and ensure our full part in world affairs for a better livelihood. Countries, where politics have worked, are those with conscientious and strategies for achieving what they need.

As a developing country, the president and those in the corridor of power at the time of his reign should familiarize themselves within their mandates and responsibilities, including strategy in dynamic world of modern diplomacy.

Under the present circumstances and atmospheric condition of things in the country, wise and mature citizen of the nation are to be stronger in their resistance to any dictatorship and violation of fundamental human rights; thus, abruptly ignore such a personal or provoking situation.

Nevertheless, the dialogue and freedom of expression and sincerity of purpose should also be constantly maintained.

We have the Almighty living God, the creator, there is always the need to think deep on personal consciences and sins we commit; more of a necessity are also the prayers of the religious leaders in the country to tackle inter-religious conflicts because conflicts might lead not only the African countries to untold heavy problems and dangers but any country to more disaster that might be difficult to overcome for long time.

It is also pertinent to note that good leadership goes with love and sincere humble service. The efficient and effective service in this constant changing world of ours is a sine-qua-non; the language of love covers all areas of dissension, ethnicity and boundary dispute. What spans deep divides and cultural conflicts in modern African multi-cultural nations and Nigeria regions boarders more on lawlessness, disunity, lack of true love, corruption, egoism and selfishness and lack of creativity.

When all these abnormalities we have seen and enumerated so far are taken into consideration and put under check, the issue of human rights and human dignity and righteous living and ipso facto the better growth of a nation will be a thing of reality.

6.2

CONCLUSION

To pacify the situational anomaly in the country, both the ruler and ruled should be conscientious, recognize the common humanity, the rights of the citizenry and to see to the fact, that every human being-the rich and poor as well as the weak and strong deserve a peaceful happy existence.

Nigeria is not a syndicate of moral cowardice but stands as a giant colossus of morality. What spans deep divides and cultural conflicts in modern African, Nigeria is more of self-infliction. Though African continent or third-world countries are not a syndicate of moral cowardice but remain the giant colossus of morality. In adequacy of creativity and attitudinal behaviorism contributes its quota in the African problems.

The life of ordinary Nigeria counts also less in the economic concerns and this could be upgraded by the government of the day. What are we to do under this hemisphere? Justice, human rights, equity, merit, fair-play should be the greatest priority and focus of any progressing nation, state or community as the fundaments leading man objectively to the protection of basic rights.

The equivocal signification of righteousness, ideal life, justification of one's action ought to be maintained because regarding the principles of justice, what is unjust is unequal!

What is equal is universally accepted even without the support of any logic or an argument. We should acknowledge the fact that the policies that might have performed economic miracles or fruitful successes in other societies have continued to fail and to work actively in Nigeria, an example is SAP (Structural Adjustment Programme), and other reforms. Justice and fairness could be well practiced in different states or regions in Nigeria according to Thomas Aquinas doctrine of justice and human rights. Restoring Human Rights in Nigeria today has channelled its attention towards exploring, exposing, unravelling, highlighting, digging out as well as proffering panacea out of this doleful and crippling menace in this contraption nation.

The dream is to have a promising pearl packed with enormous sensational treasures for our moral, social, intellectual and legal edification. The Church and society today are in a busy struggle for a reasonable integral Human Rights and the issue of Justice not only in Nigeria-Africa continent but the whole world generally. On the ground of Human consideration is ever worth-while because as earlier explained, mercy compliments justice.

The nation, however, could come-up to higher magnitude of excellence when moral, God-fearing politicians and the educated public realizes and accept the challenges cum the core criterion facing them plus having the lust to achieve once again or further more, the name wonderful great Nigerian nation. However, it can be more profitable, that any morally dubious and Godless personality dare not rule any nation for such an individual will not be able to handle the affairs of the nation properly. Nigerians and any other African country should be careful and selective in choosing any of their leaders and cabinet members needed to be in the helm of affairs in the country. Motivation wise, Nigeria as a multi-religious country needs a steady harmonisation for unity, more innovations, and survival.

The nation should remain rightfully consistent and steadfast in their call for a civilian and democratic government in the African continent.

Above all the correct applications of the law as opposed to the arbitrariness is a thing of importance.

It will be honorable and praiseworthy if the United Nations, UN, Amnesty International, Human Rights Watch, the US government, NATO, European Union, EU, and African Union, AU, among others, as well as men and women of good conscience around the world, should make more efforts concerning the African continents governments and her security agencies to think more on how to stop the mysterious death that often happen in some countries, regarding terrorism in any form, be it from any body or the Islamic-Muslim groups that is spread every where in various nations for example, Al Qaeda, Taliban-Jihads, Boko Haram, Salafists groups etc, and to take the issue of conflicts resolution in various countries as their prime agenda.

It is the impartial resolution of dispute arising from conflicting claims and is very closely linked with morality which is the standard of behavior based on the principle of right and wrong. Equally, it cannot but has its connotation on the idea of fairness, equity, tolerance and accommodation.

Good government leads by example.The Agenda of Inter-Religious Dialogue is the intensive bid to promote 'love and brotherhood' among the different religion in the country. Religion and society peace pact are evermore necessary. To be dedicated, patriotic and honest in rendering good services is never without sacrifices and sufferings. It is hoped and expected that waste and prodigality should be outlawed.

Frugal style of life is sometimes lived in our yet developing country. Honesty is to be practiced with public probity, and above all, dedication and public accountability should always be welcomed. A good and honest foresighted man, who will treat the people right, will be loved, cherished and honored. Only good leadership could be a noble heritage of good government for its successor and for the maintenance of a stable administration in the State.

Looking for the way forward is the most urgent necessity amidst orgies of circles of terrorisms, violent bloodbath, killings, kidnappings, seemingly endless radical Muslim-Boko Haram-Terror-Networks cum the recent Fulani marauding herdsmen bringing in various States like Agatu town in Benue State, Ukpabi-Nimbo town in Enugu State, February and May 2016, etc, the homicide escalation with their Cattle prowlers (nomads) urging the whole nation to "Cry-Wolf." This very scenario needs a serious immediate affirmative action as these problems do affect heavily the nation's developmental growth and progression and could lead to ethnic warfare.

The focus then is to minimize general hardships or difficult livelihood, economic diplomacy should among other things be the top priority coupled with promotion of democracy, the rule of law and stability of the government not only in Nigeria but also in Africa as a whole to imitate other developed nations of the world. This will no doubt enhance commitment to professional excellence. It should be the intention of the government in power to inject vigor and dynamism to the nation's foreign policy.

Finally, the best option for the Nigerian populace is to be foresighted and be looking ahead in order to come up to the excellent expected level like other developed nations in the world. The future indeed, rests largely on the continuing vigilance of Nigeria's civil society to correct any negative malaise, e.g the issue if early child marriage, an old man of 25, 50 and 57 years marrying a young girl of 9, 10, 11 and 13 years of age should stop, no matter the unreasonable and unhealthy personal reasons or any religious irrational crazy excuses. Allah means God and he wants that holy and good things should be done well to his glory and good of mankind, moral-sanity, righteously and human historicity.

Equally the problem of child's prostitution, drug addiction and gangsterism should be constantly looked into by the government of the day and be stopped abruptly.

With the sure return to civilian rule, it could still be possible for a great majority to entertain much hope in their own country. Actually, what to do about the several lasting problems for urgent attention like: the endemic radical and pandemic harvoc of the Islamic-Muslim Taliban, Boko Haram (ISIS)Terror-Neworks; of which almost three thousand innocents people have died since 2009 as kicked-off by Nigeria Muslims; and since then ensued, the bombings and damages, the Kidnapped and its mysterious disappearance in Sambisa Forest the over 290 Chibok Girls at night in the Secondary School dormitory in Chibok town of Borno State caused by Boko Haram from Islamic States Insurgents the Fulani Herdsmen-Normads, the Niger Delta Avengers Militants reacting against the President Buhari's type of government, the Unstoppable Radio-Biafra-Daily News seeking for Biafra freedom and independence and acting as guard-fly hot critique-agent against the past and present government failings and corruption saga cum the Fight for the Freedom of Biafra by the members of the IPOB, (Indigenous People of Biafra) and MASSOB (Mass Actualization for the Sovereign State of Biafra), etc, etc. Equally, sequel to the array of unguided contempt and constant ridicule of the rule of law by the present government (executive arm), at all levels of the government, therefore, much credence should be given to the resilience to the country's judiciary under certain dispensations. Lawyers should dispense justice with tactical intelligence, fairness, spirit of dynamism and human face. What is majorly needed among other things is the political will to place a greater accent on the dignity of human person in Africa-Nigerian nation, as well as respect for citizenship rights. Justice and good administration and neglect of human dignity and violation of Human Rights and freedom are what the Nigerian government should always watch out to correct.

This means that both the ruler and the ruled should rededicate themselves to a better task and a hard working spirit that is aimed more seriously at nations building and in all truism with concrete actions, justice, righteousness and mutual harmony for the progression of the country. Actually, there should be no excuse for any waste of time, and life of idleness.

The test of humility and human patience is a necessity with the intention of bringing peace or the goal of creating peaceful and happy environment for the common good of one another.

It is also praise-worthy that the Federal Government intensifies the assessment of their efforts and high-level of collaboration between Nigeria and development partners, the World Bank, EU-European Union and the UN-United Nations which aimed at supporting the government in its short, medium and long-term efforts towards building and sustainable recovery in the North East. There should be time to impose sanctions on erring nations whenever necessary and might help to avoid repetition of their failures and mistakes. As mentioned earlier in the foregoing Chapters the International Security Council, Federal Security Watch and Agents; and other detectives should also quietly often control and monitor what is going on in various Mosques on Fridays or daily-hours prayers sections- (*Wudhu and Salat al Zuhr*) from Imams, Islamic theologians and Psychologists. They ought to and should be preaching more all about that a peace nations develops more greatly and lives more happily because we belong to God and our lives belong to God who alone has right to end our existence in this earth. There should be an urgent need to improve Human Rights records. The saving and protecting one's and another's life in every place is for all to adopt this most important urgent maxim of *Live and Let Others Live in peace!* What is neutrally and objectively meant here is all about wordings and expressions used in Mosques and also in Churches on Sundays; and in Conferences or any gatherings, concerning utterances from the type of preachings, doctrine or indoctrination the Imams in and Priests in Christian Churches deliver to from their pulpits to their congregations or audiences on daily, weekly and monthly or yearly bases.

Above all the fundamental rights of every man, justice, and meritocracy, egalitarianism and equity; fair-play and should always neutrally have a human face to play the key role in human nature with its existentialisms for all and sundry in our today's transient and ephemeral earthly hemisphere. The African continent-nations generally constant efforts to imbibe and practice the moral excellence of virtues are the watch word for their expectancy and achievement of an ideal society.

Bibliography

References (From Lexicons, Encyclopaedia, Directories and Dictionaries)

Aquinas, T., Summa Theologica, Ia- Iiae Art 90. trans.by Fathers of Dominican Province, Sullivan Daniel, J., and W. Benton English Encyclopaedia, Britanica, Chicago 1952.

Schwarz C., / G. Davison et al., Chambers 20th Century, Dictionary, New Edition, Clay Ltd,. London Press, England 1993.

Code of Canon Law (CIC), Latin, English ed. Trans. By CLSA, Libreria Edittrice – Vatican City 1985.

Müller. J., Is There Still a Terrorist Threat? Real Politic and Terrorism Webster new World dicationary- Second Edition en//con// wwwhtp. London 2004 .

Oszmanczyk. E. J., Encyclopaedia of the United Nations and International Agreements, Philadelphia/London 1985.

Runes, D. D., Dictionary of Philosophy, New Jersey 1981.

The New Jerusalem Bible (NJB), Darton Longman and Todd., Verbum Bibel Kinshasa 1985.

The Penguim Dictionary of Sociology, Abercrombien, et al., London 1974.

Vatican Council II, Pastoral Constitution on the Church in the Modern World., Guadium et Spes, nr. 25, Dec. 7th, London 1965.

Websters Encyclopaediae, Unabridged Dictionary of the English Language, (ed.)1989.

Other Works (All Sources in the Chronological Order)

Abba, J.B.C., The Contemporary Nigeria, Our Fate, Glories, Woes and Prospects, Independent Series Vol. 1. Enugu, Nigeria 1997.

Aduba , N., The impact of Poverty in the Realisation of Fundamental Human Rights in Nigeria, Jounal of Human Rights Law and Practice, Vol. 3, Nos. 1,2, 3, December 1993.

Anyadike, O. O., "The Barrister" a Journal of the Law Student (Lawsa), U.N.N, Enugu Nigeria 1988.

Agbakoba, O.,/ IBE, S., Travesty of Justice, The Human Rights Law Services, An Advocacy Manual Against the Holding Charge, Lagos 2004.

Akehurst, M., A Modern Introduction to International Law, London, 1971.

AlanL, W., What does it Mean to be Human? A New Interpretation of Freedom in World History, New York 2001.

Alice, H. H., Human Dignity, New York 1979.

Arendt, H., The Human Condition, 2nd (ed.) Chicago - London 1998.

Argyle, M., / HENDDERSON, M., The Anatomy of Relationships, Penguim, Harmondsworths 1985.

Aristotle, Ethics, Great Britain 1976.

Aristotle., Politics, Great Britain 1981.

Araujo, R. J., "Justice as Right Relationship: a Philosophical and Theological Reflection on Affirmative Action" , in *Pepperdine Law* Review, 448-450, 474-476, London 2000.

Azinge Epiphany., The Concept of amnesty and Its Place in Human Rights Discourse 3, Vanguard News Paper Oct. 2013 p. 39, and the UN Human Rights Review, Nigeria has Examplary Record, Innocent Anaba says the Federal Government.

Barber B., Strong Democracy: Participatory Politics for new Age. Berkel: University Press, California 1984

Bardo, F. (ed), Universal Declaration of Human Rights, United Nations, New York 2009.

Brain, B, Theories of Justice , Los Angeles 1989.

Brain, B, Justice as Impartiality, Oxford 1995.

Bayertz, K., Sanity of Life amd Human Dignity, Dortrecht, Deutschland 1996.

Bortner, M. A., Deliquency. An Age of Crisis, New York 1988.

Berm, K. G., Dignity and Human Rights, Schoten, Deutschland 2002.

Bourke, U. J., Ethics, A Text Book in Moral Philosophy, New York 1966.

Clartke, P.B., West Afrika and Islam, London, 1982.

Dowrick, F. E., Human Rights, Problems, Perspective and Texts: Saxon House United Kingdom 1979.

Civil Liberties Organisation, Annual Reports on Human Rigths in Nigeria, Lagos 1993.

Conklin, A., Colonialism and Human Rights, A Contradiction in Terms? The Case of France and West Africa, 1895-1914, in The American Historical Review 103, 2, New York 1998.

Development and Peace. Basic Princilples and Orientations 1982.

Donnelly, J., Cultural Relativism and Universal Human Rights in Theory and Practice, London 1989.

Extracts From the Constitution of the Federal Republic of Nigeria, in: C., (ed.), Africa Contemporary Record: Annual Survey and Documents 1979-1980, New York, London 1981, C60/C75.

Eyo, I. E., Understanding the Psychology of Ethnicity and Prejudice, Nsukka, Nigeria 2003.

Eze, O. C., Society and the Rule of Law (ed.), Nigeria 1987.

Eze, O., Human Rights in Africa, Lagos 1984.

Ikenga-Metuh, E., Comparative Studies of African Traditional Religions, Onitsha, Nigeria 1987.

Federal Republic of Nigeria, (1999), The Constitution of theFederal Republic of Nigeria 1999, Lagos, Federal Government Press.

Feldman, D.I., et al. (eds.), International Law, Mosco 1990.

Fagothey, A., Right and Reason: Ethics in Theory and Practice, Ohio 1989.

Flannery, OP., Vatican II Council, Concillia and Post Concillia Documents, Dublin 1975.

Franz, W., Die Religionen und die Meschenrechte, Muenchen, 2000.

Fromm, E., the Anatomy of Human Destructiveness, New York 1974.

Füller, L., Morality and Law, cited in More Essays in Legal Philosophy, New York 1971.

Gardner, J.P., Human Rights as general Norms and a States Rights to Opt Out, London 1997.

Godwin, R. E.,/PETIT, P., (ed.), Contemporary Political Philosophy, An Antology, London 1977.

Hilary, H., Rights of the Religious in the Church in The Nigerian Journal of Theology, Vol. 8 No. 1, Enugu 2003.

Harold, P., Nobel Lecture, Art, Truth and Politics, Real Politic und Terrorisms, Germany 2001.

Higgins, J., Man as Man, Mary Land, USA 1948.

Hinsch, W.,/Jansssen, D., Menschenrechte militärisch schützen; ein Plädoyer für humanitäre Interventionen, München 2006.

Hodgson, D., Human Rights to education, Alderschot, Deutschland 1998.

Hobes, T. Leviatian (ed.), Macpherson, C. B., England 1978.

Hobes, T., Body, Man and Citizen, New York 1972.

Howar, R., Human Rights in Common Wealth Africa, New Jersey 1986.

Humana, C., World Human Rights Guide , 3rd Edition, New York 1992.

Ibhawoh. B., Human Rights fand Cultural Relativism: Reconsidering the Africanist Discourse, Netherlands Quarterly of Human Rights 19, 1, Canada 2001.

Ibhawoh, B., Human Rights fand Cultural Relativism: Reconsidering the Africanist Discourse, Netherlands Quarterly of Human Rights 19, 1, Canada 2001.

Ibhawoh, B., Imperialism and Human Rights, Colonial Discourse of Rights and Liberties in African History, Canada 2007.

Ike, O. F., / EDOZIEN N. N., Understanding Africa, Traditional Legal Reasoning Jurisprudence and justice in Igboland, As Basis for Culturally Rooted and Sustainable Development, Enugu Nigeria, 2001.

Igwe. O., Politics and Globe Dictionary, Enugu, Nigeria, 2002.

Iwe, M.S .S., Christianity Culture and Moral, Portharcourt, Nigeria 1979.

John XXIII., "Peace on Earth" (Pacem in Terris), in the Great Encyclical, New York 1963.

John Paul II; On the Hundreth Anniversary of Rerum Novarum (Centesimus Annus), Liebreria Editrice Vaticana 1991.

John Paul II, On Social Concern (Sollicitudo Rei Socialis), in The Encyclicals of John John II Our Sunday Visitor, Inc. Huntington, Indiana 1996

Justice, Peace and Human Development, A priority for the Church in Nigeria Lagos 1999.

Justice Indifference of Humanity; Restoring Human Rights in Nigeria Today 11th Edition, Onitsha, Nigeria, 2012.

Human Rights, A Compilation of the International Instruments (United Nations Publication, Sales No. E.78. XIV. 2).

Human Rights Organisations in Nigeria: An Assessment of Nigeria human Rights Ngo Community. Copenhagen: the Danish Centre for Human Rights-Evaluation and Reviews of Partnership Programmes Series, Lagos 2001.

Human Rights (Civil, Social, Economic and Cultural): Their Place and Protection in the Future Political Order- the Nigerian Bar Journal, Vol. 21, No.3, Lagos 1986.

Jhiroux, J. P., Ethics-Theory and Practice, California 1977.

Kenya, A., On Aquinas, New York 1980.

Kenny, J., The Catholic Church in Tropical Africa, 1945-1850, Ibadan, Nigeria, 1983.

Kolm, S.C., Modern Theories on Justice, New York 1997.

Kretmer, D., The Concept of Human Dignity and Human Rights Discourse, the Hague 2002.

Leo XIII., On the Condition of the working Class (Rerum Novarum), St. Pauls London 1942.

Mac Donald, M., "atural Rights" in J. Waldron., (ed), Theories of Rights, London 1984

Madiebo, A., The Nigerian Revolution and the Civil War. Forth Dimension Enugu, Nigeria 1980.

Maier, K., This House has fallen: Nigeria in Crisis, Penguin, London, 2000.

Daniel Jordan Smith, A Culture of Corruption: Everyday Deception and Popular Discontent in Nigeria, Princeton University Press, Oxford, 2007.

Maritain, J., The Rights of Man and Natural Law, London 1959.

Maritain, J., The Rights of Man, London 1982.

Marcci, C., (ed.), Serving the Human Family; the Holy See at the Major United Nations Conferences', Path to Peace Foundation, New York 1997.

May, R., / NORTON, W., Power and Innocence, A Searching for the Sources of Violence, New York 1972.

Maurus, J., It is Hukan Relation that Counts, Better Yourself Books Bombay 1997.

Manda, P. Development and Human Rights: The Role of International Law and Organisation, London 1985.

Marx. K., The Marx- Engels Reader, New York: W.W. Norton, 1978.

MC Dermott, N., Opening Address to the International Conference on Human Rights Education in Rural Environment, Lagos-Nigeria 1985.
Mofokeng, T., The Cross in the Search for True Humanity: Theological Challenges Facing the South Africa Church, Voices from the Third World XII, (1, London 1989.
Moltmann, J., On Human Dignity, London 1984.
Niebuhr, M., Moral Man and Immoral Society, London 1963.
Novak, M., Liberty and Social Justice, Rescuig a Virtue, Notre Dame 1993.
Obi, L., The in Human Abuses, in "African Concord Magazine" Vol. 2 nr. 38 Ikeja, Nigeria 1988.
Obuna, E., The Root of Violence, A Moral Evaluation of the Nigerian Biafra War, Rome 1985.
Ogbu: O. N., Human Rights Law and Practice in Nigeria: An Introduction CIDJAP, Enugu 1999.
Ogilvy, J. A., Self and World, Chicago 1973.
Okechukwu, S.N., The Right*to Life* and the Right to Live. Ethics of International Solidarity. Peter Lang Publisher, Frankfurt 1990.
Omoroegbe, J. I., A philosophical Look At Religion, Lagos 1992.
Pieper, J., Justice, Trans., by Lynych, E. L., New York 1955.
Pescke, C. H., Christian Ethics, Vol. I. Doublin 1979.
Peters, D, "On Human Rights in Economic, Social and Cultural Rights Context and the Judiciary in Nigeria" Journal of Economic, Social and Cultural Rights, vol. 1 No. 5, Enugu 2002
Pogge, T., World Poverty and Human Rights, Cambridge, London 2005.
National Association of Social Workers, (NASW Code of Ethics. Washington, D.C. NASW Press, 1996.
Norwitz, J. H., (ed.), Pirate, Terorrists and Warlords, Armed Groups and the Law, Article by Craig H. Allen, USA 2009.
Nherere, P., The Philosophical, Moral and Historical Basis of Human Rights in (1997) Human Rights Theories and Practices: Summaries of lectures delivered at the African Human Rights Camp Zimbabwe 1996.
Obi, L., The Human Abuses, in "African Concord Magazine" Vol. 2, nr. 38 Ikeja -Lagos Nigeria 1988.

PERIODICALS/REVIEW/ARTICLES, REPORTS/ JOURNALS AND MULTIMEDIA DOCUMENTS, WEBSITES AND ENCYCLICALS

Pontifical Commission "Justitia et Pax" The Church and Racism: Towards a More Fraternality Vatican City 1988.

Pontifical Council "'Cor Unum, World Hunger, A Challenge For All: Development in Solidarity, Nairobi 1996.

Rawls, J., /Fremans, S (ed.), Collected Papers, on Justice and Reciprocity, Justice as Fairness, Distributive Justice and Fairness to Goodness, Cambridge London, 1999.

Rawls, J., Justice as Fairness, in Bioethics, Refugees-Magazine on Human Rights Declaration, England 1989.

Rawls, J., Theory of Justice, London 1988.

Rawls, J., A Theory of Justice , (rev.ed.), Oxford 1999.

Romelt, J., Menschenwürde und Freiheit; um die Erklaerung der Menschenrechte: Ein Symposium, Zurich 2006.

Rousseau, J., The Social Contract, (ed.), by Lester, G., New York 1977.

Reichert, E., Social Work and Human Rights, Foundation for Policy and Practice, New York 2003.

Rousseau, J. J., Discourse on Inequality Among men (ed.), by Crocker, L. G., Washington 1971.

Ryde, A., Benin and the Europeans: 1485-1897, London,1977.

Sabine; G.H., A History of Political Theory, 4th (ed.) Illinois 1973.

Sandel, M., Justice: What is the Right Thing to Do? London 2009

Siehart, P., The International Law of Human Rights, London 1997.

Scruton, R., A Dictionary of Political Thoughts, New York 1982.

Shivji, JI. I., The Concept of Human Rights in Africa, Council for the Development of Economic and Social Research in Africa-Codesria London 1989.

Social Work Speaks, National Association of Social Workers policy Statements , 2000-2003. 5th ed. Washington, D.C. – NASW Press 2000.

Schweidler Walter., Die Angst und die Kehre. Zur strukturellen Verbindung Heidergers mit Kierkegaard, in Zeitschschriuft für Philosophische Forschung 42 (2), Freiburg/ München, Germany, 1988.

Report of Committee of Experts on Human Rights to Committee of Ministers, (Council of Europe, DH-73. Adopted on 9 Nov., 1973.

St.Augustine., The City of God, Henry Bettenson, trans., New York: Penguin Books, USA 1986.

T,N. Tamuno., "'Traditional Methods of Crime Detection and Control,"' in Nigeria, Orita: Ibadan Journal of Religious Studies XXVI, nos1, Lagos 1994.

The Declaration of the Rights of Man and the Citizen in: Cahn, S.M., (ed.), Classics of Modern Political Theory, New York, Oxford 1997.

United Nations Charter and Universal Declaration of Human Rights (U.N.O.), Department of Public Information: Preamble, Chap.VII, Actions with respect to the threats to peace, breaches of Peace and acts of agression, Art. 1- 52. Research Approaches, New York 2006.

United Nations Body of Principles: For the Protection of all Persons under any Form of Detention or Imprisonment. UN Document A/43/49 1988.

United Nations on Human Rights. (Collection of International Instruments) New York 1988.

United Nations Center for Human Rights: Mannuals on Human Rights Reporting United Nations Publ. New York 1991.

United Nations Organisation on Human Rights: Questions and Answers, United Nations Departments of Public Information, New York 1988.

United State, Department Web Site: http://www// gpv/s/ et/r/s/ rpt/fto/ 2001/ 528.htm. Peter Fischer, International Terrorism and Mental Health"Exeter University, Journal of International Violence, Vol. 23, No. 42008 SAGE Publication, U.S 2001.

Utomi. P., Boko Haram, "'I saw it Coming,"' Sun Newspaper, Nov. 13, 2011, p. 2 "'Senators Demand OBJ Trial, "'Sun, Dec. 1. 2011

Van der Ven, J. A., Dreyer, S. J., et al, Is There a God of Human Rights? The Complex Relationship between Human Rights and Religion: A South African Case, Boston 2004.

Vanier, J., Our Journey Home, Rediscovery A Common Humanity beyond Our Differences, trans. By M. Parham London 1997.

Vincent, R.J., Human Rights and International Relation, New York, USA 1986.

Vossentkuhl, W., Die Möglichkeit des Guten Ethik im 21 Jahrhundert München 2006.

Walzer, M., (ed.), Towards a Global Civil Society, Britain 1995.
Wengert, T.J., Human Freedom, Christian Righteousness, New York 1988.
William, J., Education and Good Life , New York 1991.
Wronka, J., Human Rights and Social Policy in the 21st Century- A History of the Idea of Human Rights and Comparison of the United- Nations Universal Declaration of Human Rights with United States Federal and State Constitution. Rev. ed. Lanham, Md., America, 1998.
Weber, L. J., "Common Good" in The Modern Catholic Encyclopedia Collegeville, Minnesota 1994.
Wellman, C., "A New Conception of Human Rights" in Kamenka, E & Tay, A. E., (ed.), Human Rights ... England 1978.
Young, H. J., God and Human Freedom, Trends , London 1983.
http://www.boston.com/news/nation/articles/2008/04/25/bringing_iraqis_to_thetable, April 2008.
http://www.uffl.org/volii (2000).
http://www.ask.if.common.good./com/usk.(2011).
Sun Newspaper March 7, 2014.
Sun Newspaper March 15,2014.
Vanguard Newspaper, March 10, 2014.
Vanguard Newspaper, March 15, 2016.
Sun Newspaper April 19, 2016.
Sun Newspaper September 08, 2016.
Numbers and Percentage of Muslims in African Countries ... https://muslimsinafrica.wordpress.com/numbers-and...
Boko Haram: Cameroonian authorities shut mosques ... Who are Nigeria's Boko Haram Islamist group?
24.11.2016 – *Boko Haram* promotes a version of *Islam* which makes it "haram", ... freed in October *2016* following talks involving the militants, the *Nigerian* ...
www.cnn.com/2014/06/09/world/boko-haram-fast-facts/; www.bbc.co.uk/news/world-africa-13809501
Viewing Fast Facts on *Boko Haram* to get information on the militant *Islamic* group based in *Nigeria*, whose purpose is to institute Sharia, or *Islamic* law. ... *Boko Haram Fast Facts. CNN Library. Updated 1:28 PM ET*, Mon October 31, *2016* ...
Nigeria: Boko Haram , Borno State – Genocide Watch.

genocidewatch.net/category/updates/byregion/africa/ … /nigeria/

Nigeria-One of the girls kidnapped by *Boko Haram* more than two … - Here's a look at *Boko Haram*, a militant *Islamic* group working out of *Nigeria*, … *Nigerian* Girl Abducted by *Boko Haram* from Chibok Girls Is Found … 18 May, *2016* LAGOS, www.cnn.com/2014/06/09/world/boko-haram-/

www.premiumtimesng.com/.../187365-boko-haram... *Boko Haram* terrorists storm village in Cameroon, kill 8October 22, 2015 … *Muslims* constitute about 20 *percent* of Cameroon's total *population* of 20.5 … . Before Imam Buhari's *100* day honeymoon is over you are likely to take …

Islamic Terrorism: Why There Is None in Japan *chersonand-molschky.com/ … /islamic-terrorism-japan …*

Gumi: Boko Haram is 100% Muslim problem |The Sun News *sunnewsonline.com/gumi-boko-haram-is-100-musli …*

Most dislike ISIS in Muslim countries |Pew Research Center *www.pewresearch.org/ … /in-nations-with-significant …*

http://nymag.com/news/politics/48675/ The Independent Lecture at Trinity College, April 13, 2000.

http://www.independent.co.uk/news/world/europe/independent-lecture-delivered-by-nelson-mandela-719364.html (2000).

About the Book and Author

A scientific work on critical inquiry majorly on the nucleus and whole gamut of the thoughts and scholasticism of Thomas Aquinas classical philosophical synthesis and his insights and quest of his and Christian theology on Justice and Human Rights as a panacea or desired urgent solution to racial justice, abuse of human life and human rights for the Africa Cultural Conflicts Resolution of today. Dr. JoeBarth Abba focused also on the ethico-moral, neo-welfares, socio-anthropological and psychological-systematic dialogue on the cultural-conflicts resolution social teaching of the Church, human rights and righteous living, equity and fairness for the Afro-Nigeria dimensions to understand people's natural inclination and efforts for the peace and happy life. Steady necessity for discursive dialogue for the seemingly endemic Islamic Muslim fundamentalist groups, Talibans, Al-Quaida and Boko Haram insurgents etc; who engages in various styles of killing and bombings; and holding on to the horrible menace of innocent souls.

Extra-Focus on: Reviewed Pan-Africanism seen as epitome of the African Forum and Promotion of Negritude henceforth to avoid any logical fallacy or categorical error for peaceful co-existence. DDr.JoeBarth Abba meant that what spans deep divides and cultural conflicts in modern African, Nigeria is more of self-infliction. The African continent or third-world countries are not a syndicate of moral cowardice but remain the giant colossus of morality.The problems are engrossed on Conflicts of Niger Delta Avengers, Biafra Independence, Lawlessness, Disunity; Terror-Networks, Boko Haram, Al-Quaeda, Talibans, Jihadism, Wars, Racial-Injustice, Corruption, Confusions, Anti-Pro-Life and Human Rights, Poverty, Self-illusions, Backwardness and Egoism. The root-causes call for urgent resolution as it touches under development and backwardness but could stop if Africans should stop repetition of their past mistakes and reflect greatly on the meaning of self-deception to live more godly.

Prof. Dr. Wilhelm Vossenkuhl,
University, Munich, Germany

A type of book we always long to read for peace and joy in any nation, Father DDr. JoeBarth Abba touched many areas amidst orgies of circles of terrorisms, Islamic Insurgents with key solutions for psycho-dialogical ways on cultural ethnic tensions for conflicts resolution.

Gerhard Ludwig Cardinal Müller,
Vatican, Rome

JoeBarth C. Abba, Dr. theol. Dr. phil. (LMU, Munich), Germany, M.A., phil. M.A., theol. B.A., B.phil., B.th. (Rome) Extra: B.A. Journalism and Public Relations (USA), P.D.G. Ed. Dipl. (Nig), Foreign Modern Langs. & Office Admin., the European Scholar hails from Iheaka Town Nsukka in Enugu State, West-Africa, Nigeria; a linguist, talented brainy Catholic Priest of the Archdiocese of Onitsha, Versatile Researcher in Human Development, a Lecturer/Guest Lecturer national and internationally, and a Priest people often looked for as: Youth Counsellor, Spiritual Retreat Preacher, Poet; Author of several books and articles in different disciplines.

Philosophie

Donatella Colantuono
Vernünftig glauben?
Gemeinsamkeit von Religion, Metaphysik und Wissenschaft bei Bernard Bolzano
Bd. 107, 2016, 224 S., 29,90 €, br., ISBN 3-643-50774-7

Laura Böckmann; Andrée Gerland; Malin Elsen; Karin Amos (Hg.)
Per Absurdum
Das Absurde als Lebensentwurf und Denkmodell. 11 Versuche
Bd. 106, 2016, 230 S., 34,90 €, br., ISBN 978-3-643-13461-5

Gerd Pohlenz
Die Relationismusfalle und die verschleppte Weltkultur
Zur Lage der Philosophie, Band II. Mit weiteren Facetten und Übungen zur Theorie zweier polar-komplementärer Weltaspekte und ihren geschichtlichen Kontexten
Bd. 105, 2016, 864 S., 89,90 €, br., ISBN 978-3-643-13440-0

Ulrich van Sutum
Ewig leben ohne Gott
Logik und Physik vs. Bibel und Koran
Bd. 104, 2017, 88 S., 19,90 €, br., ISBN 978-3-643-13343-4

Ursula Weitkamp
Selbst bestimmt leben
Bd. 102, 2014, 144 S., 29,90 €, br., ISBN 978-3-643-12655-9

Inge Künle
Das Selbst und der Andere bei Paul Ricœur und Amartya Sen
Zur Identität des fähigen Menschen
Bd. 101, 2014, 312 S., 34,90 €, br., ISBN 978-3-643-12607-8

Martin Mohrenz
China
Christentum im Aufbruch
Bd. 100, 2014, 96 S., 19,90 €, br., ISBN 978-3-643-50573-6

Alexander Neupert
Staatsfetischismus
Zur Rekonstruktion eines umstrittenen Begriffs
Bd. 99, 2013, 448 S., 29,90 €, br., ISBN 978-3-643-12336-7

Stefan Köchel
Das Gesetz des Realen
Lacan – Merleau-Ponty – Adorno
Bd. 98, 2013, 216 S., 24,90 €, br., ISBN 978-3-643-50508-8

Clemens Janisch
Theorie der fremdverschuldeten Unmündigkeit
Bd. 97, 2013, 136 S., 24,90 €, br., ISBN 978-3-643-50503-3

Giovandomenico Davoli
Heidegger und die Frage nach dem Sinn von Sein: das Dasein und das Nichts
Bd. 96, 2013, 304 S., 29,90 €, br., ISBN 978-3-643-12161-5

Kathrin Flottmann
Zur Chancengleichheit von Kindern auf dem Bildungssektor
Eine vergessene Aufgabe der Philosophie
Bd. 95, 2013, 216 S., 24,90 €, br., ISBN 978-3-643-12156-1

Martin Mohrenz
Konfuzianismus
Philosophie, Ethik, Geschichte und Gegenwart
Bd. 94, 2012, 104 S., 19,90 €, br., ISBN 978-3-643-50420-3

Wolfgang Gärtner
Philosophische Impulse: Recht und Gerechtigkeit von Aristoteles bis Habermas
Eine Einführung in die Ethik der Gerechtigkeit
Bd. 93, 2012, 184 S., 24,90 €, gb., ISBN 978-3-643-11616-1

Leonhard Weiss
Hegels Geschichtsphilosophie und das moderne Europa
Bd. 92, 2012, 192 S., 19,90 €, br., ISBN 978-3-643-50389-3

Walter Szostak
Weltgeschichte, Verantwortung und Selbstsorge
Über den Geist der europäischen Moderne
Bd. 91, 2012, 208 S., 19,90 €, br., ISBN 978-3-643-11569-0

André Kamphaus
Wie wird man, was man ist?
Eine Auseinandersetzung mit Nietzsches Vorstellung von Selbstverwirklichung
Bd. 90, 2012, 208 S., 19,90 €, br., ISBN 978-3-643-11568-3

Thomas Bernhard Seiler
Evolution des Wissens
Band II: Evolution der Begriffe
Bd. 89, 2012, 376 S., 29,90 €, br., ISBN 978-3-643-11377-1

Thomas Bernhard Seiler
Evolution des Wissens
Band I: Evolution der Erkenntnisstrukturen
Bd. 88, 2012, 336 S., 39,90 €, br., ISBN 978-3-643-11376-4

Erika Erber
Achtsamkeit und Intersein
Der Buddhismus bei Thich Nhat Hanh
Bd. 87, 2011, 256 S., 24,90 €, gb., ISBN 978-3-643-50328-2

Domagoj Akrap
Erich Fromm – ein jüdischer Denker
Jüdisches Erbe | Tradition | Religion
Bd. 86, 2011, 272 S., 24,90 €, br., ISBN 978-3-643-50323-7

Hilmar Lorenz
Kants kopernikanische Wende vom Wissen zum Glauben
Systematischer Kommentar zu Vorrede B der Kritik der reinen Vernunft
Bd. 85, 2011, 456 S., 34,90 €, br., ISBN 978-3-643-11298-9

Tina-Louise Eissa
Frage und erkenne
Philosophische Dialoge über Wahrheit, Erkenntnis, Wissen, Weisheit, Objektivität und Glückse(e)ligkeit
Bd. 84, 2011, 312 S., 29,90 €, br., ISBN 978-3-643-11266-8

Brigitte Buchhammer
Feministische Religionsphilosophie
Philosophisch-systematische Grundlagen
Bd. 83, 2011, 400 S., 39,90 €, br., ISBN 978-3-643-50316-9

Martina Schmidhuber
Der Prozess personaler Identitätsbildung und die Rolle von Institutionen
Eine philosophisch-anthropologische Untersuchung
Bd. 82, 2011, 216 S., 19,90 €, br., ISBN 978-3-643-50282-7

Roland Stastny
Erkenntnis und Gabe
Eine experimentelle Philosophie des Zusammenlebens
Bd. 80, 2010, 216 S., 19,90 €, br., ISBN 978-3-643-50171-4

Marie-Luisa Frick
Moralischer Relativismus
Antworten und Aporien relativistischen Denkens in Hinblick auf die weltanschauliche Heterogenität einer globalisierten Welt
Bd. 78, 2010, 320 S., 29,90 €, br., ISBN 978-3-643-50147-9

Horst Heinze
Die psychologische Weltformel
Mysterium und Martyrium der Sprache in der Zeitlosigkeit
Bd. 77, 2010, 392 S., 49,90 €, br., ISBN 978-3-643-10491-5

Ulrike Stammerjohann
Beschreibung, Argumentation, Kontext
Darstellung und Vergleich von Argumentationstheorien
Bd. 76, 2009, 152 S., 19,90 €, br., ISBN 978-3-643-10423-6

Daniel Stolarski
Die Mathematisierung des Geistes
Algebra, Analysis und die Schriftlichkeit mentaler Prozesse bei René Descartes
Bd. 75, 2009, 160 S., 19,90 €, br., ISBN 978-3-8258-1876-0

Marian Nebelin; Andreas Deußer (Hg.) unter Mitarbeit von Katarina Barthel
Was ist Zeit?
Philosophische und geschichtstheoretische Aufsätze
Bd. 74, 2009, 120 S., 19,90 €, br., ISBN 978-3-8258-1874-6

Monja Elisabeth Art
„Liebt einander!“
Die Vereinbarkeit von Homosexualität und christlichem Glauben
Bd. 73, 2008, 200 S., 19,90 €, br., ISBN 978-3-8258-1735-0

Tina-Louise Fischer
Menschen- und Personenwürde
Über die Notwendigkeit eines neuen Würdebegriffs
Bd. 72, 2008, 120 S., 19,90 €, br., ISBN 978-3-8258-1486-1

Philipp Schaufelberger
Emmanuel Lévinas – Philosophie des “ich”
Gravierende Spuren menschlicher Freiheit
Bd. 71, 2008, 272 S., 25,90 €, br., ISBN 978-3-8258-1129-7

Thomas Marti
Anthroposophie – heute noch modern?
Ideen – praktische Arbeitsfelder – Perspektiven. Eine kritische Würdigung
Bd. 70, 2008, 160 S., 19,90 €, br., ISBN 978-3-8258-0724-5

Frank Koren-Wilhelmer
Auf der Spur des Du
Personalität zwischen Immanenz und Transzendenz bei Martin Buber und Kitaro Nishida
Bd. 69, 2007, 184 S., 19,90 €, br., ISBN 978-3-8258-0368-1

Bettina Fröhlich
Die sokratische Frage
Platons *Laches*
Bd. 68, 2007, 280 S., 29,90 €, br., ISBN 978-3-8258-0185-4

John-Stewart Gordon
Bemerkungen zum Begründungstrilemma
Bd. 67, 2007, 80 S., 14,90 €, br., ISBN 978-3-8258-0135-9

Ferdinand Maier
Das anthropologische Prinzip. Zweiter Band
Pragmatische Epistemologie. Natur und Religion bei Feuerbach
Bd. 66, 2006, 320 S., 49,90 €, br., ISBN 3-8258-9952-7

Karim Akerma
Lebensende und Lebensbeginn
Philosophische Implikationen und mentalistische Begründung des Hirn-Todeskriteriums
Bd. 65, 2006, 520 S., 39,90 €, br., ISBN 3-8258-9744-3

Franz Gmainer-Pranzl
Heterotopie der Vernunft
Skizze einer Methodologie interkulturellen Philosophierens auf dem Hintergrund der Phänomenologie Edmund Husserls
Bd. 64, 2007, 424 S., 34,90 €, br., ISBN 978-3-8258-9546-4

Wolfgang Gärtner
Von der Nikomachischen Ethik bis zu Habermas: Philosophische Impulse
Bd. 63, 2006, 160 S., 16,90 €, br., ISBN 3-8258-9341-3

Ferdinand Maier
Das anthropologische Prinzip
Ludwig Feuerbachs Neue Philosophie
Bd. 62, 2006, 536 S., 39,90 €, br., ISBN 3-8258-8936-x

Stefan Diebitz
Seelenkleid
Beiträge zu Phänomenologie und Theorie von Angst und Scham
Bd. 61, 2005, 184 S., 19,90 €, br., ISBN 3-8258-8933-5

Peter Strüver
Ethik, Ästhetik, Normalität und Vernunft
Über die (gewollte/ungewollte) Einengung menschlicher Erkenntnis
Bd. 60, 2005, 408 S., 29,90 €, br., ISBN 3-8258-8847-9

Annette Schlemm
Wie wirklich sind Naturgesetze?
Auf Grundlage einer an Hegel orientierten Wissenschaftsphilosophie
Bd. 59, 2005, 312 S., 27,90 €, br., ISBN 3-8258-8723-5

Eva Marsal
Person
Vom alltagssprachlichen Begriff zum wissenschaftlichen Konstrukt
Bd. 57, 2006, 384 S., 34,90 €, br., ISBN 3-8258-9221-2

Martin Mumelter
Proust for President!
Rettet uns künstlerisches Denken?
Bd. 53, 2004, 136 S., 19,90 €, br., ISBN 3-8258-7735-3

LIT Verlag Berlin – Münster – Wien – Zürich – London
Auslieferung Deutschland / Österreich / Schweiz: siehe Impressumsseite

Eduard Langwald
Das ANDERE sagen
Studien zu Martin Heidegger und seinem Werk
Bd. 52, 2004, 368 S., 34,90 €, br., ISBN 3-8258-7504-0

Christine Pernlochner-Kügler
Körperscham und Ekel – wesentlich menschliche Gefühle
Bd. 51, 2004, 296 S., 24,90 €, br., ISBN 3-8258-7492-3

Stefano Cochetti
Differenztheorie der Metapher
Ein konstruktivistischer Ansatz zur Metapherntheorie im Ausgang vom erlebten Raum. Herausgegeben von Constanze Breuer
Bd. 50, 2004, 312 S., 24,90 €, br., ISBN 3-8258-7470-2

Eva Bartsch
Geschichte und Fiktion
Bd. 49, 2004, 152 S., 19,90 €, br., ISBN 3-8258-7468-0

Reinhard Glöckner
Wie Menschen als Person leben
Ein Blick auf den Mechanismus der Verdrängung in den Spannungsfeldern von Verantwortung in Freiheit und Gerechtigkeit
Bd. 48, 2004, 80 S., 14,90 €, br., ISBN 3-8258-7400-1

Birgit Olayiwola-Olosun
Verantwortung bei Jonas, Aristoteles und in der Philosophie der traditionellen Yorùbáreligion
Bd. 46, 2003, 96 S., 17,90 €, br., ISBN 3-8258-6874-5

Gabriele Münnix
Zum Ethos der Pluralität
Postmoderne und Multiperspektivität als Programm
Bd. 44, 2. Aufl. 2010, 264 S., 24,90 €, br., ISBN 978-3-8258-6629-7

Ludwig Kröner
DEUS ET ESSE
Eine Spurensuche
Bd. 43, 2003, 232 S., 20,90 €, br., ISBN 3-8258-5743-3

Thomas Eggensperger
Der Einfluss des Thomas von Aquin auf das politische Denken des Bartolomé de Las Casas im Traktat "De imperatoria vel regia potestate"
Eine theologisch-politische Theorie zwischen Mittelalter und Neuzeit
Bd. 42, 2001, 224 S., 25,90 €, gb., ISBN 3-8258-5252-0

Matthias Rühl
Schopenhauers existentielle Metaphern im Kontext seiner Philosophie
Bd. 41, 2001, 256 S., 30,90 €, gb., ISBN 3-8258-5001-3

Ursula Sigismund
Denken im Zwiespalt
Das Nietzsche-Archiv in Selbstzeugnissen 1897 – 1945. Mit einer Einführung von Dietrich Wachler und unveröffentlichten Aufsätzen von Max Oehler
Bd. 40, 2001, 336 S., 25,90 €, gb., ISBN 3-8258-4865-5

LIT Verlag Berlin – Münster – Wien – Zürich – London
Auslieferung Deutschland / Österreich / Schweiz: siehe Impressumsseite